Educating
Alice

Educating *Alice*

ALICE GREENUP

HarperCollins*Publishers*

HarperCollins*Publishers*

First published in Australia in 2013
by HarperCollins*Publishers* Australia Pty Limited
ABN 36 009 913 517
harpercollins.com.au

HarperCollins*Publishers*
Level 13, 201 Elizabeth Street, Sydney NSW 2000, Australia
31 View Road, Glenfield, Auckland 0627, New Zealand
A 53, Sector 57, Noida, UP, India
77–85 Fulham Palace Road, London W6 8JB, United Kingdom
2 Bloor Street East, 20th floor, Toronto, Ontario M4W 1A8, Canada
10 East 53rd Street, New York NY 10022, USA

National Library of Australia Cataloguing-in-Publication entry

Greenup, Alice.
  Educating Alice / Alice Greenup.
  978 0 7322 8810 5 (pbk.)
  978 1 7430 9840 0 (ebook)
  Greenup, Alice.
  Rural women – Australia – Biography.
  Country life – Australia.
  Rural conditions – Australia – Biography.
  Urban-rural migration – Australia – Biography.
  Australia – Rural conditions.
994.404092

Cover design by Matt Stanton, HarperCollins Design Studio
Cover photography by Stuart Scott
Typeset in 11/16pt Sabon LT by Kirby Jones
Printed and bound in Australia by Griffin Press
The papers used by HarperCollins in the manufacture of this book are a natural, recyclable
product made from wood grown in sustainable plantation forests. The fibre source and
manufacturing processes meet recognised international environmental standards, and carry
certification.

5 4 3 2 1   13 14 15 16

For Sally
My friend, my muse, my mentor, my shining light, my sister.
So many books, so many memoirs and so little time.
Here's one for the trip home. My love forever,
Alice

Alice had not the slightest idea what latitude was, or longitude either, but she thought they were grand words to say.
Lewis Carroll

Foreword

Across the table, Alice Greenup's shining eyes and radiant smile dominated the celebratory dinner for winners of the 2006 MLA (Meat and Livestock Australia) and *Australian Women's Weekly* Search for Australia's Most Inspiring Rural Women, of which I was an instigator and judge.

Now Alice has shared her remarkable journey with disarming honesty and at times confronting candidness. Her story is a must-read, an emotional feast. The Modern Melbournian Miss was never going to fit the mould upon marrying into a well-respected, long-established pastoral family. However, my fellow city convert and her land-entrenched man have survived against the odds and, through dogged determination, Alice has forged her own pathway to become a highly acclaimed rural leader. *Educating Alice* reveals the many intricate and challenging layers of life on the land, at a time when Australian farmers, who feed and clothe the world, remain undervalued. Passionate and unconditional love of land, livestock and each other are at the very heart of the lives of Alice and Rick – and that of my family too.

Terry Underwood OAM, author of *In The Middle of Nowhere*
Riveren Station, Northern Territory
November 2012

Prologue

The old cow glances up; unperturbed by my sudden appearance she resumes grazing, selecting the sweet new shoots of grass in preference to the dry tasteless stalks of last summer. Her three-month-old calf is playing further down the hill, where the gully opens up into a creek flat. He frolics with his three playmates; they chase each other through the long grass, skipping over rocks and logs of ironbarks that died in their prime, their demise hastened by fifteen years of drought. The landscape bursts with renewal after a wretchedly dry spring.

Better late than never, good January rain has liberated us from the treadmill of drought – for how long is uncertain, but for now the water is still seeping from the hills, keeping the ground moist, the grass lush and the creeks trickling, and lifting our spirits with its promise. Our dams are full. There is a good body of feed, the calves are strong and sappy and the cows' udders are bursting with creamy milk. It's going to be a ripper of a branding season.

Unaccustomed to water on the ground and flowing gullies, my horse snorts and paws at the strange phenomena. His body is tense. He twists and agitates as I urge him to cross a gully. The water is shallow and clean. I can see the bottom. But he is a young horse and at three years of age, born into the middle of the worst drought in living memory, he has seen little rain. Flowing water to him is as terrifying as a snake. His body is in flight mode. I rub his neck and talk to him, giving reassurance. It's the first morning of what is going to be a long week, mustering 700-odd cows with calves, with plenty of gullies and rivers to cross; he might as well get used to it.

Squeezing with my thighs, I urge him towards the grazing cow. He makes up his mind and commits himself, lurching forward, clearing the gully easily with a metre to spare. I land roughly in the saddle, his sudden leap taking me by surprise. He snorts again, still unconvinced that the water is safe. I tilt my weight forward, he takes my cue and we head up the rocky bank, his powerful hindquarters thrusting me to the fore of the saddle.

Seeing my proximity, the cow moves off quietly down the gully towards her calf. She lets out a warning, a low moan that tells him to stop playing and return to her side. Around the ridge the other cows stir and mirror her movements, meandering down the gully like rivulets merging to become a stream of cows.

'Mac, go back.' I accompany this command with a long low whistle to send my dog to the lead to block the cows' momentum. A cream short-haired border collie, Mac stands out in the landscape and is easily spotted snapping at the cows, his pale coat contrasting with the deep reddish-brown of the herd, gleaming in the sun. The calves are getting their first education in respect. Step out of line and before they know it a cream blur will be nipping their soft brown muzzles. They soon learn there is safety in numbers and it's prudent to toe the line.

The CB radio strapped to my chest crackles into life. 'You copy, Alice?'

'Copy, Rick.'

'How many cows have you got up there?'

I contribute my tally and he calculates that we have them all – 120 in this mob. A rendezvous point is arranged.

'Mac, come behind.'

My cows amble off to join the rest of the herd. Mac and I guide them by positioning ourselves on the wing of the mob, nursing them through the trees towards a clearing where the other stockmen, Shane and Lachlan, are converging with their respective mobs, gathering the cows and calves with Rick's in a corner of the paddock so we can get an accurate count. We have been riding for three hours and have completed the paddock in good time, with all cows accounted for. We're pleased to be so far along by mid-morning; to have mustered the cattle before the fresh, crisp air makes way for the stifling, sticky heat that builds as the shadows of the trees and hills shorten and the sun rises high into the sky. The cattle walk better in the cool and it's much easier going for the calves.

It's a long walk for them back to the Jumma stockyards – seven kilometres or more. There's little point in us all going with the cattle, which are now relaxed and content and can be handled by two riders and a couple of handy dogs, so Rick sends Shane and Lachlan to muster an adjoining paddock while we walk the first mob back to the yards. We hand over our CB radios so they can stay in touch with each other – we won't need them now; the hard part is done. The cattle are well controlled and we've done this trip many times. The rest will be a breeze.

I offer to swap horses with Shane as his looks tired, having taken a much longer route around the perimeter of the paddock. My bay gelding is a strong young horse and still fresh.

'Nah, she'll be right. Thanks anyway.'

'See you at the yards then.'

With that, Shane and Lachlan gather their reins, urge their horses forward and trot into the distance.

Rick and I make our way back through the trees without speaking. We are lost in our thoughts. I don't disturb his contemplation; I presume he is planning the logistics of drafting the cattle four ways in the inadequate, crumbling timber yards built at the turn of the century, held up by Cobb & Co's, the wire twitches that have been holding outback Australia together for a hundred years.

Separated cows and calves call to each other, and the forest sounds are swallowed up by bleating calves and their mothers' replies – a deep moaning bellow, each call as distinctive to the other as the voices of any mother and her child. The mob meanders down a track bordered by a World War II-era barbed-wire fence. Recycled into duty in the bush after the barricades were dismantled around Brisbane, it's now a rusty, brittle barrier held up by split posts cut on the property decades before, hewn from ironbark trees that were felled with an axe and split with an adze and crowbar long before the days of chainsaws.

Rick is riding Roxy, a three-year-old bay mare. They are positioned on the rear wing of the mob while the dogs control the lead, finding that delicate balance between keeping the mob together yet allowing the cattle to walk freely down the roughly graded track. It's a good time to relax before the physical demands of drafting and branding.

I'm sitting loosely in the saddle – my reins long, my grip light, marvelling that this is called work. The scenery is as good as any bushwalking hotspot – people pay good money to experience a moment like this.

I bring up the tail, urging the calves that are trailing behind to catch up to their mothers with a quiet 'Tch tch', and head off the track to coax two wayward cows back to the mob. My gelding weaves through a dense thicket of immature blue gums, picking his way over the sandy gravel and between granite rocks. And then—

Jesus Christ.

Searing pain like a hot knife slices into the back of my skull and engulfs my body.

Why am I on the ground?

I can't move my head. It feels as if it's been bolted to the earth.

'Alice!'

'Alice!'

'Alice, can you move? Can you hear me?'

Rick crams something under my head.

'I'm going to roll you onto your side. Tell me if it hurts.'

Don't touch me! I scream. But no words come out. I am still, as still as death, except for the blood pulsing from the gash near my throat.

'Alice, I've got to go and get help. Stay there, I'll be right back,' Rick assures me.

The agony dissolves into strange calmness.

Moving hurts. Don't move. Stay as still as you can.

Blackness. Sweet blackness.

'Alice, can you hear me?' Rick is back by my side, wiping my face.

I try to shuffle my right foot one centimetre to the left. I wonder if it moved.

Sweet blackness.

Then a woman's voice: 'She hasn't been conscious much.'

Who's that? What's she doing here? Where did she appear from?

Someone sticks a needle into my arm.

'Alice, can you tell me who the prime minister is?' another voice, male this time, asks.

'Paul Keating,' I whisper.

Paul Keating held office from 1991 to 1996. It is 2003.

My head feels as if someone has taken a blunt axe to it. I wish I could move. I try to turn my head.

Oh my God ...

My skull is glued to the spot, my neck seems powerless to do its job. Movement is nearly impossible and infinitely more agonising than the pain in the back of my head.

'I won't move her in a vehicle in this country. It's too rough and we could do more damage.' I don't recognise the authoritative male voice. 'I'm going to call in a chopper.'

Good idea. Keep me still.

More sweet blackness.

I can no longer hear the cows. They've wandered off. It's so silent. My eyes are closed. *Just lie still*, my body tells me. When I am still, I drift into a quiet place where there is no pain. My sensory inputs have shut down. Proprioceptors, which send signals to build up a concept of my position in space and on earth, have been told to stand down while my body does the work of constricting veins, reducing blood flow to all but the major organs, and sending deceptive messages that all is well. So while I am tranquil and still, all is peaceful and calm.

Motionless, I lie on Jumma's sandy earth. I am immersed in her. The busy entomological world is alive around me. I can hear the scurrying of beetles through the grass, but I'm not concerned about what may climb on me, bite me. I am as comfortable as the grey logs all around me. Nothing bites a log. The log doesn't feel the prickles of the grass, a sharp edge of a granite rock. Neither do I.

The presence of others brings searing pain. They bother me with questions, movement.

Let me be. Jumma is my soothe.

Hassled, bothered by humans to engage with their world, I reluctantly re-emerge from the sweet blackness into the pain. I come and go.

Helicopter blades slice through the eerie quietness. The sound of the beating air reverberates off the mountains, getting closer and louder until it is deafening and I can feel the wind whip around me.

I'm unperturbed by the grip on my arm and the cold prick of steel as a large needle slides into a vein. An oxygen mask is placed over my face, easing my breathing. My head is lifted a few millimetres to glide a neck brace on. The pain is cruel. I want to vomit. I surrender. I am lifted onto a stretcher in perfect sync by many pairs of hands, my spine and limbs stable.

My stretcher is carried to the helicopter and fastened down. Rick kisses my forehead.

'You'll be fine, Alice. Just hang on. I'll meet you at the hospital soon.'

Our closest major hospital is 250 kilometres to the east. With little ceremony and no time for sentimental farewells, the helicopter blades start turning and the sound is deafening.

There's a swinging sensation as we defy gravity and rise high above the tall ironbarks and hills. I've always wanted to fly in a helicopter. I long to sit up and look out the window and see our land from this perspective. Then it grips me.

I'd be lucky if I can ever sit up again.

Part One

Don't be afraid to take a big step if one is indicated.
You can't cross a chasm in two small jumps.

DAVID LLOYD GEORGE

One

If I trace it right back to where it began – how I came to be on that horse, on that mountain, on that day – I can pinpoint one moment, one decision made in the time it takes for a camera shutter to capture an image, when my life changed forever. All because I changed my mind.

I made a decision that being happy would be my compass from that point forward. And being happy meant some things had to change. Although outwardly it looked the same, in that moment my world made a quantum leap and started spinning on a parallel axis.

It was like a weight off my shoulders: everything I carried – the disappointment of others, my own disillusionment, and the feeling of tightness I had developed in my chest – it all evaporated. Now I just had to tell Mum. It wasn't going to sound pretty any way I framed it.

I practised out loud: 'Mum, I'm quitting uni.

'What am I going to do? Well, after I've saved some money, I'm going to join Gary travelling around Australia.

'How are we travelling? Um, on his motorbike ...'

From there my mind ran on, preparing rebuttals in various imaginary arguments – and contemplating where I could sleep that night to avoid frostbite.

But the real conversation was even harder than I'd imagined. And when the hour of my departure came, Mum barely acknowledged me. A cool 'Goodbye' was all she could summon. After so many years of it being just the three of us – and since my brother Doug left home, just the two of us – I guess I was letting the team down by ignoring her advice and clearing out. She was pissed off with me and not afraid to let me know it, even though we wouldn't see each other for an indefinite period of time.

A few months had passed since I'd first told her my plan, so she'd had plenty of time to get used to the idea, but Mum, I felt, was being pathetically protective. 'Get over it,' I'd told her, with that certain lack of respect well-known to parents of teenagers.

I had just turned eighteen and I wanted – hell, I *needed* – to do this. It would give me time and distance to gain clarity, a sense of purpose and the career direction that I sorely lacked. What was her fucking problem? The plan was flawless. Apart from the fact there really was no plan.

The invitation from my brother's best friend, Gary – two years my senior and infinitely more worldly – to travel with him had been compelling to say the least. It was the excuse I could hinge my escape on. And for the record, we were just mates. I didn't have boyfriends.

Although there *was* one guy I had a serious crush on – you know, stolen kisses, anguished, respectful restraint, hot crotch type of crush – but Jamie was half-hearted. Our friendship meant too much to him ... blah, blah, blah. I hoped some time apart might give him some 'perspective' – code for: he will realise how amazing and independent I am, and come in search of me, proclaiming me his one true love.

Just us.

Forever.

He would say, 'You complete me.'

I would nod, my eyes glistening with joy, and be enfolded in his arms. There'd be an intense yet soft kiss, his tongue thrusting deep into my mouth, exploring. Our revelation of each other would expand to meet my body's cravings. Delightful satisfaction and discovery would surge through us.

The standard teenage fantasy, in other words. The reality was that it had been a game of cat-and-mouse for too long. I was the cat. An ineffectual one at that. Now things were changing. No more cat for me.

So I left. To find my purpose; my path. To find myself.

The world around me looked and felt like the sausage factory I worked in – piles of perfect little frankfurters, uniform in size and colour, being moved along the conveyor belt and packed neatly into cans. But no matter how they tried to squish me in and no matter how much I tried to oblige by bending and contorting, the truth was evident: all the ramming in the world wasn't going to make this sausage fit. So I quit. I quit my job at the sausage factory, my university degree, my tribe and my life. I intended to return to Melbourne eventually. But for now I was sausage meat busting out of its tight skin and that was all I was certain of.

All the possessions I could take had to fit into a small pannier. So the eclectic wardrobe I treasured, with its long flowing skirts, tall high-heeled boots, scarves and huge earrings (not to mention my favoured heavy make-up), was cast aside for one that included little more than Gary's spare leather jacket, black leather biker boots, jeans and t-shirts. A matt black one-piece bathing suit would do double duty paired with a scrunchable black skirt for nightclubs.

Gary had the other pannier and the remaining space on the motorbike was dedicated to a two-man tent, basic cooking gear, water and food.

And so on a chilly July morning in 1990, two weeks after my eighteenth birthday, I shoved my thick plait of mousey brown hair inside the jacket, pulled on the helmet Gary lent me and straddled his 1500cc Yamaha, shivering. Then I wrapped my arms around Gary and we headed west – to the mecca of motorbike devotees, the Great Ocean Road.

The frigid salt air was fresh and tantalising, resurrecting senses deliberately dulled from closing mind and nostrils to inner-city Melbourne.

Gary opened the throttle and tested out his new bike on the winding coastal road, leaning into the curves.

I am so cool.

But thrill turned to terror as Gary channelled Wayne Gardner, treating each curve like a chicane and trying to beat some invisible stopwatch. Three hours from Melbourne and I was hugely pissed off with my companion. I prayed that I wouldn't return to the city in a body bag: my ego wouldn't be able to bear the 'I told you so's in the afterlife.

Leaving Victoria we continued west beyond Adelaide, then north through Port Augusta into the heart of Australia, past Maralinga, that radioactive wasteland of particular significance to the indigenous locals and the handful of others who worked there from the mid-1950s to the early '60s. The government had erected fences to keep people out, but the fatal legacy of the British nuclear tests had already leached into the earth and her people and – unbeknown to me – my family. But I digress. The shame and disgrace of Maralinga is not the point of this memoir, although soon enough I would learn that it wove its ugly thread through my family's cloth.

The never-ending highway stretched to the horizon with a monotony that was unsettling and contrasted starkly with the urban landscape I was used to. The outback was spectacular in its unrelenting flat landscape of sandstone hues, with little to break up the vista apart from the odd roly poly bush or decomposing roadkill to rekindle one's sense of smell. I was awed by the vastness and grateful for the frequent petrol stations that kept the harsh and unforgiving desert at bay, fuelling our bodies and bike. I wondered how people could live so far away from a city.

Two weeks later we arrived in the heart of Australia, the outback's capital, Alice Springs. Here, Gary and I agreed to part ways, finding we had less in common than at the outset of our adventure. I returned his leather jacket and helmet, stuffed my belongings into a garbage bag and we wished each other a safe journey. I'm sure he was equally relieved to be free of me.

I had no companion, no transport and no backpack, but I had my quest – to find my life's purpose – and my rock-solid teenage confidence and naivety to see me through. I'd become a master of frugal living and my meagre savings were holding up well. I figured I could stretch my travels out for another couple of months, so I bought a second-hand backpack and hitched a ride to Darwin.

After a few weeks there, however, my bravado wavered. Despite my conscientiously applied program of sunbaking, sightseeing, pool-playing and Happy Hour hopping, I was no closer to discovering my calling. I was at the great T-intersection of the top end of Australia – and my life.

At a T-intersection, there are four choices: left, right, park the car or reverse. Reversing was not an option, so this translated to: do I escape left, to that spectacular West Australian coastline of sparse population, staggering scenery and reflective isolation; right, east to Queensland – a safer, less exotic option with more employment options, or linger in Darwin, get a job in a pub and call myself a local in five years' time?

Fate intervened. A letter arrived from Jamie. He was travelling up the east coast and wanted to meet up with me.

Hah! Knew it! The mouse wants to play …

I hitched a lift east to Townsville with some grey nomads, then a week later thumbed another lift south. Awash with a hormone-induced surge at the idea of reuniting with Jamie, ignoring all sense, I tossed my gear onto the leather seat of an immaculate Kenworth truck, grabbed the chrome side rail and hoisted myself up into the cab. Heading who-knows-where with a total stranger, and no-one expecting me.

Rows of flames lit up the horizon and the air filled with the smoky sweetness of burning cane fields. On the road, however, the night was black and dense, with no house lights to serve as beacons of safety and refuge. Somewhere out there were people, but it would be a long way to run for help.

Around midnight we stopped on the deserted highway for a rest. I rolled my sleeping bag out on the rippled steel tray of the flatbed trailer and shoved my jumper under my head, leaving my shoes on just in case I needed to run. It was hard, cold and uncomfortable. All my reserves of adrenaline were on stand-by as I concocted various escape plans, keeping my ears pricked for any sounds from the cab where the driver slept, my body tensed to feel any motion. Sleep was out of the question. Three long, cold, dark hours later, a thump and grunt shook the cabin and a great hulking outline climbed down the steps for a dingo's breakfast – a piss and a good look around.

'You right to go?'

The truck wheels devoured the last 300 kilometres of bitumen and as the first streaks of dawn appeared we approached the outer fringes of Mackay. This was my stop, even though the truck was going further south, to Yeppoon and Jamie.

During a homesick moment the previous week I'd called Dad and was now regretting it. Phone calls home often caused setbacks, sometimes to my plans – as in this case – but mostly to my emotional state. On this occasion Dad had asked me to stop at Mackay and visit his friends, who ran a backpacker hostel there.

The funny thing was, I hardly ever called Dad. Mum and Dad had been divorced forever – well, since I was four, anyway. Dad rarely asked anything of me and I rarely did as I was asked – boundaries that we both accepted as the norm for our fractious father–daughter relationship, cultivated by fourteen years of tense divorce and obligatory every-other-weekend visits. But some fragment of dutiful daughter DNA must have overridden my eighteen-year-old 'it's all about me' attitude, because I agreed to drop in on his friends, thus surrendering my perfectly good truck ride.

I simmered at the recollection of the phonecall. If I hadn't called Dad last week to tell him my plans, I'd be in Yeppoon by lunchtime, where Jamie and his embrace awaited.

The wide streets of Mackay were quiet except for the rumbling purr of the Kenworth as we navigated our way to the hostel. We found it easily on the edge of town, and there I was deposited with backpack and sleeping bag. My teeth were clenched as I watched him drive off. 'Dad'd better appreciate this,' I grumbled to the kerb.

I dragged myself up the path littered with tiny ochre leaves from a sprawling poinciana in the front yard, unravelled into the slumbering hostel and grabbed an empty bunk. My reckless adventure had left me exhausted and I fell into a deep sleep.

Emerging sometime around noon I introduced myself to Dad's friends, Una and Bob, the owners of the hostel.

'Stay as long as you want,' they offered.

'Thanks, but no thanks. I've really just dropped in to have a cuppa and say g'day, then I'll hitch a ride south. I want to be in Yeppoon this afternoon. A friend's expecting me.'

'Alice, please stay at least one day. We've got some news ...' Una hesitated, her lips quivered.

Crap. What is it now?

I looked past her shoulder into the huddle of backpackers playing cards and wondered if any of them were heading south. I was barely listening, impatient for her to finish talking so I could arrange a ride, as she continued, 'I'm sorry to be the one to tell you, but it's all happened quite suddenly. Your dad has a tumour on his spine.'

For a moment I just didn't believe her. To me, with all the narcissism of an eighteen year old, it felt like an elaborate conspiracy to undermine my adventure and plans to get laid.

'When he woke up yesterday he was paralysed from the waist down. He was taken to hospital. They're operating tomorrow.'

I had to admit it: paralysis and surgery were extreme ways to get my attention. My resolve rattled, I considered what my next step should be. Finally I agreed to stay one night in Mackay.

That evening I joined the other backpackers for a barbecue dinner. The cheap wine and cheerful bronzed bodies with German, Dutch and Swedish accents were a welcome distraction from the town where I wanted to be and the bed where I should have been. Someone got out a pack of cards and a hand of euchre was dealt, another cask of wine was drained, and before long I'd put the day behind me and was shimmying into my sleeping bag, thinking Mackay wasn't such a bad town after all.

Despite my efforts to stay numb, the wine was unable to stop the image of my father dragging himself to the phone to call the ambulance playing over and over again in my head. I couldn't turn the clock back. I had to move forward into the nightmare. I contemplated how I could get back to Melbourne and see Dad.

Sleep would not be my friend and allow me an escape, so I was grateful to watch the darkness at the windows uncurl. Gradually grey light suffused the room, as if nothing had changed in the world, but my emotional plane had undergone a metamorphosis.

The dorm slumbered on while I began the process. I hauled myself out of my bunk and into the communal kitchen, made myself a cup of tea and slice of toast, and opened my book where I had folded down the ear of the page the night before. The words didn't go in. I re-read the chapter. And again.

One creaking bunk at a time, the rest of the hostel awakened and the kitchen filled with bodies and the bustle of people making plans. I half-heartedly tuned in. Then my ears pricked as I overheard a conversation.

'—it's out on a cattle property teaching kids.'

'Will you apply for it?'

'No. It doesn't start for a few weeks. I don't want to wait that long.'

As I waited for them to get their breakfast my heart raced. From a logical perspective I needed work and I was ready for a real outback adventure – a cattle station would be perfect. But there was more, something beyond reason. It felt as if this conversation was a private letter addressed to me.

Finally they sat down at the table with their bowls of cereal.

'Excuse me,' I started. 'What's this job you were talking about?'

'A governess position.'

'A what?'

'You know, a governess – teaching kids on a property in the middle of nowhere.'

'Do you mind if I apply for it?'

'No, go for it. Here's the number.'

I was already tipping out the coins from my purse into my hand as I hurried out to the payphone in the hallway to call.

By coincidence, the employer, Sharon, was coming to Mackay that very day and agreed to interview me. I slipped into the shower and got to work on making myself presentable.

Yet when I met Sharon, a slim, fit-looking woman in tight jeans belted at the waist, crisply ironed shirt tucked neatly in and not a crease in sight, I felt shabby and unkempt in my crinkled op shop shirt, knee-high skirt and black canvas Volleys. We discussed my schooling, background, experience with children and work history, and within twenty minutes – I presume given an acute lack of applicants – I'd got the job, a nine-week contract starting in a month's time, in early October.

Spinning on my heel, grinning like I'd won the lottery, I grabbed my stuff, said goodbye to Bob and Una, promising to be back in October, and hitched a ride south. Five hours later I was in Yeppoon.

Jamie had always been painstakingly backwards in revealing his true feelings, so I waited patiently for his next move, shrugging off my concerns that the embrace I had dreamt of for three months was cooler than I'd expected.

We took champagne, Kentucky Fried Chicken and sleeping bags down to the beach. The evening was perfect for romance: soft moonlight, a warm seaside breeze and a deserted beach all to ourselves. Sitting together in the dunes, Jamie and I watched the gentle waves of the receding tide stroke the fine sand, their white foam like luminescent whipped cream. The moon cast a dreamy hue on Jamie's tanned skin as he turned to me, the light bright enough to illuminate the crystalline blueness of his eyes, but dim enough to dissolve all trace of vulnerability.

This is perfect!

I leant forward, my heart taking off as I tried not to breathe fried-chicken fumes too heavily into his face. I wanted to be composed and sexy for this long-awaited kiss.

'Alice, there's something important I want to tell you; something I've wanted to say for a long time.'

My heart pounded faster as I prepared for the yearned-for words I knew would allow us to move on from best friends to lovers.

'Yes, Jamie,' I purred, leaning closer.

'Alice, you probably know what I'm going to say ...'

'Maybe, but say it anyway.'

He paused. I was desperate to hear him say those words ...

'I'm gay.'

The music in my head screeched to a halt as if someone had dragged a needle across an old vinyl record. I recoiled.

'*Gay?*'

'Yes, gay.'

'Are you sure?'

'Yes, I'm sure.'

To say I was shocked would be an understatement. I felt stupid. I hadn't seen it coming, but I should have. It seemed so obvious with instantaneous hindsight.

I'd been blinded by my attraction to him: blond, blue-eyed, great body, tanned, the way his body swayed and his long fingers danced over the keyboard as he played Beethoven's 'Moonlight Sonata', his perfect white teeth, his sensitive funny manner ... but oh, gay. It explained so much.

The revelation spread through me like a sponge soaking up red wine. But no amount of squeezing would extract this knowledge. He was gay and my fantasy was over. My idyllic teen romance had washed away with the receding tide, leaving an unmarked stretch of sand.

While I was drinking champagne and eating fried chicken with Jamie, Dad was rapidly deteriorating from post-operative complications. Jamie offered to drive me back to Melbourne.

Three days later I walked through my wrought-iron front gate. The familiar squeak of the spring latch was music to my ears. I had notched up more than 10,000 kilometres since leaving home. Winter had slid aside for spring. The limbs of the crabapple tree in our front garden, which were bare when I left, were smothered in crimson buds and soon would be a mass of deep pink blossom.

I unpacked, showered and went to the hospital.

Surgeons had removed a tumour strangling Dad's spinal cord after he'd woken paralysed from the waist down. They'd concluded the cancer was a souvenir from Australia's atomic testing range, Maralinga. Dad worked there as a nineteen-year-old technical assistant, walking the footprint of each nuclear explosion, measuring the strength of radiation from ground zero outward after every detonation. I understood what 'Maralinga' meant, having seen what the atomic testing left in its wake: nothing. Maralinga is not a place, it's a sentence.

Over the next week, Dad's life hung in the balance as seizures racked his body, exploding with terrifying intensity. They strapped his limbs to the bed for his own safety and the safety of the nurses he was trying to attack, convinced they were part of a conspiracy – a symptom of the madness that was engulfing his mind by the hour. He actually died during one seizure, but was revived. Machines kept him alive as the doctors worked blindly trying diagnose the problem, racing against the clock and the marching, hidden enemy. Eventually the complication was resolved. Dad's life, which had been tenuous for days, was finally stable. He was given a reasonable prognosis and he would walk again.

Three weeks later, with Dad out of the woods and assigned to a program of radiation and chemo, his healing and physical therapy underway, I repacked my bags, and boarded a bus heading for Mackay to pick up my travels where they had left off.

I gazed out the window and felt my chest ease as the city untangled, as buildings merged into farms, great spans of wheat superseded manicured lawns and scattered sheep and cattle replaced seething crowds.

Gazing at the straw-coloured plains of central Victoria, I reflected on my ambitions for myself and knew I came up short. I was meant to have worked out what I wanted to do while travelling. But after months of hitchhiking, traversing thousands of kilometres of the continent, countless card games, numerous Happy Hours, nightly billiards tournaments and living on what seemed to be my last dollar for weeks, I was no closer to finding my calling. I had no bloody idea – not a clue. And apparently my time was running out.

Questions like '… and what do you want to do now, Alice, now you've had your little trip?' sent me into a cold sweat. The implication was clear.

Like, it's over.

Like, I'm meant to settle down.

Like hell!

I could easily have been trapped in Melbourne, seduced by guilt and reason and people who wanted 'what's best' for me, and settled back into familiar ways and familiar friendships. The job back in Queensland was the perfect escape plan. It was just what I needed: solitude, a steady income, a fixed address for two months, time to get my head in order. Time to find my compass.

I wasn't planning on starting the rest of my life, just putting the other one on hold a little longer.

Two

The four-wheel drive wound its way around steep hills forested with tall eucalypts. The precarious descent on the other side of the range signalled we were crossing from the lush eastern hinterland to the western grazing country, one hundred kilometres inland. Passing cars were far and few between. *Hitchhiking would be tricky out here.*

My interview at the backpackers had been hurried and scant of detail. I had a mere smudge of an understanding of what I had signed up for. Back in Melbourne I'd been unperturbed by my ignorance and blissfully confident. My smugness had been palpable – until I exchanged eastern watershed for western and then my smugness fell sharply away, leaving only giddy trepidation.

I'd deposited myself in the middle of nowhere, not knowing a soul and with no independent transport, and committed to working on an isolated cattle property for nine weeks. Not to mention that I was broke; so broke I couldn't afford to get back to Melbourne with a face smeared in humble pie if it all went pear-shaped.

My chutzpah faltered as it dawned on me what I'd done: I was indentured until my first pay cheque. I wondered if I'd got it wrong – maybe being trapped in Melbourne was better than being trapped on a cattle station after all.

Shit, what have I done?

Sharon talked me through the job as the mountains levelled out onto a flat straight highway. 'You'll have your own quarters but will eat meals with us. You'll teach our two kids – Ned is seven and in grade three and Alicia is five and in first grade. Their curriculum is provided by the School of the Air. Every day at 11 a.m. you'll tune into the School of the Air radio for an hour, when the kids talk to the other students and their real teacher. You don't need to know much else, just keep them working through their books.'

We turned left off the highway, where a wooden sign that said BOROONDARA was all that denoted the property entrance, and continued down a winding dirt track for an inordinate amount of time. Sharon rounded a bend and dropped down a gear to cross a steep gully. 'That's the Boroondara River,' she informed me, as we crossed a cement causeway.

I scanned up and down the gully searching for signs of water, wondering if it would be rude to point out that only sand snaked between the grassy slopes.

'Last year we had great rain and this river flooded. No-one could get in or out for three weeks,' Sharon recounted wistfully, a hint of a smile tilting up the corners of her mouth.

'You're kidding me!'

My inner drama queen speculated whether I could leap out of the moving vehicle without breaking my neck. I figured that I could walk the ten kilometres back to the highway by lunchtime, hitch a ride on a passing road train and be back in civilisation by nightfall, but there was still that sticky issue of no cash to get back to Melbourne. Sharon interrupted my calculations.

'We're here.'

We rounded a clump of eucalypts and the forest opened up to a cleared landscape dotted with houses and cattle yards. To the left sat an older, single-storey white house of generous proportions, surrounded by expansive green lawns accented with garden beds full of the flame-orange darts of strelitzias. Three peacocks idled through the garden, the male's tail in full spread, displaying his turquoise and jade plumage. Large shady trees, together with (as I learnt later) an ample supply of underground water to feed the constant rat-chat-chat of whirring sprinklers, created a cooling microclimate that protected the plants and the house.

'That's the main house – where Peter and Jane Hughes live, they own the property. Our house is down the hill,' Sharon qualified before I got my hopes up.

A huge set of timber yards sat to the right of the track, next to a row of stables, also timber. A dozen horses grazed near the track. My heart skipped as I wondered if I would be able to ride the horses. Like most little girls, I had dreamt of one day having a horse, and felt confident that I could swing up onto any of these mounts bareback and gallop into the sunset.

Past the yards, Sharon pointed out a grey besser block building to the left as the jackaroos' quarters. 'And that's where we live.' She indicated a building about a kilometre down the track from the main house and yards. A minute later we pulled into their carport. The house was a simple modern fibro construction set in a fenced yard devoid of trees or garden. A lone hibiscus bush suggested a desire for more.

The recently built schoolroom and teacher's quarters were set three metres behind the house. The classroom had the basics you'd expect: a teacher's desk and two smaller desks for the students, and a reading corner. A two-way radio dominated one corner – a substitute for real classmates. The teacher's quarters comprised a single bedroom and en suite that was connected to the classroom by a passageway lined with cupboards full of craft and teaching supplies. Sharon left me to unpack and settle in. 'It'll be okay,' I told myself. I could tolerate anything for two months. I was no stranger to working; I'd had plenty of experience as a children's camp leader, supermarket check-out chick, factory worker, house cleaner, waitress – in the scheme of things, this governess job seemed very civilised.

I joined Sharon, her husband (the head stockman), Mark, and the kids for a dinner of roast beef, vegetables and stilted conversation, then retired to my quarters. Fifteen minutes later, I heard the sounds of the family settling down in the adjoining house. One by one their lights went out. I was gobsmacked. I didn't know anyone who went to bed this early.

I had no TV, no radio, no friends, no phone. To ward off the threat of cabin fever I took out my sketch pad and drew the pink hibiscus flower I'd picked up off the ground.

I wrote a letter.

Showered.

Washed my hair.

Arranged my clothes in the drawer, again.

Read my book.

Bereft of any more inspiration I too went to bed. The quiet stillness was unfamiliar to me. My ears strained against the auditory vacuum.

I thought how different my childhood was from the one these kids were experiencing. Doug and I were nearly the same age as Ned and Alicia when Mum took us and left. Having grown up on a busy main street in Melbourne, the clamour of the city was the background noise of my life, peppering each moment with ambience: the whoosh of passing traffic twenty-four hours a day, hollering drunks ambling home from the pub down the road and stopping to urinate in our driveway, barking dogs warning off the intruder. These sounds had crooned me to sleep for more than a decade. In fact, my earliest memories are of a house filled with noise; a noise more unsettling than drunks walking the streets abusing barking dogs and complaining passers-by. This drunk was in my home, arguing with his wife. Unable to escape the fury, unable to sleep, I used to slide deep under the covers on my apple-green bed, lying still and flat as if I wasn't there. The solid brick walls of our Californian bungalow in the leafy seaside suburb of Brighton kept the roaring decibels private from the outside world.

Anyway, life goes on and now I was my own person on my own adventure, and no longer beholden to my parents. Dad had made that clear when he handed over the last sockful of gold coins – his deliberately irksome ritual of saving up the monthly alimony by putting his change into an odd sock each night after leaving the pub. I remember the final transaction as though it were yesterday. It was the day after I finished my year twelve exams, I was seventeen. His tipsy grin as he stood on the front porch and the bulging navy-blue sock dangling from his outstretched hand punctuated my transition from dependence to liberty.

'Tell Jill that's the last one. You're on your own now, kid.'

I welcomed the independence and figured it bought me the right to make my own decisions – even the less prudent ones.

As I lay in the bed in that quiet room on a cattle station in the middle of God knows where, I thought about the choices we make and the choices that had brought me here to this outback station. I'd read somewhere that we choose our parents. I had pissed myself laughing at the time. I think most people do.

At first I wondered why I didn't choose my friend Katie's parents. It sure would have been a cruisy trip. They were married. Happily, it seemed. Katie didn't have to go and visit her father every other weekend and hang around his smelly drinking friends with their pickled noses and dumb jokes. Katie's mum didn't work. She was always on the school cake stall, at every sports day and always at home after school cooking up batches of pikelets. Katie's trajectory would probably take her along the tribal path of her female elders – a path that leads to a pristine world of designer clothes, tennis on Mondays, netball on Tuesdays, lattes on Wednesdays, shopping on Thursdays and drinks with the girls on Fridays. I wondered what Katie would think of being in the middle of nowhere on a cattle station instead of cocooned in her Laura Ashley bed linen. I bet she'd like it. So I get it now. I chose my parents well.

A cow lowed in the distance, her moan clear in the gentle night breeze. A finch settled her chicks back to sleep with a soothing trill. My mind drifted.

I woke early, refreshed.

Class started at 8.30 a.m. Alicia held out until the afternoon to test the new governess.

'Alicia, it's *those* shorts, not *them* shorts.'

'We don't say it like that here. We say *them* shorts.'

'Well, I've been employed to help you learn English, so it's *those* shorts.'

'Well, you talk like you've got a plum in your mouth and we ain't like you,' she proclaimed defiantly, hands on her hips. 'It's *them* shorts.'

With an English mother, my 'plum' stood out more than ever on this northern Queensland cattle station. However, I'm sure it wasn't just my plum that caused Alicia to wrinkle her freckled nose at me. It wasn't hard to understand that she'd had limited contact with people other than her immediate family and the station staff. For her, I had no credibility. I talked like a foreigner and dressed like a city slicker – I wore shorts instead of jeans; she'd probably deduced that I couldn't ride as well as her; I didn't know anything about cattle – duh! – and, above all, I was the nemesis who stood between her and being outside mustering with her father.

I let it drop and made a mental note to pick my battles carefully with my youngest charge.

Class ended at the scheduled 3 p.m. and Sharon offered to show me around the station. 'The men are working at the main yards today ...'

Pause button; did she say 'men'?

I know this will sound dumb, but it's the truth – and consistent with my general naivety – that it hadn't occurred to me that there would be men here, except of course Sharon's husband and the station owner. *God knows what I'll find*, I thought. I had no romantic notions about men who worked on the land. My blinkered, city-based world view had not allowed for such concepts.

'... We're going up for smoko,' said Sharon. 'Do you want to come?'

I did another double take: *Smoko?*

I'd hoped my self-imposed exile would help me quit smoking. I was amazed that smoking was not only allowed in this workplace, but that they apparently encouraged everyone to stop work at the same time to have a cigarette.

'Sure!'

As we arrived at the yards I noticed Mark and four young men standing next to the stables, horses tied up alongside them.

The kids rushed up to the men, making a beeline for one in particular. 'Take your hat off, Rick! C'mon, show us,' the kids taunted.

Rick looked around sheepishly then broke into a luminous grin. He lifted his hat a fraction and the kids squealed with delight, dissolving into giggles as they glimpsed his freshly shaved head – a souvenir from the weekend, I presumed.

'Guys, this is our new governess, Alice,' said Sharon. 'Alice, these are the jackaroos, Willy, Brett, Tom and Rick.'

Rick looked straight at me and our eyes locked as he broke into another melting smile, his hand darting up to the brim of his wide tan cowboy hat to lift it up a couple of centimetres in a charming, genuine gesture that was clearly second nature.

'G'day, Alice.' Straight white teeth shone through a dust-caked face, signalling a hard day's work. Hazel eyes twinkled with mischief.

I'm sure the others said and did much the same, but I didn't notice – my mind had gone blank and my knees weak. I know it's a cliché, but clichés are born for a reason, and if you've ever experienced instant attraction then you'll get it: the brain is momentarily short-circuited and the legs go numb from the knees down. It's an emotion that is etched into every cell of one's being, invoking a response that is physical, emotional and, at some level, spiritual. But hell, I was eighteen; I wasn't looking for a soulmate. All I wanted to know was *How do I get me some of this?*

We meandered over to the main house as a loose group. I smothered a smile as I watched Rick trot ahead as if he had a bee stalking his bum while the other jackaroos moved more slowly, in a rolling, relaxed saunter. With bowed legs that looked as if they'd been sculpted from plasticine – custom-built for riding horses – Rick resembled a character from a cartoon Western.

Leaving their boots at the door the jackaroos filed into an extension off the main house, a large room dominated by a long wooden table that would easily sit sixteen people. Plates of homemade cakes and biscuits graced the table and we filled our mugs with black tea from a large teapot. Banter bounced around the room and a plump cook bustled in and out of an adjoining kitchen, making sure everyone was tended to. I was introduced to the gardener and one of the station owners, Jane. Hoping to remain inconspicuous, I sat at the end of the table and attempted to follow the conversation, occasionally stealing glances at Rick, who seemed oblivious to my presence. He was absorbed in a story Willy was telling about how a young horse had bucked Tom off earlier that day, much to the delight of everyone in the room – even Tom, who proudly displayed his torn shirt. I failed to see the funny side;

I could imagine nothing worse and was bemused by the lack of concern for Tom or his shirt.

'Where are you from, Alice?' Jane's sudden question sliced through the conversation, bringing with it an unwelcome silence as all eyes turned to me, either out of manners or curiosity to hear what came out of this girl's mouth.

I cleared my throat, quickly putting down the tea cup I'd just brought to my lips. 'Melbourne.'

Someone snorted. I hoped my uncharacteristic brevity would discourage Jane and I picked up my cup for a second attempt, but she was undeterred.

'And how did you come to be here?'

'Um, I was backpacking around Australia and … I just heard about the job …' I stumbled over the words, wondering where the confident, bulletproof backpacker had gone.

'Do you have any qualifications?'

'Well, I finished year twelve last year, and I've worked with kids a bit.'

'Oh.'

My CV, aired publicly for all, hardly seemed to impress. I ached for Willy to resume taking the micky out of Tom.

Fortunately for me, at that moment the men got up in unison, thanked the cook, put away their mugs, headed to the door and pulled their boots on. No-one had smoked a cigarette yet. It dawned on me that 'smoko' was simply Outback for 'afternoon tea'.

I followed the stockmen back to the yards, where they were shoeing horses ready for the next day's work. Climbing onto the timber yard rails, I watched with fascination as Rick wrapped a long piece of tan-coloured leather, shaped roughly like one-sided trousers, around his waist. He looked as if he were getting ready to play cowboys and Indians, but no-one else seemed to see the funny side. In fact they were all strapping them on, so I chewed the inside of my cheek to contain the smart-arse joke blistering to escape from my mouth.

'What are those for?' I asked Rick, thinly disguising a smirk.

'They're chaps. They protect my jeans from tearing if a horse pulls its leg back.'

'You know, they wear something similar in the gay bars in Melbourne – black and white ones.'

Rick burst out laughing. 'Hey, guys, you hear that? The gays in Melbourne wear chaps in nightclubs!' It felt good to make him laugh. I relaxed a bit.

'Why'd you shave your head?'

'Seemed like a good idea – I don't go much on hair.'

'What did you use?'

'Horse clippers.'

'Nice.'

'Better than letting Willy at me with a pair of scissors.'

Rick worked methodically, lifting the horse's feet one by one, holding them between his legs and nailing the steel horseshoes into place. The well-mannered horse stood quietly as Rick deftly cut away old hoof and whacked the nails in, trading insults and jokes with Willy as he worked.

'Doesn't it hurt?'

'Nah, they're just like fingernails. As long as you don't cut too much away or put the nails in the wrong place, they don't feel a thing.'

The pretence of watching the shoeing was a helpful cover while I absorbed every aspect of this jackaroo as he bent over the horse's legs, engrossed in his work – his strong jaw, tight buns in denim jeans, his balanced proportions, slight frame and muscular, athletic build made for a nice piece of eye candy and I made sure I got an eyeful before Sharon signalled that it was time to head back.

The next day I was invited for smoko again. 'They've been mustering today,' Sharon told me as we drove up the hill. I nodded without really understanding. Smoko had begun when we arrived. I stifled a giggle at the metal spurs fastened onto the boots lined up at the door – as I was reminded of the punks and bikers that frequented one of my regular haunts in Melbourne. The jackaroos' spurs were dirtier and had a spiky ring at the back. I wanted to comment on the similarity and ask what they were for, if not to look cool in the mosh pit. But for once I kept my own counsel, helped myself to a cup of tea and some cake, and settled down at the table.

My desire to get Rick to notice me soon overrode my shyness and I braced myself to attempt conversation. *Here goes …*

'So, Rick, what were you rustling today?'

The table broke out in raucous hilarity. The blood and heat rose in my face. *Hell. What was wrong with that delivery? What's so funny?*

'Rustling is when you steal cattle, Alice. I think you mean mustering,' Willy spluttered.

I forced a laugh too. *Why won't this floor swallow me up?*

Rick filled the void left by my gaffe, explaining, 'We're doing a branding muster, Alice.'

I didn't know what a branding muster was, but there was no way I was going back for a second dose of humiliation. I figured it was best if I shut up.

Smoko over, I was invited to watch the branding. The men drifted back to the yards where cows and calves, divided by a timber fence, bellowed to each other. The calves were manoeuvred through a series of consecutively smaller yards until being driven up a narrow fenced laneway – 'a race', they called it.

'Steer!'

'Heifer!'

They sang out to each other as they drafted the calves through the yards. I didn't know what a steer or a heifer was: in my world all of these brown-eyed, four-legged creatures were just called 'cows'. This scene required its own manual, dictionary and thesaurus.

One by one, each calf was caught in a cage-like steel contraption, which Sharon called a 'cradle', at the end of the race. The cradle was then laid down so the calf was on its side. The men worked wordlessly and efficiently as a team, each in his role. I hovered discreetly, straining my ears to pick up this foreign tongue; struggling with the language, the innuendoes and the inside jokes. 'Check his fly's done up!' Willy taunted with a larrikin grin as Rick climbed out of the race after pushing a stubborn calf up into the cradle.

One stockman branded, a second castrated, a third cut the horns off and a fourth injected a vaccine near the shoulder. Trickles of blood ran down the calves' heads and from their scrotal sacks. I was shocked. *The poor little mites!*

Before my emotions got a full head of steam, I noticed that as soon as the men released a calf, it bounced up, trotted back to its mother, found a teat and contentedly sucked, butting its head against her udder, willing her milk to flow faster – apparently more distressed by the separation than the barrage of treatments it had just endured.

Keeping my distance from the branding, I stayed back down the race and, following Sharon's lead, helped to push the calves up. The grey powdery dust from the stirred-up yards and the smell of burning hide filled my nostrils. A couple of hours later the last calf was branded. My clothes, more suited to strolling on a beach than yarding cattle, were filthy.

I returned to my quarters to wash the smell and dust away. As I scrubbed my clothes in the shower, brown water swirled around my feet. Muddy black mucus streamed from my nose and I wiped my ears three times before the face washer came away clean. I couldn't recall ever being so dirty. I couldn't wait to do it all again.

The next afternoon, we were back at the yards. The guys had knocked off already, having completed the day's branding early. I drifted over to watch Rick riding one of the station stockhorses. Rick trained the horse quietly. His jaw clenched with concentration as he cantered the mare in gentle circles, first one way then the next. He adjusted his weight – signalling his intention to the horse – then lifted the reins, pulling softly as she slid into a stop and backed up. Settled, he rubbed her neck to assure her she'd done well.

I was impressed: the horses I'd ridden on trail rides either wouldn't go or wouldn't stop once they got going. This animal was of a different ilk. It even had a reverse gear!

'Tch, tch.' Rick urged the horse forward. They eased into a relaxed trot, working as a team. His hands were light on the reins as he guided her movements with his legs. He was so intent on the horse that he didn't notice me on the rails.

'How long have you been riding?' I called out.

Startled, he looked up, his concentration broken. 'I guess since I was old enough to sit on one.'

'What are you doing with this horse?'

'Getting her ready for the weekend.'

Focusing on the horse again, Rick resumed training. I watched a little longer, fascinated by both horse and man. Devoid of anything further to say, fearing that I would seem like a crazy stalker chick and with little encouragement from Rick for continued conversation anyway, I climbed down from the rails, offered a 'See ya' over my shoulder and meandered the kilometre of track back to my quarters.

I still had eight and a half weeks to go and I was climbing the walls. I'd read a book, drawn three pictures and written eight letters, and was only halfway through my first week.

There had been talk at smoko earlier about the Clarke Creek Gymkhana on the weekend. It seemed that everyone from the station was going but me. Rick was giving Tom a lift in his ute, Brett had made other plans, and Mark, Sharon and the kids were taking the station truck with everyone's horses. I'd been told it would be too cramped if I came too. Like Cinderella, I was not invited to the ball.

But it seemed that I too had a fairy godmother – one with long gangly legs, a wry smile and faded Wranglers who smoked rollies while granting wishes. My relief didn't seem to be shared by Sharon, however, given her lack of enthusiasm as she told me that Willy had a spare seat in his ute, which was mine if I wanted it.

You betcha. Anything would be better than being left on a cattle station all weekend with the cook and the gardener.

Friday afternoon the station staff loaded up the horses, hay, saddles, spurs, bridles and bits and piled into their respective vehicles. I threw my sleeping bag and backpack in the back and jumped into the passenger seat of Willy's white 1971 HQ Holden ute, complete with mag wheels and stickers boasting of B&S (bachelors' and spinsters' ball) conquests that obscured sixty per cent of the rear window. Willy took off, howling a convincing 'Yee-ha!' as he fishtailed out onto the gravel track, one hand on the steering wheel while the other snapped a tape into the cassette player, filling the cab with the twanging sounds of Slim Dusty. I grabbed for the dash and the 'Oh shit!' strap hanging from the roof to keep myself upright.

'Willy, do you actually like this music? It's so ... so ... ding, ding-a-ling.'

'Alice, out here we like both kinds of music – country *and* western!'

Laughing, he turned the volume up full bore, ignoring me as I covered my ears to block out his enthusiastic accompaniment to 'Leave Him Out There in the Long Yard' while he put the pedal to the metal, leaving a billowing tail of dust in our wake.

We arrived at Clarke Creek as the sun was setting. The sportsground was an oval clearing in dense virgin forest. A corrugated iron shed open on three sides with a concrete floor provided a bar and servery. Everyone else busied themselves unloading horses, setting up electric yards, filling buckets with water and putting out hay while I sat at one end of the shed reading a book and feeling like a fifth leg. Broken-hearted ballads crooned in the background.

I joined the jackaroos when they congregated at the bar after setting up their makeshift stables. Even out here in a dusty clearing in the scrub they appeared well groomed and in their outback finest – freshly shaven with tidy hair and clean, ironed shirts. The guys I hung out with in Melbourne prided themselves on looking and acting grungy, with long hair, week-old stubble and shirt hanging out – and that's when they went out. These country boys wore uniform garb – large-brimmed Akubra hat, a blue or checked shirt tucked into Wranglers, brown leather belt and brown top boots. It seemed individuality out here was expressed by the colour of your hat and the check on your shirt. I felt as if I'd been dropped into the middle of a cheesy American cowboy movie – but the cowboy hats, the dust, the spurs, the bandy legs and the music were all for real. With my long hair, skirt and singlet top, I would have blended in better at Woodstock than in a Western. The only jeans I owned I'd bought for riding the motorbike. I didn't own a hat of any description, I wore sandals or loafers and I couldn't recall the last time I tucked in a top. Chameleon I wasn't.

The stories got taller and taller with every round. I relaxed and felt welcome despite the MADE IN MELBOURNE brand stamped on my forehead, and my strange version of the English language which had me pronouncing 'dance' as 'dahnce', to general amusement.

Where had the cute cowboy with the to-die-for smile been during all of this? Yes he was there, being low key, enjoying his mates' jokes, keeping his distance. Mind you, I was getting zero vibe. I stole fleeting looks and each time my stomach felt like a clothes dryer changing direction. Once I thought I might have caught him glancing at me. A little later, as our glances crossed paths, our eyes snagged.

Hmm, was it my imagination or did his smile widen just a fraction?

He'd done nothing extraordinary, yet by 9.30 p.m. I'd become quite smitten just by watching him interact with his mates. When the banter paused, Rick stood up, announcing, 'I'd better go water the horses'. I jumped up – a little too fast – blurted, 'I'll help!' – a little too loudly – and raced to catch up as he strode off to the stables.

We filled the horses' water buckets and gave them some hay. The light from the shed and the sounds of laughter and music spilled out into the night. I dawdled, trying to delay our return to the group, scouring my mind for conversation. I asked him about the spurs and why they wear them. He laughed when I told him about the spurs worn in Melbourne.

God, it's a nice laugh.

'Your town sounds pretty wild to me.'

'You should come and visit. Have you ever been to a city?'

'Yeah, Brisbane. And Sydney once – for rugby camp. Now that *was* a wild town – we went to Kings Cross for a look. Jesus!'

He stepped closer. I stayed absolutely still, so as not to startle the prey.

'So,' I prattled on nervously, searching for something, anything, to say to monopolise his attention, 'what's the story with these cowboy hats everybody wears? Is it to be cool, to look like John Wayne?'

'What?' he laughed. 'No. They just keep the sun off.'

Argh, so obvious, yet I had to ask. I came from a culture of sun-worshippers basting their bodies in Reef Oil – it was 1990 and hats had yet to make a comeback as mainstream attire.

'Honestly, I didn't know they were for real.'

He chuckled and stepped closer. 'What did you think they were for?'

'I thought they were just worn in cowboy movies.'

Our chitchat stalled as the situation dawned on him and his eyes registered a comprehension that if he made one more move, just a little bit closer ...

He leaned in towards me. The electricity leapt between our bodies. I lifted my head.

Our lips connected. It was a wonderful kiss. None of the 'which angle do I approach from?' awkwardness or the 'mismatched mouth' kiss or the 'accidental chin' kiss. And there was no *Oh no! Is he going to be slobbery?* or *Oh no! Am I too slobbery?* It went like clockwork – the perfect first kiss. Delicious. Musky. Sweet.

We pulled apart. 'That was nice,' he murmured.

'Mmm.'

'We'd better get back.' He grabbed my hand and we walked back to the shed, letting go as we approached the crowd. With unspoken agreement we sat back opposite each other, our eyes meeting without the earlier shyness and our wide smiles the only clue to our secret.

By midnight, the crowd had sloshed its way through litres of rum and Coke and dissipated back to the trucks. Rick and I rolled out his swag and my sleeping bag on the ground behind the makeshift horse yards. I was already wondering how he felt, needing reassurance. Was the kiss an accident? Was he trying to think of an escape route and I was one of those chicks who didn't get the hint? After all, I'd done most of the groundwork. So I ran some background checks before getting any closer.

'So were you playing hard to get, earlier?'

'I wasn't really thinking about you, until you came outside.'

'Why? Weren't you keen?'

'Oh I was keen all right – I just never thought anything would happen.' My heart and ego launched into the ionosphere.

'Why?'

'Oh well, you were Willy's.'

'What?'

'Willy had first option.'

'I beg your pardon!'

'Well, you came with Willy.'

'Willy gave me a lift, Rick, I hardly knew him before that – you know that!'

'Yeah, doesn't matter – he had first option. He'd washed his car before picking you up.'

'You're kidding me? Bloody hell, Rick. Doesn't the girl get a say in it?'

'Oh well, you did, didn't you?'

Our laughter travelled through the slumbering showgrounds.

'For Christ's sake, shut up, you two!' an unappreciative audience in a nearby truck hollered, sending us into muted giggles.

The sky was a deep black and with no street lights to compete with, the Milky Way was putting on a hypnotic display.

'Look at the stars, Rick. I've never seen so many.'

'The what?'

'The stars, Rick! They're stunning. Look at them.'

'I slept in a swag all last year working out on the Barkly Tableland and never once looked at the stars. You get a bit over them when you sleep under them every night.'

'I s'pose you don't look at sunsets either?'

'Not really. But I quite like watching the sun come up.'

'Jesus, Rick, you're on your own with that one. The only sunrises I see are when I'm coming home from nightclubs.'

'You don't know what you're missing out on, Alice. Dawn's the best time of day.'

My gag was hidden in the darkness. 'Best time for sleeping ...'

'You can get plenty of work done before it gets too hot. Speaking of which, you'd better wear a hat tomorrow or you'll be sore.'

'But I don't own a hat, not even a cap.'

He laughed again. A human without a hat was an anomaly out there. 'You can wear my hat.'

'Won't you need it?'

'I have a good one and a work one. You can wear my good hat tomorrow.'

The hours ticked away like seconds as we laughed and kissed and laughed some more, until glimmers of light diluted our Milky Way. Cradled in his arms, my head nestled into his chest, the strong steady beating of his heart lulled me reluctantly to sleep.

Three

No sooner had my eyes closed, it seemed, than I was woken by noise and action. But beside me there was silence. No warm arm cradling me. An empty swag.

The cheerful delusions of the night before were scattered like neat rows of skittles. I chided myself for falling for a smiling, hat-tipping cowboy after one kiss. Blood sent my décolletage a prickly hot red – my trademark of embarrassment. *Bugger, I thought he was different.*

A voice needled inside my head. *What were you doing kissing him, getting all swept away like that for a guy you'd only just met? You just made a right fool of yourself – in front of everyone.* I knew that voice: it was that of my cynical, fearful, self-appointed guardian, who'd entrusted herself with the duty to keep me safe from the type of harm that love does. She'd vowed when I was four, and every year since, that she'd make sure a man would never hurt me the way I'd seen Mum hurt. She was like a genie who escaped from her bottle at the first whiff of pheromones.

I had no options. I was stranded until Willy wanted to leave, so I'd have to drag my mortified arse around this outback excuse for a sportsground all day. And even then, back at the safety of my quarters, I would have to endure his rejection for the next eight weeks.

Turning to gather up my belongings, I saw an immaculate tan Akubra sitting on top of my backpack. His 'good' hat, he'd called it last night. And, just like a pancake flipped over, it was okay. We were okay. I was okay. The genie was sucked back into her bottle.

I smiled gratefully, for my preserved feelings as much as for the hat. My sense of trust crept forward a few millimetres. *Perhaps I'd found a lost tribe of gentlemen.*

I looked around the grounds and spotted him in the distance warming up his horse. No longer lingering for the sake of avoidance, I scrambled into a t-shirt and shorts and grabbed the Hat, trying to remember the correct way to put it on, which he'd shown me the night before. Willy had told me that if you messed up a cowboy's hat you'd be swiftly excommunicated – or something like that. Either way it was an emphatic warning concurred with by all at the bar. Although at the time I'd thought, *Get your hands off it, boys – they're just hats*, now I pressed gently on the crown of the Hat, as demonstrated. It was not the time to be estranged from the tribe.

Despite the early hour, the sun was warming the grounds, bringing with it a hot bite to the wind, and I was grateful for the Hat. I joined the idling crowd watching the gymkhana events, shrugging off Sharon's cool reception. I hoped that the comfortable amiability that came easily in the darkness between Rick and me would survive the glare of daylight and the locals.

Rick was now on the course, manoeuvring his horse around barrels and over little jumps made of white wooden slats. With his course completed he spotted me on the sidelines, the Hat perched awkwardly on my head pleading for him to rescue it. Even from that distance, with his face shadowed by the brim of his working hat, I could see a broad line of white teeth gleaming. He cantered over, dismounting in a swift move.

'Someone slept well. I see you found the Hat.'

'Yeah, thanks. You sure you don't want it back?'

'No. You'll need it and it suits you.' He adjusted the brim down over my eyes. 'That'll keep the sun off better. Do you want to get some breakfast?'

'Sure.' I was ravenous. Rick led his horse as we walked back to the shed, a metre of sparse dusty ground separating us. I held the horse's reins and patted her on the neck while he ordered steak burgers and sausages wrapped in bread.

Sunday afternoon stampeded unsympathetically towards us. As dusty dirty clothes were thrown into bags and the homeward-bound trucks were loaded up with tired horses and competitors, I rejoined Willy and his ute. A kilometre down the road Willy let me know where I stood and what I needed to keep in mind if I were to remain welcome in this man's world.

'A girlfriend should know her place, Alice. First comes the mates, then the ute, then his hat, dogs, horses and last of all the girlfriend. Get that right and you might just stick around. Jump the queue and you're history.' The lips smiled at me, but his eyes meant business.

'Well then, I'll just have to be his mate.'

'Girls can't be mates, Alice.'

'We'll see.'

Our drive back to Boroondara was more subdued than the outward bound trip. I was dropped off right in front of my quarters – any chance of a final embrace or quiet moment with Rick had been thwarted.

Willy wasn't the only one unenthusiastic about the liaison. Sharon made her disapproval clear and laid down some ground rules, which I accepted, to keep the peace – and my pay cheque.

'I don't want you spending time with him alone, Alice.'

'What about weekends?'

'Weekends are your own time. I can't tell you what to do on your weekends. But during the week you must be in the presence of other staff at all times. And when the kids and I come home in the afternoons I expect you to do the same. There will be no lingering up at the stockmen's quarters. Are we clear?'

'Crystal,' I nodded.

But I thought it was bullshit. This would have to have been the greatest limit placed on my freedom since I was fourteen. However, with food, board and wages all at the mercy of the fun police, I was not in a position to argue. So I bit my tongue and got stuck into teaching while Rick went mustering. We hadn't discussed what was going to happen once we got back to the station anyway so, while I was prepared to stick to the rules, the truth was I didn't have a better offer. I was back to being an island in the sea of station life that went on around me, like swirling currents that never scooped me up into their flow.

The jackaroos worked long hours that week trying to get some of the bigger paddocks branded before the rain set in. Mark got home in the dark most nights so I knew the jackaroos would have too. The smitten teenager part of me who was high on pheromones reassured herself that there was no chance of seeing Rick when the men were working such long days. She held the fort for Monday and Tuesday, but by Wednesday the genie was back with a reality check: *He's just not interested.*

And as a final nail in our courtship coffin, Rick had a second job on most weekends at another property called Sondella, more than a hundred kilometres away, near the mining town of Moranbah. The maths was pretty clear-cut – there was not a lot of room for a hanger-on in Rick's life. I had enough male friends to know how their minds worked and how they pull the pin after meeting a girl. The weekend job would offer a convenient out. I would get to keep my pride and he got his escape route. I accepted the facts, and tried to let go of the tickling ripples I felt in my stomach when I relived that first kiss and the way his eyes shone at me across the crowd.

Thursday night I was lying on my bed reading and was interrupted by Sharon knocking on my door: 'Alice, Rick is here.'

See? the smitten teenager gloated to her cynical opponent, *I told you.*

I'll believe it when I see it, the genie sneered, ignoring the tight chest and drumming heart. She didn't want to see anyone hurt by this fling – after all, it could never work; he came from another world. Someone had to be sensible.

Despite the inner misgivings, I scrambled to the door and soaked up the delicious, long-awaited sight of him.

No hat. His hair had grown to a dark shadow and with his shapely head, aquiline nose and strong angular jawline he looked better than I remembered. He'd clearly showered and shaved and in a navy polo shirt tucked into shiny new navy jeans he looked crisp and edible, like a wholesome apple. In Melbourne those jeans would've been a deal-breaker for me, I had to admit. He wouldn't have got past my first perusal – I would have judged him as not my type: too straight, a bit of a dag. But his tanned, well-muscled forearms revealed a physical strength that was not at all daggy and I thought he looked fine. Just fine.

'Hi, Alice. You got time for a walk?'

He remained distant, a couple of metres away at the entrance of the carport. I stayed cool. Smiling ... friendly ... detached ... unfazed.

'Sure.' Pulling on my sneakers, I joined him outside.

We meandered up the driveway, chatting about our respective weeks, comparing his scraps with horses and mine with the kids – some broken spurts of laughter, but no way as comfortable as the weekend. With the light fading we reversed our steps back to my quarters. The casual exchange became stilted and awkward.

'Um ... So that's your news?' he concluded, with a tone that sounded like a mixture of boredom and impatience to get back to his quarters.

And there, ladies and gentlemen, is his wind-up ... I prepared myself for the 'I really enjoyed last weekend, but ... I already have a girlfriend/I don't have time for a girlfriend/it's complicated' speech. Or perhaps that old favourite: 'I think it's best if we just remain friends'.

'I really enjoyed last weekend, Alice ...'

I got my smile ready and composed a casual, flippant retort.

'Would you like to come with me to Sondella this weekend? I have to work both days, but there's a rodeo in Moranbah on Saturday night that you might like.'

I told you he was keen, crowed the smitten teenager to the genie. I'd misjudged the heat coming off him; I was in Fahrenheit and he was in Celcius. To avoid further false readings I would need to recalibrate.

Four

At 6 p.m. on Friday evening a red XF Falcon ute pulled into the driveway. The gleaming polished duco would surely be spoiled by the time we reached the highway. As natural as pulling on his Wranglers, the cowboy opened the passenger door and, after a brief embarrassing moment while I got up to speed with his etiquette, I got in.

The interior of Rick's ute was immaculate too. Not a speck of dust, not even on the floor mats. I noticed a small bottle of Armour Oil and a rag tucked into the driver's door pocket.

As Rick walked around the front of the car, my eyes were trained on this living specimen from the lost tribe of gentlemen. Only one year older than me, he seemed infinitely more mature and self-assured. He backed smoothly out of the driveway, shifting into first gear, guiding his ute up the road with respect. James Blundell crooned on the tape player – dulcet tones; country, but without the twang. Rick's tapes were stacked in a case, not spilling over the dash like Willy's. There was only one Slim Dusty tape, thank God. Half an hour later our hands brushed on the console. The hairs on my arms prickled.

Conversation was easy and relaxed. A thick deep wound on his thumb looked painful and I suggested he should bandage it. He couldn't even remember doing it – I would've taken myself to Outpatients. The back of his hands were aged beyond their nineteen years, stained with work and pitted with scars from sores that wouldn't heal while he worked in stock camps in the Northern Territory. 'Barcoo Rot', he called it, with just a hint of pride, as if it were a mark of initiation to some exclusive club instead of a sign of a diet that had been lacking in fresh fruit and vegetables. The palms were rough and calloused. I drew his attention to their desperate need of moisturiser.

'You need callouses, otherwise you get blisters,' Rick objected. 'You've got to get the blisters first to build up into callouses, then your hands won't burn when you're branding or blister when you're swinging off a crowbar digging holes all day.'

I looked at my right hand as it lay on the dash. It was soft and buttery, a dent between index and middle finger from constant writing. I wondered if I'd ever even had a blister on my hands. I did get blistered feet from my favourite pair of black stilettos, and from the pointe shoes I used to wear for ballet.

'We used to soak our toes in methylated spirits to harden them up for ballet. Have you tried that for your hands?'

'No, I'll give it a go, thanks for the tip.'

Night had fallen before the ute finally slowed and Rick turned off the highway, his headlights illuminating a track concealed among the gnarled black outlines of brigalow trees. I was disappointed to see the lights of Sondella, and marvelled that an hour had passed so quickly and comfortably.

We pulled up in front of a wide timber house elevated a metre above the red earth. A broad verandah beckoned above sweeping steps. The silhouette of a tall man filled the doorway and a voice boomed out: 'What took you so bloody long?' I flinched but Rick just grinned.

He guided me onto the verandah and introduced me to Jeremy and Robyn. Jeremy's large hand devoured mine in a strong handshake as I strained my neck to meet his smiling blue eyes. Robyn and I launched into an easy conversation about how a girl from Melbourne came to be at Sondella. I was given a tour of the house and discovered I was among kindred souls in a treasure trove of antique furniture and books – their custom-made bookshelves spanned two entire walls. I was in love.

The sun had set hours before, but the gentle late-spring air allowed us to remain on the verandah, reclining in squatter's chairs, chatting. Our laughter travelled on the night breeze, evaporating into the sparse scrub. There were no sounds to serve as a backdrop to our voices, at least none that I was used to: no-one at an adjoining table telling stories or calling for the bill, no music, no sirens, no distractions. The warmth emanating from the house and the lively conversation of our hosts conferred a sense that this was the centre of the universe rather than just a lonely outpost.

Looking eastwards, a fringe of trees just visible in the light cast from the house swayed beckoning in the breeze, and beyond them was the consuming darkness that was Sondella. No other houses, no lights of passing traffic, no other people for miles. I could feel the land drawing me into her magic. I was tranquil, yet exuberance hummed like a base note through my body. I found the solitude captivating. The shift in me was barely perceptible as this outback landscape cast its spell and began to awaken something potent inside me.

Finally, with an early start in the morning, Rick manoeuvred towards retiring for the night. A long rectangular block of demountable quarters for contractors sat fifteen metres from the main homestead. Robyn offered us our choice of shared or separate rooms. Due to the unspoken agreement regarding PDAs (public displays of affection) there had been nothing but flirting since our sweet kisses a week earlier.

'Where do you want to sleep?' Rick asked, placing the ball in my court as hope gleamed in his eyes.

In a jumble of nerves I picked up my bag and walked into Rick's room – 'But just so we can talk, okay?'

'You're making the rules,' he smirked, evidently pleased with how the game was playing out.

We rose early. After devouring ample servings of steak and eggs – which I was told I would need to fuel me for the morning ahead – three of us squashed into Jeremy's ute.

There was an unspoken understanding between driver and passenger: as Jeremy slowed down approaching the first gate, Rick's door was open and he was gone in an instant, jogging to the gate ahead of the ute.

'See that, Alice? That's the first law of the bush. The passenger always gets the gate,' Jeremy instructed me. 'It doesn't matter if you're the Queen of England – the passenger *always* gets the gate … unless of course you have a broken leg; then you have an excuse. But it would have to be pretty badly broken,' he added.

The ute wound its way around squat scrubby wattle trees and between stands of taller black-barked brigalow. The red sandy soil was sparsely covered with grass. After half an hour of driving I had not sighted a single bovine shape.

'So where are all the cows?'

'We run the cows at about one cow to ten hectares out here. There's about a hundred cows in this 1000-hectare paddock.'

Feeling safe and unjudged in Jeremy's company I bombarded him with all the questions that had been plaguing me.

'Okay, talk me through it – I call them all "cows", but you have lots of names for them. They all look the same to me, just big and little versions of each other.'

'Oh Alice, there're calves and weaners, heifers and cows, and steers and bullocks – and of course there are the bulls.'

'What's the difference between a cow and a heifer?'

'When does a heifer become a cow?'

'When does a steer become a bullock?'

'Is a bullock like a bull?'

'When does a calf become a weaner?'

Patiently Jeremy answered my questions.

'But apart from branding, what do you do? Don't the cows look after themselves?' I persisted.

'You'll see,' he laughed.

Jeremy and Rick grinned at each other as we pulled up in a paddock beside a collapsed barbed wire fence.

'Today, Alice, you will learn the art of rolling barbed wire,' Jeremy announced.

Rick handed me a pair of gloves and showed me the technique of bundling up the rusted and brittle wire that lay in a tangled mess where a fence once stood. Metre by metre we removed all signs of the old fence, filling the ute and trailer. Our progress was steady and it was satisfying to know that the legacy of our effort would be permanent. I liked to think that long after I'd gone, and become a dwindling memory of a backpacker who passed through, I'd left my mark on the landscape with the removal of each rusted roll.

When the sun was at its zenith, we found a shady tree and tucked into our packed lunch of corned-beef sandwiches, Anzac biscuits and hot black tea. I couldn't recall ever enjoying corned beef so much before, but the strong tea without milk would take some getting used to.

More spiky rolls and a few loads to the station dump later, we returned to the homestead as the sun settled behind the brigalow. My hands were a mess, having ditched the gloves after nearly throwing myself into the dump courtesy of a roll of barbed wire that caught on them. I'd managed to brace myself just before the momentum and weight of the roll pulled me out of the trailer face first into a pile of rusty old metal – a tetanus bonanza in waiting.

No time for rest, however – we had a rodeo to get to. Showered and refreshed, we arrived at Moranbah around eight o'clock.

If you've never witnessed a rodeo, you mightn't comprehend their electric energy. Even a rodeo virgin like me couldn't resist the seduction of seeing men take on ferocious beasts ten times their size and weight, David and Goliath style. The rider's hand strapped securely, the bull explodes out of the chute. The cowboys are tossed around on the backs of these monsters like a kookaburra flipping its prey. The requisite eight-second ride for a score is a fanciful notion for most of the hopeful contenders. The bull spins, knowing how to dislodge his quarry. The rider gets pulled into the vortex, his strength no match for the 'well'. The rope should release easily but it seemed that half the time the riders got caught in it, with each buck tightening the rope's grip. The rider loses balance and is tossed sideways, flailing as he desperately tries to reach the rope with his free hand to release himself. His legs and torso are hammered as the mountain of raging bull jumps over him – the four legs somehow missing all the vital body parts. After what seems an eternity (a few seconds) the rider extricates his trapped hand with the assistance of a rodeo clown–hero–lunatic.

The rider clambers to his feet, his eyes focused on the two and a half-metre-high fence nearby – salvation. He staggers forward. Seeking vengeance, the bull drops his head and charges, lifting the fleeing rider off his legs and bringing him crashing to the ground then gouging at his ribs. The clown is back to the rescue, stepping into the bull's vision to distract the murderous beast while the rider wobbles out of harm's way. Once in the clear, the rider throws his hat in the air in triumph as he limps away – no score but he got his thrill fix. The crowd cheers all three actors – the rider, the clown and, most of all, the bull. Most riders walk away. A few are carried. The occasional rider stays on for the full eight seconds. The odds are not good. After watching for a while, it was obvious to me that the men that competed in this sport were insane.

Leaving Rick engrossed in watching the bareback broncs, I made my way to the bar. 'May I have a glass of champagne, please?'

Silence descended over the bar except for the distant roar of the crowd as another gladiator hit the dust.

'What does she think – she's in a friggin' restaurant?' someone grumbled to my right.

'Sorry, Miss, you can have rum or beer.' The sniggers dissipated and the hum of conversation resumed.

'Oh, okay. Well could I please have a VB?'

Hushed disbelief swept through the bar a second time ...

'Nope. You can have a Fourex Heavy or a Fourex Gold.'

My first can of XXXX ever in hand, I rejoined Rick. 'You right to go?' he asked.

He'd acquired a large canvas bag which he swung over his shoulder and we made our way back to his car.

'What's in the bag?'

'Rough-riding gear.'

'Are you going to ride *bulls*?'

'No. Well, not straight away. I'll practise on bullocks first.'

I could feel Rick grinning in the dark as we pulled out of the grounds onto the highway. He seemed so clean-cut and sensible – who would've known he had a death wish?

Another precious day of rolling barbed wire then too soon our weekend was over and my exile was back upon us.

'I had a great time, Rick. Thanks for inviting me.'

'Do you want to come next weekend?'

'I'd love to!'

'Great. I'll pick you up around five-thirty on Friday then.'

Five

With my sights set on the following weekend, comforted by the memories of our forty-eight hours together, the working week flew by.

There were just seven weeks to go before my contract was over, when I would say goodbye to the cowboy forever, and I was already rueing the speed with which time was devouring my outback adventure. Carrying our bags and swag into the demountable quarters at Sondella on Friday night, I knew the time for playing games was over. I was swamped with fear: fear of being judged; fear of disappointment; fear of breaking the spell; fear of being too constrained and throwing away a chance of something wonderful – and fear of being too easy and throwing away the chance of something wonderful. I would have preferred to abdicate my judgment to a bottle of champagne and allow an intoxicated romp to get out of control. The cool air and lack of inebriation left me like a hare in headlights. How was I meant to turn on week-old feelings like a tap? But our time was precious and our connection amazing. The inevitability of us moving to the next level made up my mind for me: I could see no point in procrastinating further.

Humour and friendship sheltered us from awkwardness. Our lack of know-how, the fumbling and absence of finesse were irrelevant as something extraordinary took over and ignited us. We were pioneers discovering new lands, alchemists turning base metal into gold. Afterwards we lay for once without words, in awe of something that neither could have imagined. As my fingers traced the 20-centimetre-long scar that snaked down Rick's right forearm – a souvenir from a horse accident the year before when working on the Barkly Tableland, and a symbol of a man who rode hard and lived on the edge – I tried to ignore the thought that was already circling around my head.

Saying goodbye will be hard.

The weeks sped by and every weekend I took up a permanent spot between Jeremy and Rick in the ute, but didn't join them when they mustered cattle on the motorbikes. Rick knew his prowess with stock didn't extend to motorbikes, but was less able to opt out – and sure enough the bike turned out to be his downfall.

'A horse would've known better – at least they've got a sense of self-preservation,' he griped, prostrate with an icepack on his thigh. He'd ignored the cow's warning as she pawed the dusty ground menacingly. 'I called her bluff,' he told us later, 'although, turned out she wasn't bluffing.'

The cow rammed him flat to the ground, complete with the motorbike – then stepped over the entanglement of flesh and metal and cleared out into the scrub, leaving the handlebars twisted and Rick badly bruised and unable to walk.

There was little I could do to help him – after all, he was in better shape than the bike – but I was keen to step up to be Jeremy's right-hand man and prove my worth without Rick's guidance. *My moment to shine, to be needed*, I thought exultantly. So with feigned concern, I kissed Rick goodbye and jumped in the ute with

Jeremy to burn some timber heaps and check the stock waters out the back of the property.

After a few kilometres, Jeremy swerved off the track, pointing the ute towards a steep bank then nudging it up the slope. At the top I saw we'd driven up the side of an earthen ring the size of a backyard swimming pool and filled with water.

'What is it?'

'A turkey's nest.'

I marvelled to myself. I wondered how big the turkeys were – and how could turkey eggs survive in the water? 'So how do the—?'

Luckily he cut me off before I disclosed the inane question bubbling on my lips. 'They're like troughs. The water pumps up from the bore and cattle drink out of the turkey's nest,' he explained. Satisfied about the water level, he reversed the ute and continued along the rough track.

Driving with Jeremy was one of my favourite things about Sondella. The trips were always filled with stories, linked together like a barrel of monkeys, swinging me from laughter to incredulity back to comprehension, and spanning the business of the cattle, the land and the people who work it. I'd come to know when a good yarn was in the offing as Jeremy warmed to a tale, dropping the ute back into second gear, leaning forward on his great frame, his forearms resting on the steering wheel as the ute settled to a comfortable amble along the narrow grassy track.

'... This ole black fella I worked with up north just loved Slim Dusty ...' – I'd heard enough racial slurs up here to know this wasn't a baddie, but I still cringed a bit – '... he played his Slim Dusty tape over and over again until the batteries ran out and then he sat there tapping the speaker, praying for a resurrection, wailing, "Sshpeak to me, Slim. Sshpeak to me!"'

Half an hour later we arrived at a paddock the size of ten football stadiums. Heaps of fallen timber dotted the landscape, pushed into stacks three metres high and at least fifteen metres long. Jeremy pulled up alongside one end of a long heap and threw me a box of matches.

'Alice, you light the heaps at this end. Light the heap next to the car last. I'll get the ones at the other end.'

Jerry ambled off. Keen to prove my worth, I lit my heaps in record time. As I waited for Jeremy back at the ute, I glanced back to check the progress of the nearest bonfire. It had gathered momentum, the ravenous blue and orange flames were licking at the dry, crackling timber just five metres from the back of the ute. I scanned the paddock for Jeremy, spotting him way over in the distance, still walking away from me as he lit heaps.

Why's he taking so darn long?

The flames were getting bloody close and was I shit-scared that if Jeremy didn't get back soon, at the very least his ute's paintwork would be damaged; at the worst it would be a crumple of twisted metal. Through the smoky haze I could still make out a moving silhouette near the fence – engrossed and oblivious.

Bloody hell, Jeremy. Look this way. You better get here now, or we'll have a long walk back to the house.

The fire was rampant, stalking the ute, the heat beginning to curl in through the window. Straining my eyes, I could see Jeremy's distant outline getting larger as it strode towards me, long arms waving madly – and the meaning of his gestures suddenly dawned on me.

Shit. He wants me to move the car.

My trusty pushbike had served me so well in Melbourne, I'd never had the inclination to learn how to drive. It hadn't occurred to me that a little driver education would have gone a long way in terms of useful life skills. My best friend from school, Nikki, had tried teaching me to drive the summer before in her Leyland P76. We went camping when school finished and she gave me a ten-minute lesson in the car park at one of the surf beaches – truth is, I remember singing Cold Chisel's 'When the War is Over' at full pelt rather than the driving lesson. That was ten months earlier. Desperately I clawed back some remnants of that lesson from the bowels of my memory as I slid into the driver's seat, trying to recall the function of the three pedals.

I turned the key in the ignition. The ute lurched ahead with one huge bunny hop and conked out. It may not have looked pretty, but it moved us one metre in the right direction. I turned the key again. The ute pitched forward two metres. Five barbaric manoeuvres later, and I'd moved the ute out of harm's way. Delighted with my rescue of the ute and first solo drive, I flopped back in my seat and recalled the art of breathing, urging my heart to slide back its rattling pace.

A voice boomed through the window. 'Bloody hell, Alice, you could've burnt the bloody ute! Can't you drive?'

I looked out sheepishly at Jeremy's dumbfounded face. I don't think he'd ever come across such incompetence – let alone allowed it under his roof.

'That's no good, mate, you've gotta learn how to drive.'

The incident was retold by Jeremy with relish and forgiving hilarity at lunch. Rick was astonished at my well-rounded driving ineptitude. He knew I didn't have a licence but it never occurred to him that it meant I couldn't actually drive. Bush folk learn how to drive before they can touch the pedals; the licence is a mere formality.

In the ensuing weeks, Jeremy and Rick applied themselves to another aspect of my outback education – driving lessons.

Six

While wonderful amusement for me, our weekend jaunts at Sondella could not compete with the lure of the recently acquired rough-riding gear, and rodeos were regularly inserted into our weekend program.

Rick started on bullocks – 600 kilos of thumping flesh. After hitting the dirt a couple of times, he found a rhythm, often taking home prize money. Like a junkie that needs to up the dose, he craved more and bigger fixes, and was soon jumping out of the chutes on saddle broncs, bareback broncs and eventually the ultimate high: 800-plus kilos of bull.

The rough rider spends hours behind the chutes in preparation for the rides – limbering up, stretching, preparing the rope and saddle with resin, helping mates with their rides and channelling adrenaline from any source. As I watched and waited during all this preparation, I felt like a goldfish flapping around on dry ground, waiting to be rescued and tossed back into its preferred environment. Sensing a waning of my confidence the genie drifted out of the bottle where she had been concealed, waiting. Doubt and self-flagellation were her calling cards. She whispered in my ear as I watched him. Watched *them*.

The smile that I thought was just for me was doled out in generous quantities. Rick was liked by everyone. It was impossible *not* to like him, with his easy-going manner, willingness to jump in and lend a hand and the humility coupled with skill as he rode broncos and bulls. It was evident that I wasn't the only one charmed by this cowboy. Jealousy fermented, reacting with the froth of insecurity.

I wondered why he was with me. I wondered this often. Would he tire of the novelty? How long would he enjoy playing the teacher, the outback ambassador, the tour guide? There were cowgirls at the rodeos – real ones in rhinestones whipping their paint horses round barrels, lassoing calves, carrying flags, singing in tune to Slim Dusty and Johnny Cash. Ready-made mates. They seemed to know the right things to say. I on the other hand had a tendency to blurt out whatever thought or observation was passing though my head. Rick told me I made him laugh (which was true: we laughed from sun-up to sundown) so perhaps with my sarcastic sense of humour and passion for partying, my appeal was that I kept Rick amused.

I certainly worked hard enough to fit in. My vocabulary and familiarity with the nuances of this foreign land and its inhabitants expanded with every passing day. I'd learnt that 'handy' meant useful and when Rick asked me if I wanted to have a 'bogey' I knew he was asking if I wanted to take a shower, not blow my nose. I worked out through context that 'waddy' was a Rickism he'd picked up in the Barkly from his Aboriginal co-workers and adapted to mean 'strange', and when he told me he was so hungry he could 'eat the arse out of a low-flying duck', I understood that he was suggesting we get something to eat. I studied the tribe's culture and applied myself, proving my value at every opportunity. I never walked to get a gate when I could trot – 'I can't stand it when people poke over to get a gate', I'd heard Rick say. Every comment and behaviour was filed, noted and mimicked. I was moulding myself into 'a half-handy type', Rick had told me. I'd beamed at him and longed for the day when I would simply be 'handy' – no half, just full-bottled 'handy'.

And so the lessons continued.

Another weekend, another rodeo, another sinking return to Boroondara and Sharon's disdain for my weekend adventures. Nevertheless, back at the station the genie kept silent. There, it was just Rick and me. No rodeos. No one hundred per cent certified cowgirls to rattle the genie's bottle.

Of course there were always Willy, Brett and Tom – all hell-bent on taking the piss out of me and whenever possible setting me up as the fall guy for some inside joke. So despite my accelerated lessons in outback language and living, the depth of my ignorance was continually exposed.

After seven weeks, my head was so full of romantic notions of cattle stations – men galloping horses through the hills mustering cattle; branding; taming the land by turning barren, neglected country into productive pastures – that it had been easy to overlook the primary function of a beef cattle property, which is, of course, to produce beef.

I had eaten beef for breakfast (sausages), lunch (cold corned beef) and dinner (roast beef) every day since arriving at Boroondara, but had given no thought to its source. My education was about to step up a notch, as I'd accepted an invitation to witness the slaughtering and butchering of the following week's menu.

Rick, Tom and Willy were putting the final edge on knives as I arrived at the yards after work, while a creamy yellow steer waited in a small square wooden yard adjoining a freshly scrubbed cement bay. I wondered how much blood there would be. I hoped the student wouldn't disappoint her teacher by dissolving into a tearful slump.

Rick climbed the yard fence, throwing a leg over the top rail to balance himself. Willy passed him the rifle. My muscles tensed. My breathing stopped. For once no teasing chitchat was exchanged among the jackaroos. They were quiet. Watching. The steer sniffed the rail and chewed its cud. Rick cocked the rifle and took aim. He waited. What for? The steer wandered closer. My heart beat quickly – more for myself than the animal. The suspense was excruciating; my body rigid, every fibre tense.

Shoot, dammit. Shoot! Willy waved a hand above his head to draw the steer's attention. Glancing over, its large body turned slowly to the left and its head had moved to within a few feet of the end of Rick's rifle. Unaware of the predator poised above, the steer meandered further into the rifle zone until its head was directly below the gun. Rick eased the rifle into position between the beast's eyes.

A deafening 'crack!' smashed through the silence and the animal slumped to the ground with a barely discernible 'humpf'. My body released. My breathing resumed. Now there was action.

The guys worked fast as a team, opening the gate, grabbing the beast's legs, pulling it onto the cement work bay and laying it on its side. Finding their voices again as they worked, the jibes began.

'Geez, Rick, what took you so long? Thought we'd be here all night.'

'C'mon, Tom, get over here and grab a leg – you worried about getting that pretty shirt dirty?'

The cut to the jugular was swift and clean. The blood gushed out of the wide slash, as if someone had bashed a hole in the side of a barrel of red wine. The red river of blood drained into the cement bay, pooling around the warm carcass.

Curiosity was by far the most powerful urge that consumed me as I edged closer, trying to see the action, peering over the men's backs, leaning forward, until I was nearly on top of the dead beast. Without warning, the back legs lashed out violently, kicking at the jackaroos.

Shit! We all leapt backwards.

'Look out, it's still alive. Run, Alice!'

I scrambled up the rails to escape the enraged beast bent on revenge. My ears filled with the blood pounding in my head. From the safety of my 2.5-metre-high perch I looked down to see three jackaroos falling about laughing and a very dead steer still at their feet. The final death throes – a twitch, a convulsive spasm, had offered the perfect fodder for shit-stirring.

'You bastards!' I hollered from the top rail, where I remained a little longer than necessary, just to be sure.

A two-metre steel bar, suspended by chains and supported by a 3.5-metre-high wooden hoist, was lowered and the steer's back legs hooked on. The bar and beast were raised slowly as the creamy yellow hide was cut away, each man wielding a sharp butchering knife. One worked in the front, removing the intestines and other viscera from the belly. Swiftly they transformed what had been a living, breathing, mooing beast into a red and white slab of meat.

An hour later the butchering bay had been washed down, the knives put away and the guys were heading to the kitchen for smoko, abandoning the exposed carcass. It would hang overnight, they told me.

Right there in the yards? 'You're kidding me; you're just going to leave it out here with all the dirt and dust? And flies! Doesn't anyone give a shit about maggots?'

'The maggots won't eat much,' Rick offered as consolation.

That night dinner tasted totally different and I dreamt of dingoes tearing shreds off the carcass. However, my curiosity had been piqued and I couldn't wait for the second instalment of Butchering 101.

The next day they broke up the carcass and transformed it into cuts of meat that I recognised from butchers' shops – as well as some that I didn't.

'This is the skirt.' Rick held up a thin strip of meat about half a metre long; dark, with a rippled surface. 'It's one of the sweetest cuts. The Aboriginals up at Barkly got me onto it – they know the best cuts. It comes from here – inside the ribs. A lot of people mince it – that's a crime!'

'Uh huh.' My nose crinkled despite myself as I battled to keep an expression that conveyed 'I'm cool. It's meat. I've seen meat before'.

Even though I found the butchering fascinating, the truth is I would have endured much worse than a slaughter to spend time with Rick during the week. Despite our good behaviour, our romance continued to be curtailed while at Boroondara, thanks to Sharon's prudish trimming of my activities to a standard becoming of a governess from the nineteenth century.

Washing the ute (whether or not it needed it) was our preferred way of being close. Rick's ute was the cornerstone of our courtship and the constant backdrop to the memories I was filing away in my mind. For inevitably, this affair would be just a matrix of memories: singing country music out loud as we travelled in convoy with the other jackaroos to rodeos; dancing under the stars on a dusty dirt dance floor to the tunes of Little River Band; drinking Bundy and Coke ('Mother's milk', Rick called it); midnight calisthenics under the tonneau cover – and sweltering under it once the sun came up while nursing a hangover in the unforgiving heat. A few weeks earlier I hadn't even known what a tonneau cover was – now it provided shelter in the back of the ute every Saturday night, the rooftop to my outback boudoir, so to speak.

This new world still had so much to teach me, but my contract was speeding to a conclusion. Our worlds, which had collided seven weeks before, were about to separate again – and sooner than we thought.

Seven

At the end of my final weekend at Sondella, I could only manage a tight-throated, wide-smiled goodbye to Jeremy and Robyn – we all knew the chances of seeing each other again were remote. What could I say that would convey my appreciation for their friendship and hospitality? Without them, Rick and I would have been nothing. Now we were something. 'Good mates' is what he said we were. By Willy's definition, that moved me up to the top of a man's list of priorities.

We had two precious weeks left. And then what? I had no plans beyond Boroondara; my life in Melbourne, the one I needed to return to, was the white elephant between us. Neither of us spoke about it. It was a quiet trip back in the ute.

But the genie was waiting to deliver her reality check: *You knew it would end. When the school term's over you're going back to Victoria: to the city, to uni, to real life; and he's going to the Kimberleys – on the other side of the continent, for God's sake, to a world that's the opposite of yours in every regard. There will be thousands of kilometres and countless cowgirls between you. Get real, girl!*

Our return to Boroondara was flat. We settled onto the couch in the jackaroos' common room to watch '60 Minutes'. Not talking. Prolonging. Brooding. When I could procrastinate no longer, I said goodnight and ambled the kilometre back to my quarters in the dark. The walk gave me some clarity. I resolved to make the most of the next two weeks and not mope around spoiling what pleasure could be salvaged by stewing about the imminent.

The following morning I resolved to be perky and bumbled into the kitchen for breakfast, but was met instead by Sharon's stony glare and grim mood.

'We need to talk, Alice, before class. Sit down.'

Her tone left me in no doubt that she was pissed off. I was bamboozled. How could I have upset her since leaving Friday afternoon? I did a mental checklist: quarters and classroom spotless, schoolwork up to date and submitted, kids progressing well ... stuffed if I knew what her problem was.

'You will finish up at the end of the week.'

My stomach lurched and bile rose in my throat. I'd just been robbed – swindled – in broad daylight.

'But that's a week early!'

'This is the final week of curriculum, the last week is revision. The kids can go mustering with the men that week. I want you gone by the end of this week.'

'But why?'

'Last night Rick's car arrived at 7.30 p.m. and you didn't get back to your quarters until after 9 p.m. The kids were asking where you were and we had to make up a story about you watching TV up there.'

'But I was!'

'You knew the rules. You are not to be alone with Rick on the station.'

'No, that wasn't the deal. You said weekends were my time.'

'When you get back to the station your weekends are over and you're back on our time. We expect you to come straight back to your quarters.'

What bullshit! Clearly I hadn't registered the fine print about what constituted a weekend. I seethed. 'Is Rick fired too?'

'No, he's employed by the Hugheses. You're employed by us.'

I wanted to tell her to stick her job, but the fact that I was stranded on the property until someone could take me back to Mackay, my need for another week's wages and my desire to see Rick a few more times – however fleetingly – forced a more dignified response. So I sucked it up and continued with the week as planned.

At the end of the first torturously long day, I wandered up the road to the stockyards and found Rick. He sat beside me on a fallen tree behind the yards and held my hand in silent disbelief as I told him I'd been fired. We concocted a plan. It was the first time we had planned anything beyond a weekend in advance. I agreed to base myself in Mackay at the backpacker hostel and find casual work until he finished the season. It would give us another five weekends together. Five weeks, before the next inevitable goodbye.

I was resolved to put the bad ending behind me – the blight on my reputation would not follow me, I reasoned. After all, I was just a girl from Melbourne; nobody of relevance, just a backpacker passing through. In two days, let alone two weeks, no-one would care that I was terminated or why. I would just be another forgotten governess with no evidence that I was ever there – unless perhaps Alicia remembered to say 'those shorts' instead of 'them shorts'.

An uncomfortable week living and eating with the people who had fired me at last drew to a close, and the sweet sound of gravel crunching under tyres of perfect air pressure as the XF pulled into the driveway put a smile back on my face.

Rick and I retraced the route back to Mackay; up the dirt driveway, past the jackaroos' quarters and then the main house, over the causeway and finally past the waterholes that the kids and I had walked to on hot days for a picnic and swim. I marvelled at how scared I'd been of the distance of Boroondara from 'civilisation' – the same distance I now regarded as an effective filter keeping the world at bay.

I took a permanent bunk at the Mackay backpacker hostel with Dad's friends Una and Bob and within a week had found work waitressing and renovating boats at the shipyard.

Rick and the ute did a lot of driving over the next few weeks, collecting me on a Friday evening and returning me each Sunday afternoon. Those slivers of time were like breakwaters rapidly constructed to protect the fragile foundations of the 'thing' between us from erosion.

Our weekends were like bookends to my brooding and musing about my future. Christmas was looming and, with it, Rick's return to his family property, 800 kilometres south of Mackay, where he would do his family's branding before leaving for a ten-month stint in the Kimberleys once the wet was over. It seemed our affair had run its course. With Rick gone I would have little to keep me in Queensland. I couldn't escape the thoughts that stayed with me as I served beers and sanded back boat hulls. I wanted something more than hopping from one casual job to another. At some point I would have to return to my fate, tie myself to some university degree and try to compose a direction for my life. I felt the old familiar sense of a noose tightening, but I took a deep breath and blew out the fears – if I was going to go back and study, then it would be of my own doing, in something that excited me or, at the very least, stood a chance of leading to something that would excite me.

We'd arrived at our last weekend together. We lay by the pool at the hostel, the water beading on our bodies after a swim. My eyes were closed as I concentrated, willing time to stop before he left. Rick rolled over, looked at me and said quietly (quiet, I suspected, from lack of conviction, rather than the calm self-assurance of a man declaring his love and devotion). 'Alice, I want to be with you. You could stay in Queensland. I could look after you.'

Poor man – even I could see it was a desperate scramble away from a hopeless dead-end. Heat and hormones had got to him.

'Good on you,' I laughed. 'And how long before the novelty of that wears off?' But his words rang in my ears as I rolled the idea around and found my mind drifting ... imagining ... Maybe ... What if ...?

'Well all I know is, I don't want it to be over.'

'Come on, I know you won't want me hanging around in the Kimberleys. Anyway, I'm going to try and get into a uni degree after summer.'

'You have? Since when? Back to your arts degree? I thought you hated that.'

'Good God no! I'm thinking about a degree that lets me work with animals and the kind of people I've met up here, and gets me out onto the land a bit.'

How could I explain that those eight weeks of rolling barbed wire, pushing calves up branding races and all the other outback lessons had given me a sense of peace and satisfaction I'd never known before? My days working with Rick had woken something within me. Of course the delight of being with him could have been the entire basis of the pleasure I found in rural life, but I suspected there was more to it: I was comfortable out there. More comfortable than I'd ever been shopping in city boutiques or partying at nightclubs. It wasn't much to go on, but I sensed it was that *something* I'd been searching for that would give meaning to the present and propel me into the future.

'Well, if I can't stop you going back to Melbourne, can I at least convince you to come to Rosevale for a few weeks?'

I agreed. As a kind of last dance, I would join him on his family's cattle property in time for New Year's Eve and stay on for a few weeks. Then I would return to Melbourne for university and he would leave for the Kimberleys once the wet season had finished. The maths was pretty obvious. Three and a half thousand kilometres would separate us for a year, and we'd only been together a handful of weekends.

You see, that was the clincher, the inbuilt sunset clause we couldn't escape. In another time, in another relationship, the sunset clause would have made the perfect out: no strings attached, no hurt feelings; just sweet memories of a holiday romance.

Chances were this outback affair would die a natural death, so why not finish the feast with some final scrumptious morsels?

Eight

'I asked Mum last night if you could come and stay. She said it would be fine.'

'Mmm. What else did she say?'

'She seemed surprised I wanted to bring a girl home. I guess bringing a girl home is a little different from bringing a schoolmate.'

'What exactly did you say? Girl's version please.' ('Girl's version' was code for 'please give me the details and specifics, leaving absolutely nothing out'.)

'I told her I'd met a top fun bird.'

'Rick! No mother wants their son to meet a "top fun bird". And they sure as hell don't want them bringing them home.'

'It's fine, Alice. She already knew about you.' My women's intuition issued a red alert.

'Have you mentioned me before?'

'Nope. But her best friend is Peter Hughes' sister. She'd heard that the governess had been fired for being caught in the jackaroos' quarters,' he explained, evidently amused at the misunderstanding.

'How is that even possible? I only met Peter once!'

'The bush telegraph – you know, the grapevine – it works well
out here.'

'Did you tell her the truth, what really happened?'

'Um, no.'

'Why not?'

'It doesn't matter.'

'Not to you, maybe!'

Fortunately I had a few more weeks before facing the reputation
that preceded me, and had lined up some full-time work to keep
me occupied for the rest of December. I'd got a casual job on a
small island resort off the Mackay coast and would work until just
after Christmas, then join Rick at Rosevale to go to my first ever
B&S on New Year's Eve. I didn't know which I was more scared of,
the B&S or meeting Rick's mum.

My new boss, Lee, managed Newry Island single-handed and
also piloted the speedboat that ferried people back and forth from
the mainland. With a large crowd booked for Christmas, I'd agreed
to be her assistant. The tasks included starting the generator each
day, cleaning the cabins, washing the linen in a copper large enough
to boil the bodies of four men, clearing away the palm fronds and
manning the bar for anyone lucky enough to be there – passing
prawn trawlers, fishermen and inspired travellers – all for the
pleasure of spending every waking moment in a tranquil paradise
and eating the most sublime meals of fresh fish and other local
produce. The board was free, however my nightly tab at the bar for
Malibu and cigarettes ran neck and neck with the small wage. The
dress code was bathers, with a sarong when modesty was called
for. Lee and I worked like navvies during the day and partied at
night, afterwards wandering down to the ocean edge with Malibus
to dance barefoot in the sand or contemplate the meaning of life.

By Christmas Day the island was at capacity, with day trippers
and overnight guests. Even my mum had made the trip for what
was going to be a memorable tropical Christmas. The turquoise

sea was calm, a gentle wisp of cloud caressed the sky. As the feast of seafood and tropical fruits was devoured inside, the sea turned dark and choppy and the wafts of white cloud were blown away by a turbulent purple sky menacing towards us. By the time we'd learnt Tropical Cyclone Joy had decided to join us for Christmas it was too late to evacuate. Hunkered down in the main building, we looked on helplessly as the wind bent the tall palms at a sixty-degree angle and the cabins flooded from the deluge of rain, drenching the guests, their luggage and personal effects. I lent out what was dry of my meagre wardrobe to our rain-sodden, stranded guests and promoted myself to Morale Manager. For two days the cyclone raged outside, but inside the main building the atmosphere was festive.

Finally a brief reprieve in the ocean swell allowed a group of us to get back to the mainland. I kissed Mum and Lee (who had become firm friends and allies) goodbye, rounded up my damp clothes and threw them in a garbage bag. They could dry later – getting back to Mackay and on the road to Rick was my only concern.

It wasn't going to be that simple. My heart sank when we arrived back in Mackay – the township was flooded with the deluge that Cyclone Joy had brought. The rain had moved inland as well, causing roads to close, cutting off the access to the north and threatening to do the same to the south.

I hitched a ride with some reluctant travellers, assuring them that it was ludicrous to delay their trip south and that they should make haste: 'Escape now or be trapped for weeks' was my selling proposition. We got to dead-ends, towns and highways that were cut off by raging torrents. We backtracked and took alternative routes. The roads were closing even as we passed along them. We crossed flooded highways, assessing the depth before easing the car across. The car stalled, once, twice, three times, from waterlogging, yet I urged them to push on: 'We can't stay here, it's the middle of nowhere – we could be trapped for days!' Options were closing fast, there was only one direction left: south, away from the monsoon.

The moisture in the air was thick. I draped my wet clothes across the brown vinyl back seat, hoping to dry what I could, but contenting myself with keeping the mould at bay.

Against the odds, after two and a half days of a journey that should have taken ten hours, we pulled into the deserted main street of Jandowae, Rick's hometown, at 1 a.m. on 30 December. There was no 24-hour petrol station or backpackers where we could sleep and freshen up, so my drivers decided to push on to the next major town. With the only other option being to sleep on the pavement – which would have made another great piece of gossip once the bush telegraph caught wind of it – I called Rick.

I sat vigilant on the kerb, the black bitumen, glistening with the rain, shining a metallic silver. Twenty minutes later there it was: the crisp pre-emptive note of a finely tuned six-cylinder engine sending a welcome shiver through me, as a gleaming red ute turned into the wide empty street.

A quick embrace swept away his incredulousness at my arrival and the hour of our reunion. His beaming smile, his powerful arms, his musky scent – all worth it.

By the time we'd arrived at Rosevale I was ravenous. Rick made me some toast with peanut butter and a cup of tea. I wasn't concerned about my bedraggled appearance; I'd been wearing the same clothes for three days – the freshest and driest of my wardrobe – while the rest lay crumpled in the garbage bag at my feet, still damp. But who cared? I had literally crossed flooded rivers for this man – who wouldn't be impressed with that?

My self-congratulation was short-lived. A foreboding figure shuffled down the hallway in a pink dressing gown, arms crossed, her diminutive frame no match for the energy she was exuding at two in the morning.

'Meet my mum, Peg,' said Rick.

'So you must be Alice.' The low pitch and elongated vowels oozed unmistakable disdain.

Since travelling, intoxicated with my emancipation, I'd come to think of myself as a young woman more worldly than my eighteen years. But in that moment, frozen to this woman's cork-tiled kitchen floor, I shrank from her scanning eyes, feeling like a fifteen-year-old bad influence caught breaking my curfew.

I was efficiently shown the guest room and offered the shower – no surprises there – then fell into bed, thankful that exhaustion would put paid to scathing self-appraisal.

Tonight I will sleep and tomorrow I will dazzle ...

Nine

The room was bright – too bright – when Rick knocked on my door.

Shit, what time is it? I'd slept so soundly, there was no need to check if a pea had been placed under my mattress – no, I think they'd already concluded that I was no princess, even without the pea.

'Good morning. Sleep well? I thought I should wake you before the day's over.'

Shit. Shit. Shit!

He walked to the window, pulling up a blind to reveal a sweeping lawn bordered by tall shady gums and an understory of manicured shrubs which screened the house from the thousands of hectares of pasture and crops surrounding us.

'Get dressed and come and meet everyone. They're all busting to meet you.'

Rick lent me some dry clean clothes. Washing would be first on the agenda.

Everyone else had finished breakfast long before. Rick pulled a plate of shrivelled rissoles from the oven and poured me a lukewarm cup of tea from the teapot to wash it down. He introduced me to his elder brother, David, and younger siblings, Peter and Sally – twenty-one, fifteen and thirteen respectively. They all shared Peggy's dark hair and eyes in varying shades of brown and hazel. Beautiful smiles and good teeth were evidently signature family traits. They put me at ease as they discussed everything and nothing, dancing around topics that served their main intention of taking the piss out of each other. It was easy to see that the four siblings were good mates.

Rick's dad, Grahame, wandered into the kitchen wearing a faded royal-blue work shirt and patched denim jeans. The fastidiously sewn patches so consumed the remaining denim, it wasn't clear where the patches ended and the original fabric began. Grahame's tall, broad, 1.8-metre stature, blue eyes and light flaxen hair contrasted with Rick's smaller, slighter build and dark features, but the outward slant of the brow that lent a kindness to their eyes was a perfect match.

'Dad, this is Alice.'

'G'day.'

'Hi, Grahame.'

'Alice who?'

'McKiggan.'

'Hmm.' It meant nothing to him.

'From where?'

'From Melbourne.'

'Oh. Right.' It still meant nothing to him.

No-one asked for surnames in my Melbourne social circle, but in the country your surname is your calling card and everyone is linked somehow – you just have to dig a little. But the McKiggans of Melbourne meant nothing here, and no amount of digging could put my surname into a meaningful context for Grahame. He asked me a few questions about my trip and the cyclone, then cleared out again – back to work, mumbling something about fixing a pump. I didn't know if he was friendly, shy, bored, dismissive, or distracted, or maybe all of the above.

Rick gave me a quick tour of his home. Built in the late sixties, the house was shaped like a wide V, spanning the hill. Peg and Grahame's bedroom was at one end. A bathroom, Sally's room, the guest room and a formal dining room completed the left wing. The family room and kitchen were in the middle and the right wing housed the 'boys' room', an office, a sewing room, and a breezeway filled with the various fridges and freezers I came to learn are a signature accessory in the country. The freezer section led to a double carport and a laundry the size of a large kitchen.

For the rest of the morning Rick showed me around the property, the cattle yards and the bull selling complex. He introduced me to his grandfather, known as Gaffer, who, having been widowed a few years before, lived on his own in the original century-old homestead near the yards. At a fit seventy-two years of age, Gaffer was still very involved with the running of the cattle station and the stud for which it was renowned, despite his knees no longer obliging him and forcing him off a horse and out of the paddock. Inviting us in for a cuppa and biscuit, he took me around the old house, proudly showing off the volumes of stud records in his office – forty years of meticulously recorded and transcribed pedigrees.

'David does most of this on the computer now. But I like to keep my records up to date. You know what's what with paper. But these computers are a different matter altogether.'

At lunchtime the table was extended for the interloper, yet it still felt crowded. I felt like a tennis spectator as I watched the verbal toing and froing. Rick laughed at my new-found reserve. Truth is, at first I didn't know how to get a word in edgeways. But after a couple of days I got into the rhythm, my gregarious nature came to the fore, and I was soon throwing my two cents' worth into the conversation and introducing my well-honed knowledge of card games to the after-dinner program.

Rick's family was just how I'd imagined life with a large family would be, and reminded me of the family I'd spent every afternoon of my youth with: *The Brady Bunch*. My own experience was so different: my brother Doug had moved out of home when he finished high school three years earlier, leaving just Mum and me. Between my schedule of work, netball, ballet and study and Mum juggling full-time and part-time jobs, we rarely sat down at the table together. Instead we often ate on the run, grabbing a plate of the stir-fry that sat on the stove awaiting passers-by.

Even the food was different: plain but hearty – and lots of it. At Rosevale, breakfast was cereal, rissoles, sausages and eggs, and even gravy. The cooked breakfast was Grahame's domain. The frying pan sizzled away while Grahame disappeared into his office to make phone calls, pay bills and conduct other secret cattlemen's business – I acquired a taste for his well-done rissoles. Lunches were cold meat and salad, and dinner was an ample meal of roast beef or steak and vegies, or corned beef with white sauce and mashed potatoes. And a constant supply of freshly baked biscuits and cakes took up prime real estate on the kitchen bench.

The kitchen and the laundry, with their respective piles of potatoes for peeling and Wranglers for washing, proved to be handy venues to endear myself to Peg and get to know the woman who'd raised the man who'd captured my heart. It was clear that Peggy's bustling, diligent efficiency was the backbone of the operation, allowing Grahame and the kids to get on with the running of the properties with little thought about where their next meal or patched pair of jeans came from, or why there was always a homemade quiche in the freezer ready to defrost at the unexpected arrival of a client or old acquaintance. Even Sally had the blood of the stockmen pumping through her veins, leaving Peggy to 'man' the fort alone.

After a few days, having served as Peg's evening kitchen hand and gained some confidence in her domain, I took a bold step, offering to cook dinner and give her a well-deserved night off. Opting for a simple foolproof recipe, one of my childhood favourites that shouldn't offend Grahame's conditioned palate, I chose macaroni cheese with bacon.

I'd only ever made macaroni cheese for one or two people – but really, how hard could it be to cook for seven people? I just needed to increase the quantities ...

6 p.m. I look confident as I set to work on my pièce de résistance, caramelising the onions and sautéing the bacon.

6.05 p.m. Start the roux for the white sauce.

6.10 p.m. Burn the butter.

6.15 p.m. Add the flour and realise things have just gone from bad to worse.

I should have aborted then and there, or at the very least called in the cavalry. But no, I was determined to fly solo. As well as being out of my depth quantitatively speaking, my IQ had apparently plummeted on the correlated inverse gradient with the pressure of impressing Rick's family.

Too much bloody flour! I panic. I don't cook off the roux properly.

Maybe it'll work out.

6.20 p.m. I add the milk.

Cripes, it's still thickening!

6.23 p.m. Add more milk.

It'll have to stop thickening soon!

6.28 p.m. Add yet more milk. Still gluggy. But I'm committed. I go all out and finish the two-litre milk carton. I have just used up all their milk. There are no corner stores. We'll have to defrost another carton – and that won't be soon enough to save this sauce. *Fuck.*

6.35 p.m. The saucepan is full. But it's a gooey paste, the texture of clag. I hope that the caramelised onions and bacon provide sufficient flavour to mask the white sauce catastrophe – more like a tan sauce thanks to the burnt butter.

Shit. I haven't cooked enough onions and bacon!

6.40 p.m. Add more salt.

Maybe some pepper will help?

6.45 p.m. With no escape, I serve my meal to the family.

Everyone politely partook of my abundant offering. I was conscious it was a variant from their usual steak and vegetables, but I had hoped to open a Pandora's Box of culinary opportunities with my macaroni special. I had my first mouthful and tried to hide my disappointment. *Maybe they won't notice. It's the first time I've made it for them – they might like it.*

Their eyes flitted around the table as each mouthful went in. The pained silence was finally broken by Sally: 'I really love what you've done with the pasta, Alice.'

I relaxed slightly and for a moment allowed myself to think that maybe I'd pulled it off, as she noisily smacked her lips.

'Especially the way it sticks to the roof of your mouth,' she concluded.

Laughter erupted around the table. Peter got up to make some toast and a chorus of 'Whack some in for me' followed, as someone else scoured the shelves for baked beans and sardines. I'd screwed up dinner but my rite of passage felt complete as they took the piss out of me. I felt like family.

Ten

I refer to the family en masse because that's how I saw them: as a cohesive unit; an entity in its own right with its own belief system and opinions on everything – from what constitutes a sensible men's haircut (and for the record there is only one style that qualifies –a 'Number 3' all over) to the most practical family car (a white Ford Falcon station wagon), and from the merits of aluminium window frames over labour-wasting painted timber to the right and proper way to breed bulls. The family had a resonance, a rhythm, a character of its own that put paid to my notion of 'family' as merely shared heritage and a conglomerate of genetic traits.

The family's annual pilgrimage to the breeder country they called Benroy, to do the branding muster, was upon them, and guess who got a team jersey? Everyone was invigorated. Branding at Benroy was like a working sabbatical for the family. Benroy was old school: living rough, sleeping on old army cots in a slab shed; no phone, electricity or running water. The only toilet was a long-drop inside a corrugated iron tank with a hinged door cut into the side and bogeys were a swim in the nearby waterhole. There was no scope to be precious about frogs, spiders and snakes out there.

On the first morning, the men and Sally loaded the horses onto the truck in the dark and drove to Benroy to start the muster. Peggy and I stayed behind and finished packing up the supplies – enough food to feed a mob of ten for a week.

Peggy didn't ride and seemed content with her lot – she knew that without her, there was no show. I was miffed at being kept behind for mere 'women's work' – especially when Rick told me it was the most useful thing I could do. It made sense that someone should stay and help Peg, but I was desperate to go mustering. Despite the fact that my accumulated hours in the saddle (from trail rides) wouldn't even come close to what the Greenup kids would have racked up by age four, I was confident about my riding skills and felt I'd be more useful in the paddock – after all, what's so hard about riding a horse and getting some cattle in? However, I stifled my inclination to sulk, suspecting it would do nothing to further my cause, and set about helping Peg.

At the hut we unpacked supplies, lit the fire in the cast-iron wood-fired stove and made up the beds, disturbing four generations of mice that had enjoyed the warmth of the old horsehair mattresses over winter. Peggy showed me how to fuel up the kerosene fridges and light them. Fridges that had not been used since branding twelve months before chugged into life. I filled the huge old cast-iron kettle with water. It would bubble on the wood-fired stove twenty-four hours a day providing hot water for washing and endless pots of tea. Five monster watermelons were rolled under the tank stand and covered with wetted hessian sacks.

On cue, as the first billy was boiled, a distant bellowing filtered out of the hills, echoing off the steep gully walls. The chorus got louder and louder, teasing me with anticipation, until at last a lone stockman trotted around the base of the steep hill, followed by a trickle of cows and calves. Their rich red coats gleamed in the early morning sun, the long ears of the calves bobbing and wagging as they walked, reminding me of four-legged gremlins. The last of the mob spilled onto the track and the rest of the stockmen came into view, bringing up the tail and keeping the wings in order. I ached to be among them.

The peace that had been speckled with the pottering sounds of unpacking and making tea was now shattered with the proximity of ninety-odd cows and calves bellowing for each other and the sounds of stockwhips cracking in succession, like a round of rifle shots. A blur of stockmen cantered up and down the wing, concentrating on keeping the mob tight. I raced towards them to get a better look. Someone yelled at me to get out of sight before I spooked the cattle, so I hastily beat a retreat behind the nearest large gum tree, from where I could peek out and watch as the mob was yarded.

After a smoko smorgasbord fit for a king – fruit cake, cherry shortbread, peanut biscuits, watermelon and that black billy tea that I still hadn't acquired a taste for, nor the technique of straining out the tea leaves with my teeth – the cattle were drafted up. The cows and calves were yarded together in a large cooling yard where they could settle and have a drink before being worked through a series of smaller yards. Each calf was scrutinised to determine its fate and drafted by sex and grade.

Rick found me a vantage point where I could watch and be out of the way but within earshot so he could explain what was going on. The calves that made the grade were destined to be bulls and breeding heifers, the ones that didn't would be sold into the meat trade. He explained they would all be branded with a 'Q' to denote the year plus an individual number: odds for females, evens for males, to keep track of them and their pedigrees.

After drafting Rick gave me a job in the back yards working alongside him to bring the calves up for branding. The efficiency and speed with which the men moved was intimidating – there was no time for a breather; everyone worked flat out to process the cattle and reunite the calves with their mothers as quickly as possible.

With the last of the calves in the holding pen, I relaxed, pleased with myself and for being of use. Rick gave me a wink from across the yard as I made my way back to the branding race. Then he suddenly yelled, 'Get out! Now!'

I couldn't see any imminent threat, unless the two bulls fighting in the next yard were something to be concerned about. *Surely I'm safe where I am? They're there; I'm here behind a two-metre-high post-and-rail fence.*

'*Get out!*' Rick screamed again over his shoulder, as he raced for a whip.

The bulls smashed through the old rails into my yard, their crazed intention to destroy each other rendering the ironbark timber yards and anything else in their path a helpless casualty at the mercy of their combined 2000 kilos of fury. I'd already swung my leg over the fence into the adjoining yard, and leapt to safety as the bulls spun blindly, their heads locked in a wrestle of strength and dominance. Rick leapt into the yard with them, springing nimbly out of their way while cracking his whip menacingly until the bulls broke apart. When there was a lull in the battle, David swung a gate and bounded into the middle of the bulls, chasing the younger one who, grateful to escape, seized the invitation and ran out the exit.

'Keep those bloody bulls apart before they kill someone!' Grahame yelled. The guys separated the bulls by four yards and still the older bull kept his eyes trained on the competition, warning that there wouldn't be an escape next time. The danger averted, branding resumed with little sign that the drama had occurred, except for Grahame grumbling under his breath that, 'The bloody yards will need fixing before the next mob comes in.' However I was still shaking, my bravado checked – clearly this cattle job required more than just romantic notions.

That night, sitting on a hotchpotch of wooden chairs around the scrubbed wooden table, its legs in tins to keep out the white ants, I ate one of the best meals ever – the smoky charred flavour from the old wood-fired stove permeated the roast beef, vegetables, and raisin duff self-saucing pudding.

Atop one of the rusty fridges, a battery-powered radio chattered in the background while dishes were washed and stacked away and a huge full moon chased away the residual light of dusk. Old enamel pannikins were grabbed and filled with water to brush teeth, each person finding a spot away from the campsite to spit out the toothpaste. No later than 8 p.m. all bodies were settled into their respective swags on the stretchers and asleep within minutes.

My slumber was interrupted by Rick whispering nearby: 'Alice, wake up. Get dressed.' I puckered my lips for a kiss, but he had already whisked away into the darkness, leaving me to toss on some clothes in the dark and catch up. There was barely a pre-dawn hue on the horizon; it couldn't have been much after 4 a.m.

We made our way to the bush-style tack room – a simple lean-to, with a ten-centimetre-diameter timber rail suspended along the length of the roof for hanging the saddles. Wires with hooked ends threaded over the roof beam supported an array of bridles and halters. Rick collected several halters and bridles, looping some over my shoulder. We had about four each, including a bridle for me. *Yay!* As the first shreds of light peered over the horizon, we caught the horses and tied them to the various trees around the hut, to be saddled after breakfast.

Unspoken understanding gelled this mix of family and stockmen, like a school of fish connected by unseen forces, knowing their place in the squad and the direction they must swim in. As the barbecue sizzled everyone was occupied – filling up the kettle, cooking breakfast, cleaning up, wetting down the hessian sacks for the melons, watering the horses, cleaning hooves.

'Old Jack' arrived while we were scoffing a batch of Grahame's burnt rissoles. He was greeted with a chorus of 'G'day, Jack', and easily won me over with a tip of his hat at our introduction. The caretaker of the Greenups' breeder country, the seventyish stockman lived in a house on a block adjoining Benroy that the Greenups also owned, called Cardowan. His bent body, crinkled face and arthritic hands belied his athleticism and strength, nor did they dissuade him from riding a spritely dark bay filly. She shied nervously as he pulled up alongside the verandah, pawing the ground as he leant out precariously so Peggy and Sally could plant kisses on his leathery old cheek. 'He's just like "Clancy of the Overflow" – an absolute legend,' Sally told me under her breath as we washed the breakfast dishes.

I couldn't wait for my first muster, the excitement causing most of my rissoles to have already found their way into the long drop by the time we were ready to mount up. I'd told Rick I could ride, and I meant it – I really thought I could – however, the simple fact that I couldn't saddle or bridle my horse was a bit of a giveaway that I had my ambitions and capabilities a tad mixed up. To my dismay, I was assigned Fawn to ride – a painfully slow, safe and sensible fourteen-hand pony. I wanted to be like the cool cowboys. I wanted to ride the pretty, athletic-looking quarter horses. I wanted to go fast. How hard could it be?

The horses were saddled and mounted and all hands congregated beneath the apple gums. In their Akubra hats, checked cotton shirts, Wranglers and spurs the men and Sally looked as if they'd all been plucked from the same carton. Each man carried a stockwhip. It was a postcard moment.

Rick laughed as he glanced at the floppy leather hat that I'd picked up in a Mackay op shop. 'I hope you don't scare the cattle with that thing.'

The team moved off in unison. I dawdled behind, feeling like I was back at school, unable to keep up with the cool gang and their Sportsgirl trends while I wore whatever style Vinnies had on the day. Rick trotted ahead to open the first gate, then cantered on to the next one, opening the wire cocky gate and closing it after everyone was through. We pulled up just inside to be briefed, gathering around Grahame as he issued instructions.

'Sid, you head roun' to the *mutter, mutter, mutter* then back to the second ridge, *mutter, mumble, mutter*; Jack, you cover the back timbered country; David, you'll bring the mob from roun' the back camp, *mutter, grunt, mumble, mutter* and through the timber, *mutter, mumble, mutter.*'

Everyone mumbled their agreement and rode off in different directions, with complete comprehension of what was expected of them. I, on the other hand, was frozen to the spot.

Rick gave me his characteristic grin. 'You right to go? Just stick with me.'

He filled me in on our objective. We were to muster a 450-hectare paddock of rough hilly terrain, covered with gum trees and woven with creeks and gullies. I didn't understand how we were going to find any cattle when they were obscured by trees, rocks and topography, let alone what we were going to do with them once we'd found them.

My horse's progress through the paddock was slow, impeded by granite and sandstone outcrops. Fawn tiptoed along, unwillingly navigating the rocks, tangling vines and prickly shrubs. Rick's horse seemed to glide across the jolting landscape. I had to jig-jog constantly to catch up, my feet slipping in and out of the stirrups. My bum was hurting after thirty minutes, and I could feel my calf muscles rubbing against the leather straps of the stirrups.

'How much longer till we're back at the hut?' I asked Rick.

'Oh, we should be back around ten or eleven, so another four hours or so, I guess – depends how easily we find all the cattle.'

Holy shit. I hoped my arse was up to it and tried to ignore the stinging spreading over my calves as the loose-fitting jeans rasped away thin skin. I didn't have much choice.

We walked over a ridge and rode onto some cows and calves. Startled, they took off down a gully. Rick galloped ahead to block the lead of the cows, yelling over his shoulder, 'Stay with the tail!'

What the heck am I meant to do? They've all got tails!

With Rick out of sight, I followed the cows in the hope that someone would find me. I knew there were another seven people out there but I hadn't seen nor heard anyone since the mutterfest back at the gate. In a complete reversal of affection, I was thankful for my placid Fawn, who seemed unperturbed by our sudden isolation and continued her gentle amble towards the cows, knowing exactly what was expected of her.

Fawn and I picked our way gingerly down the gully. The last cow was just within sight. I urged Fawn into an uncomfortable trot to catch up – I knew that even if no-one came looking for me, they would come looking for the cows; those cows were my link to civilisation and I was not going to lose them. I rounded a bend and sighed with relief to find Jack and Rick sitting on their horses, yarning, with a mob of cows and calves grazing nearby.

Jack had been waiting for us. I couldn't fathom how he knew to be there and that the cows would run onto him. A qualification in outback intuition must go with the territory. Those guys could pinpoint their location and that of each other with the accuracy of satellite navigation, using such ambiguous descriptors as 'tree', 'hill', 'grass', 'gully' and 'camp' (which I discovered with disappointment meant a cluster of trees, not someone boiling a billy for a welcome cup of tea). I tried to work out how each gully, ridge, or camp differed from the next – they all looked the bloody same to me.

'Here she is,' Rick announced, already poking the mob off. We walked the cattle a few kilometres before meeting up with the others, who brought their cows into the main mob.

I rode alongside Jack and my mind filled with new questions. But my Q & A session was quickly shut down after some pointed advice from Jack. 'Alice, you've got two ears, two eyes and one mouth. You'll get on better if you use them in that order.' His advice hit its mark and dampened my effervescence. My constant chatter and questions were replaced by quiet (or quieter) observation, to, I suspect, the relief of everyone but me.

Back at the yards the cows and calves were left to rest before drafting and branding after lunch. I unsaddled Fawn and hung up my bridle next to Rick's. He pulled it back down, showing me how to do it without twisting the leather reins and so the reins hung in even lengths.

'Now you try,' he said, handing them back to me to practise. Three attempts later and I'd mastered the art of hanging up a bridle the correct way – the only way!

After lunch, sensing that I was determined to be useful – in a jackaroo kind of way, not a peeling potatoes kind of way – Rick gave me a job in the yards bringing up the calves. It was not long before my ineptitude shone. My gentle coaxing and secret belief that I could talk to animals telepathically proved vastly inadequate.

Why won't they go in there? It is so goddamn *obvious. It's a gateway: go in, you little mongrels! Why is it so bloody hard?*

I got behind them and pushed, opting to use brawn instead of brains.

Argh, the dust.

A calf knocked me over. Another calf kicked me in the thigh.

Christ, how can such a little thing have such a good kick? I just wanted to sit down and hold my leg. There may have been the hint of a tear. I was completely out of my depth. *Maybe I should just go back to the hut and peel potatoes?*

In desperation I looked up and caught Rick's eye as he paused between branding to watch me over the mob of cattle, through the yard rails and the clouds of dust. A huge smile and a swift wink came hurtling towards me – the calves were forgotten, the orchestra of bellows was eclipsed and the dust cleared as my stomach somersaulted. I held my hands up in despair but smiled back and, renewed, I stepped towards the mob again.

'Need a hand?' he called out, launching effortlessly over the two-metre-high fences. With an assertive 'Tch, tch' and some fancy arm manoeuvres, the calves filed effortlessly into the race. Rick stayed to give me some pointers and the calves loaded up the race like they knew all along what was expected of them and had just been messing with me.

'Great job. Do you want to do some branding later?'

'Um, I guess. Yes ... You sure?'

'Yup. I'll call you up when we're ready for you.'

After the stud cattle were completed and the bulk of the commercial steers and heifers were branded, Rick signalled for me to join him up at the branding furnace. Self-consciously I walked past the men, who'd stopped to swig thirstily from their water bottles, and stood beside the sweltering furnace.

'The brand must be at right angles to the hide,' Rick instructed. 'The pressure needs to be firm yet not too hard. Once you've put the brand on, count for three seconds. The hide needs to be golden when it's done, but not too burnt.' The demonstration calf was released and another brought up.

I tried not to drop the brand, but it was hot and heavy and I needed to hold it further down the shaft to get control. It burnt my hands. I could see how Rick's layer of callouses would have been handy at this point. Rick poured some cold water over the arm of the brand. 'You need a solid grip for a good brand. That'll help.'

The smell of singed hair filled my nostrils. The shiny coat of the calf was like wet glass, the brand slipped, sliding down the rump. I'd fudged it. I was mortified. A permanent screw-up for all to see for the life of the animal.

'It takes a bit to get the feel of it' he encouraged. 'The next one will be easier.'

The next calf bellowed just as I'd placed the brand on the hide, squidging it around in three different directions. *Christ, it's worse than the first one.* I wished he'd never offered, and I wished I'd never accepted. I couldn't believe Grahame wasn't intervening to stop this mutilation of his precious hides.

'If a calf bellows, pull the iron off and as soon as it's quiet, get it back on as quickly as possible – before the next bellow.'

'You want me to do another one?'

'If you're going to get the hang of it, you'll have to.'

After a few more botched attempts – each one getting slightly better as I developed a feel for the pressure, the angle and the timing – I finally left a neat, aligned, golden imprint of the red-hot symbols on the hide. Jubilantly I watched the last calf freed from the cradle skip back to its mother, sporting the fresh neat brand that I, Alice McKiggan from Brighton, city of Melbourne, had done.

The next day my puffy chest was deflated when I was again told to stay behind. The real cowboys, including Rick's thirteen-year-old sister, would be mustering a large and treacherous paddock where the cattle rush down a long, steep gorge towards the yards. It was rough going for cattle and horses, requiring whip-cracking expertise, courage on horseback, and knowledge of the land and cattle behaviour. All hands were needed, except those who required their own nursemaid. This left me relegated to domestic duties and quiet time for contemplation.

Chagrined by my demotion, I embarked on a long walk into the hills. I followed a cattle pad that wove its way up the side of a hill and soon forgot my wounded ego, marvelling at the variety of grasses and the twisting legumes weaving their intricate tendrils up the long stalks of dried grass, delicate mauve flowers that resembled a violet with pointed petals, and tiny yellow paper daisies. I gathered a bunch of large white lilies to brighten up the table at the slab hut.

A comfortable log offered a judicious vantage point from which to watch the final stage of the muster unfold while staying well out of sight to avoid startling the cattle, so I sat down to wait. An hour passed with no change. The bellowing of the cattle that had at first grown and consolidated was now stagnant in the distance. Finally a lone rider appeared at the top of the gorge, trotting down as carefully and as quickly as possible, urging the horse into a gallop at the bottom of the steep gorge along the flat slopes beneath me. I recognised Sally but didn't call out for fear of distracting her or spooking her horse – I'd learnt my lesson.

Another hour passed before the mooing moved towards me and the cattle came into view, staggering their way down the mountain. I counted the stockmen. There were two fewer than had started the muster – Sally accounted for one, I wondered what had happened to the other one.

After the cattle and stockmen had passed I returned to the hut and was greeted with exclamations of relief. The camp was astir with news of an accident and the missing city chick. A breakaway calf had bolted at the top of the gully and Rick had galloped after it. Unable to escape its pursuer the calf swerved back to its mother and the horse turned sharply in unison, slipping on a bare patch of ground and landing on top of Rick.

Rick had already been taken to the nearest hospital, so I was driven off to see him, complete with my handpicked wildflowers. Rick was aghast. 'Storm lilies? They're bloody weeds!' But my presence, my weeds and my unfamiliar ways cheered him up while we waited for the X-ray results. His leg was broken in two places and he was moved to Brisbane for orthopaedic surgery.

Rick was on a first-name basis with the surgeon, having recovered there from a horse accident while working on the Barkly Tableland the previous year. In that accident he nearly lost the use of his right arm. A steel plate and ten screws held his upper arm together and after nine months of therapy he got his hand functioning again. This time his ankle was pinned and a plate put in his leg, but his plans to go to the Kimberleys were shattered.

I stayed in Brisbane, visited him daily and returned with him for our last week together at Rosevale. Before leaving, at Rick's insistence that I needed some improvement in the practical life skills department, I sat for my learner driver's permit and passed, taking home a 'half-handy' memento to wrap up my gap year.

As good as my gap year had been, I'd been living Rick's life, and I had to live my own. I needed to become my own person, not lose myself in another. My path was clear. I booked a flight back to Melbourne. We'd said we'd write and keep in touch. You never know with these holiday flings. I wondered how long we would keep up the correspondence. But one thing I did know: I would never forget Rick and the world he'd shown me.

Eleven

At Melbourne airport my practical light cotton shirt and pants seemed out of place among the spectrum of styles around me: suits, bohemians, goths, punks, Collins Street fashionistas. I felt foreign in my homeland, and was eager to get back into my long-forgotten vintage wardrobe and be absorbed into this vibrant mosaic of a city.

I soaked in the familiarity of my home, wandering along the red-brick path that wove its way down the side of the house into a small lawn and pergola-covered courtyard. The crabapple tree was laden with tiny crimson fruit. The elegant Edwardian cottage was the first architectural love of my life, a place of solace for me and a second home for many of my friends. It was the home I had known for most of my life.

There had been another; a Californian bungalow, a couple of blocks from Brighton Beach – the perfect nest in which to raise a family. Soothing memories still tantalise with unfulfilled promises: collecting and sifting sand for our sandpit with Dad at the local beach; reading *Wind in the Willows* on Dad's lap in his throne-like red velour chair by the fireplace; my yellow daisy blinds.

To outsiders, my parents' marriage would've looked like it had the makings of a successful union. Dad had a promising career as a mathematician; Mum worked as a secretary. My brother was born in 1969 and I, two and a half years later. They had progressed from an inner-city flat to the 1920s three-bedroom brick home with a big backyard. Silver birches were planted, the walls were papered and the sand pit was built – we were the image of the perfect 1970s family.

I'm not sure when the trouble began. During the day, there were no outward signs of the nightly tirades; Doug and I would go off to school with neatly brushed hair and a healthy lunch. Until one night our family mess spilled out onto the footpath for all to see. Doug and I were woken up, bustled into our dressing gowns and bundled out onto the front porch.

'Mum's leaving. Do you want to stay here or go with Mum?'

I was four and a half and Doug was seven, but we knew the implications. Whatever was about to come out of our mouths would forever betray one parent. It was a 'lose–lose' situation. I just wanted to crawl back into my warm bed and stay in my home, with my yellow daisy blinds, and Dad's night-time stories. But Mummy was our touchstone, our caregiver and nurturer; it had to be her.

I wonder if part of him never forgave me. Was some of his anger towards Mum bequeathed to me that night as I stood on that doorstep clutching Mandy, my faithful teddy, and my precious blanket, and chose my path? Was my mutinous decision the first chink in our tenuous father–daughter relationship?

We set out into the dark, empty streets. It was a mild summer night. We were heading to a friend's house in the next suburb, about ten kilometres away – an ambitious walk with two young children and their hurriedly gathered necessities. Luckily a sedan pulled over and opened its door somewhere down the road and we hitched a ride to a friend's house, where we made a makeshift camp on their lounge room floor for a few weeks before moving into rental accommodation. It was summer 1977.

Three years later Mum found a suitable house for sale. 'Suitable' meant it was in our school zone, so we didn't have to change schools, and it was in our price range – extremely cheap. I saw a dilapidated shack; Mum saw our home and our future.

Over the next twenty years, with hard work, love, ingenuity and scrounging discards from local building sites and garage sales, the derelict was transformed into the Edwardian diamond. The original return verandah was opened up and French doors installed, the orange bedroom was painted a soft shade of olive with cream architrave, the two-metre-high grass was mown and dug out for gently curved garden beds, winding paths were laid with hundred-year-old handmade bricks and bluestone liberated from demolition sites and scrubbed clean of cement. The eighty-year-old magnolia was nurtured, a new batch of cut-leaf silver birches was planted and the garden grew outside as the walls and skirting boards were stripped inside. Furniture was scrounged and lovingly restored. Fireplaces were sanded back and breathed warmth and new life into every room. Mum was the gardener, fix-it man, wood chopper, cook, cleaner and wage earner. From an early age I knew how to pull my weight – and that husbands and fathers were surplus to requirements and largely just a source of tension.

I loved my home. It had always been my refuge and my beacon. Until now. Something was different. Something had changed; I just couldn't put my finger on it. The bricks and mortar were relatively unchanged – the cracks in the lath-and plaster-walls that had opened a few millimetres more as the house breathed on her stumps had already been hidden with another layer of plaster and paint. The natural world had blossomed and now bore the last of the season's fruit, branches stretched higher into the sky and the girth of trunks were indiscernibly wider. Continents had moved beneath us while we went about our lives on a seemingly stationary earth.

Something had short-circuited my wiring; flicked a switch. I put on my old clothes and looked much like my old self, but they just didn't sit right any more. Surrounded again by friends, family and familiar things, I felt alone and adrift. Like many expatriates I found myself in that dilemma betwixt two countries. Not of one, but no longer of the other. Wanting both.

Just in time for the commencement of first semester, I was accepted to study science, a prerequisite for veterinary science and, I figured, a good all-round first step while I worked out the finer details of my career direction and life purpose. But as grateful as I was to get a place, I found it hard to settle back into the routine of study and living at home and had to drag myself to lectures each day.

My letters to Rick groaned of the monotonous hours of study, the endless days sitting in massive lecture theatres, and the balancing of waitressing work and cleaning jobs, while I jealously coveted his 'office' in the saddle, riding the vast spaces he called a workplace.

His regular missives gave me hope that he felt we were more than 'mates with benefits'. The frequency of his letters was my salve, even if the lines lacked passion.

Dear Miss Alice,
We've been as busy as bricklayers in Baghdad this last week,
moving cattle and trying to get all our crops in. I got a third
place in the bullock ride, which paid for my nominations, but
I got thrown over the head of my saddle bronc – anyway I
learnt a lot out of it.

My translation:

My darling,
I am devoted to you and my heart beats with longing as I
yearn to be by your side ...

The occasional letter carried with it enough genuine sentiment to keep my hopes up that we would share another chapter, one day. I hoped so, because this new life of celibacy didn't appeal to me. There were boys everywhere, but I didn't see them; I couldn't shake the country and the cowboy out of my system.

As if physics wasn't enough of a shock to the system, to my horror I found I was pining for country music and a bit of ding-ding-a-ling fiddle. Incognito, I scoured music racks for Dan Seals and James Blundell like a sex addict looking for illicit porn. No self-respecting Melbourne music store stocked this genre and I found myself ordering C&W 'under the counter'. I was overjoyed when my orders came through, scurrying them away to the quiet of my bedroom. Dan Seals transported me back to the highways of central Queensland stretching into the distance, leading us to a rodeo somewhere.

The walls and the city noises closed in on me but this music brought Rick's world nearer. I needed to hang on to that world, hang on to him – to remind myself it wasn't a dream, it was real; he was real. I was stunned by the ache in my heart and the longing I felt for this man I'd spent such a short time with.

I'm good at maths. Equations should always balance and I knew this one didn't add up: the time we'd spent together relative to the feelings. The multiple distractions of work, study and reuniting with gorgeous friends who I had missed desperately were insufficient to block him out. My friends humoured me, listening for hours as I described Rick and his cowboy ways. They laughed and nodded generously as I repeated myself, not wanting to miss a detail that might help them comprehend the new world I'd discovered, its tribe and tribal culture.

I'd expected that the city would seduce me back into her fold: the dance clubs, eccentric inhabitants, dazzling lights, theatres, restaurants. But for me, her dazzle had faded. Melbourne was suffocating me. I needed to escape the 8 a.m. traffic jams, the smog and the cold, oppressive weather.

Dear Mr Rick,

Today I had a go assisting an artificial cow to give birth. They used a dead baby calf. After making sure the calf was in the correct foetal position, I placed chains around its legs and pulled it out – good stuff!

I spoke to a guy about transferring to uni in Queensland. He said it's possible and also suggested I consider agricultural science, majoring in animals. It's a four-year degree and sounds pretty full on, but I'm interested, so will find out some more.

With his brother David away at uni and Pete and Sal at boarding school, Rick postponed his trip to the Kimberleys after his leg recovered and remained at Rosevale to help as the drought took hold. He would take up the position the following year, in 1992. I applied for the transfer to study agricultural science at the University of Queensland, Brisbane campus, for that same year.

As well as our letters, Rick and I also talked on the phone every week. The phone calls were short, with little in the way of oral seduction, and usually terminated with Rick's familiar 'Yeah ... so ... that's your news' – my cue to hang up. I told myself he was a man of few words and that it was okay. Most of the time, it was. But I was desperate to see Rick again and made plans to visit him in the mid-year holidays. My high-school partner in crime, Sophie, suggested we drive to Queensland in her black 1974 Holden ute, Thelma and Louise style.

Sophie was the person who pulled me through the torrid years of high school and helped me survive the bitching and bullying. Having lived two blocks apart for most of our lives, Sophie and I had walked a thin tightrope since we were fifteen, rockin' to AC/DC and chillin' with Billy Bragg, playing snooker and swimming in her pool, blending rocket fuel and bending weekend curfews. My first and only attempt at using marijuana with Sophie left me green and nauseous and was the one point where we diverged. Drugs scared me but beckoned her.

She offered to take me up to Rosevale, agreeing to stay for a few days before visiting another friend. I was to fly back to Melbourne a fortnight later to start the second semester. Truly, I didn't consider that Sophie's toned down punk–goth style might make a stir at Rosevale. It wasn't until I caught a glimpse of the Greenups' raised eyebrows that I looked at Sophie anew. I guess she did look a tad ferocious, with her ebony dreadlocks and heavy black eye make-up. But Sophie was sweet as buttermilk, a longstanding vegetarian, a slip of a girl with the singing voice of an angel and an artistic edge. Thankfully Peggy quickly saw through Sophie's tough-girl facade and soon they were exchanging carrot soup recipes. A few days later Sophie and I hugged goodbye as she headed south on her own adventure. Sadly, our paths were never to reunite.

I stayed another week, working as Rick's shadow: putting out molasses, weaning calves, feeding hay. Before I reached Rosevale I had wondered if we would feel the same attraction when we reunited. I had even hoped the spark would be gone – it would be so much easier if we had closure. But our feelings were undiminished. The distance and time apart dissolved.

A second rite of passage was completed as I submitted to Peggy's herbal remedy for colds, registering too late why Pete and Sal had warned me not to mention a sore throat around their mother, as the concoction of chilli, ginger and other spices ripped the lining off my tonsils to the chorus of 'Oh my God, she drank it!'

Another (more useful) rite of passage was initiated by Rick. Determined to see his student driver graduate he took me into the local police station, where I sat for and got my probationary licence – to the astonishment of all who'd had the 'pleasure' of driving with me in the preceding six months.

Then I had to return to Melbourne and we were back to phone calls and letters …

Dear Miss McKiggan,

The drought is really biting now. Things are pretty hectic here trying to find enough feed for these cattle. But I am planning to come down in September after the bull sale. It will be good to see my wild girl's waddy ol' Melbourne town. Hopefully it will have rained by then. I'll write more tomorrow, gotta go to a rodeo now. See ya later.

... I'm back from the rodeo in one piece. I rode my bullock but didn't get a place. My bull spat me out the back – too strong. I was just off the points to get into the final in the saddle bronc.

Love, Rick

I jotted down words at every opportunity, usually waiting for a lecture to begin, sitting in the cafeteria eating hot chips and drinking hot chocolate to ward off the penetrating cold.

Dear Mr Rick,

It's 4.30 on Monday afternoon, waiting for dance rehearsal, trying to study. I've got a physics book and a piece of cheesecake sitting in front of me and I don't really want either ... I can't stop thinking of you and can't wait to show you my town.

All my love, Alice

On the last Saturday in September 1991, nearly a year after we'd first met, I drove to Melbourne airport in my newly acquired '69 VW Beetle to collect my cowboy for one whole week together. He'd taught me about his world, now I had seven days to repay the favour. Again I wondered if the magic would still be there. My heart pounded with nerves. The sight of his short black hair, broad smile and bowed legs made my stomach somersault with forgotten familiarity.

Spotting me in the throng, his walk became a trot until our faces were inches apart. He smelt so good. I feared my back would break as he wrapped his arms around me, squeezing the breath from my body, kissing me hard and ravenously. For a week, at least, there would be no more wondering.

Holding hands, we wove our way back to the car, my mind reviewing the signature traits I'd forgotten: his rough, calloused palms and the fast bow-legged trot that had us overtaking the ambling swarm of suits – even when he had nowhere particular to be. With Rick in my hometown, I felt like a character who'd been given a backstory, substance and context. I had a home, a city and a life. I was no longer a wandering tumbleweed – I had roots.

There were so many reasons to love Melbourne: the buildings, the food, the people. Like a six year old at her own birthday party, I was impatient to show my guest everything. Under my careful tuition he was going to taste every delicious aspect we could cram in. My town and I, together we would seduce him.

I took him home through the city, past Swanson and Flinders streets – a chance to show off his student's driving prowess with my right-hand hook turns, a traffic anomaly specific to Melbourne that allows for the trams, while pointing out the heritage architecture. We buzzed past Albert Park Lake, then down the Esplanade, with the choppy seas of Port Phillip Bay on our right looking very unwelcoming in its bleak greyness, despite it now being early spring.

'That's your beach?'

'That's Port Phillip Bay.'

'Where are the waves?'

'There are none.'

'What do you surf on?'

'We don't surf here. We windsurf.'

He gaped at the wetsuit-clad windsurfers, braced against the freezing gale, darting back and forth along the shoreline.

My program of enticement centred on showing Rick the two things that I'd missed most about Melbourne while I was away; the two things that rivalled his outback world – food and friends. Each day was a gastronomic excursion. We did Vietnamese in Victoria Street, Richmond; Italian on Lygon Street, Carlton; Lebanese in Hampton; hot jam doughnuts and seafood at Queen Victoria Market; and the requisite patisseries on Acland Street, St Kilda.

I watched him, every move and every gesture. I wondered if he could be a part of my world – even for a few years while I studied; surely he could see all that Melbourne had to offer? His eyes simmered lustfully at the selection of pastries and tantalising petits fours, glazed fruit tarts competing with chocolate profiteroles and delectable, begging-for-consumption incy-wincy lemon meringues. That is, until his stare was drawn away from the shop window and onto the footpath.

'Geez, did you see that? They're holding hands!'

'Yeah, so?'

'So? They're blokes!'

'It's not against the law.'

'I'm tellin' you, Alice, this is one wild town.'

'You just haven't seen them in Queensland because the government only decriminalised homosexuality last year. But I promise you, there are as many in your town as there are in my "waddy" town.'

We got our pastry treats and went for a walk down to the Esplanade to indulge his rubbernecking: 'Bloody hell, look what he's wearing!'

And along the pier: 'Did you see where she was pierced?'

… and up Fitzroy Street: 'Are they all prostitutes?'

And to my favourite nightclub, Three Faces, the Melbourne equivalent of 'Les Girls': 'Thanks for that, Alice. Not really my scene. But boy, can those guys can dance!'

During the days and nights we jammed in catch-ups with my friends as they clamoured to meet him. One friend who dressed like he'd stepped out of a *Vogue* fashion shoot was confused by the match, his edgy sense of style challenged by this confident outlier from the north: 'He's not the sort of bloke I pictured you with, Alice – I expected someone a little more tie-dyed and sporting a set of dreadlocks.'

I looked at Rick anew. I'd forgotten how his Wranglers, tucked-in shirts and cropped, neat, helmet-head hair would look in Melbourne. I offered to take him shopping for clothes.

'Why?'

'Because all you have is Wranglers.'

'What else do you need?'

'Well, going-out pants for starters.'

'I have going-out pants. They're my *good* Wranglers!'

Not even premium-grade flirting could get him to walk into a menswear shop. He smiled and laughed at my protestations, but he wasn't going to be cajoled or convinced that Melbourne fashion had anything he wanted or needed.

'I look normal, Alice – it's everyone else in this town who's wearing waddy clothes.'

I resigned myself to his stubborn streak, turning a blind eye to clothes that screamed 'cowboy', and instead turned my attention to our time, which was hurtling by.

Like Melbourne's fleeting summers, all too soon it was over – and once again we'd failed to exhaust the fascination with each other. It would have been simpler if the affair had lost its lustre – our worlds bore no resemblance to each other; there was no overlap, no scope for intersection.

As I drove him to the airport, I was beginning to realise that it was as if he was married and I was the mistress, and no matter how we tried, my city and I, we couldn't seduce him away from his true love. So there we were: another goodbye, another wrench.

* * *

After he'd left, I stewed on the words Mum and Dad had proffered each in their turn: 'He's a nice lad – a very nice lad – but is he really your type? He hasn't gone to uni: what would you talk about? A country life couldn't give you enough stimulation – you'd be bored once the novelty wore off. You love the theatre, restaurants – you'd miss all that. And your friends: could you live without them? And what would you do in the country? I doubt he would – or could – move to the city for you. It's best you face this now before the two of you hurt each other down the track.'

The questions had to be asked: could such an incongruous match ever work? Were we wasting each other's time, subjecting ourselves to needless pain and loneliness?

The genie sensed the doubt and fear wafting through my mind and launched a full-scale assault that lasted months, toying with my mind, showing me alternatives – and convincing me that Rick was getting *his* fair share of alternatives. The fortnightly letters and weekly phone calls continued, but rather than being a salve, their unsentimental brevity sliced away my confidence. The distance separating us began to feel vast and unbridgeable. And then one particular letter arrived to override all the others: salvation from the genie's torment, an invitation to spend two weeks of my summer holidays at Rosevale. So I rammed the genie, that negative bitch, back into her bottle.

With the first year of university behind me, exams long forgotten, and only a trifling twenty-four hours before our reunion, I twinkled through Christmas Day – a revolving door of friends and family joining our festivities. Mum gave me an Akubra hat. All present concurred: I looked rather cool in it; authentic – quite the jillaroo. My new brown riding boots were packed, along with some long-sleeved cotton shirts and jeans I'd bought at an op shop. This time I was going to blend in.

As the plane soared over the quilted interior of New South Wales, my mind swirled in opposing currents, and the genie re-emerged for a final skirmish. I could see why she was worried. I was torn between two worlds – Rick and his damned land had changed me forever.

Twelve

Another airport, another embrace.

His eyes and arms reassured me in ways that his letters never could, forcing a ceasefire in the battle that waged on between my head and my heart.

Four hours later and the horses were galloping alongside the ute as it sped down the long gravel driveway at Rosevale, chestnut blurs kicking in the air as they spun and took off in another direction. Rick pointed out a large gelding thundering past.

'That's Ambassador. You'll be riding him tomorrow.' My heart raced and I gulped – finally a grown-up big horse. *Oh my God, what have I wished for?*

At the crack of dawn I dressed and headed down to the kitchen, ready for a batch of Grahame's well-done rissoles. Sally was delighted to have accomplices to make fun of Peggy's latest health fad, a lump of slime growing in a jar of water on the bench – kombucha tea, she told me – and I laughed, falling easily back into the groove as Rick and his siblings got on their mum's case. It was hard to believe a year had passed since Rick first showed me how to brand, but here we were at the start of 1992 with a new crop of calves to mark. I was decked out in my cowboy get-up, sun-smart and ready to get dirty.

Rick took one look at me and laughed. 'What's that you're wearing?'

'My hat.'

'You look like a stock agent with that brim. I'll put a bash into it tonight.'

I was perplexed. It was a brand-new Akubra hat and he wanted to bash it? 'What's wrong with it?'

'Alice, you might as well put a neon sign on your head flashing BEWARE: CITY SLICKER.'

So that evening after dinner yet another tutorial began: Jackaroo Hat Wearing 101. Now, what I'm about to relate is top-grade insider knowledge; a kind of secret brotherhood handshake – knowledge that even the most competent TV and movie wardrobe stylists are apparently not privy to.

'Where's that hat of yours?'

I grabbed my hat and followed Rick into the kitchen where a kettle steamed on the stove. Holding my hat over the steam, he shaped first the crown and then the brim, transforming my hat as the sides were lowered and the crown lifted. Concentrating intently, he explained the art while he worked.

'Alice, your hat's your signature in the bush. It's what sets you apart from other cowboys. Australian cowboys wear different hats and styles from American cowboys; Queenslanders have different hats from Victorians and stock agents have different hats from ringers. And if you want to rile Mum, you wear a black hat.'

My heinous crime was explained. The hat comes in a box and the city person takes the hat out of the box and plonks it on his or her head. Proudly teaming it with denim jeans and checked shirt, they think their camouflage is complete. But they couldn't be more wrong: a 'box bash' is an instant giveaway. According to Rick, the genuine article takes his new hat out of the box and shapes it to give it his own characteristic bash. Country people can recognise one another from the bash of their hats – it's so distinctive the wearer can be easily identified, even in the dark or from behind, and in many cases a familial relationship can even be discerned.

'That's the best I can do with this hat. You'll still look like a stock agent, but at least you'll look like a half-handy one.'

Thanking him, I grabbed my hat by the brim, forgetting my lessons from our first date, tugging down at the front and sides. Rick's face twisted as if I'd kneed him in the balls.

'Jesus, Alice, don't hold it like that! You hold it like this, by the crown. And don't pull on the brim. This is how you put on a hat.' He demonstrated. 'And when you put it down anywhere, put it upside down or you'll ruin the bash.'

I reassured myself that at least the horse wouldn't care what I looked like. But that fanciful notion was to last about as long as my confidence in my outfit.

I was to learn that the clothes neither maketh the tribe member nor the rider. Ambassador was not fooled by my boots and jeans and was unused to having a sloppy rider who was loose in the saddle, so my gig was soon up. Fed up with his amateur jockey he bucked as we climbed a steep creek bank. Rick spotted me on the ground as I grappled with the reins, hopping awkwardly, trying to get my leg into the stirrup on the steep bank.

'What happened?'

'He bucked me off.'

'He doesn't buck.'

'Yes he does! He just did!'

'Something must have startled him.'

'Oh.' Reassured, I got back on.

Until it happened again.

And again.

And again.

And again.

'Christ, Alice, what've you done to that horse?'

I'd set a record: being bucked off five times in one muster. Each fall leaving a legacy of aching pain.

'I'll find you another horse tomorrow.'

I held back the tears as my romantic notions of this way of life wore away, rather like the inside of my knees and calves. That night as I bandaged my knees I vowed to be brave.

The next morning Rick implemented Plan B, giving me Miss Fox to ride – a large chestnut mare with kind eyes and, I hoped, the temperament to match. The next day I actually made it back to the yards in one piece. Equally buoyed, Rick started taking me on more challenging routes through the paddocks and was quick to up the ante, leading me down a death-defying cliff (okay, there may be a hint of writer's licence here) that was a shortcut to some cows on the other side of the gorge.

'You'll be right – just poke down,' he encouraged me.

'If it's all right with you, I'll walk down.'

I got off Miss Fox and started to lead her down the sixty-degree incline on a teeny cattle pad towards a creek below.

'Whatever turns you on, Alice, but I'm telling you it's easier to ride her down,' he called back over his shoulder. His mare, Warina, was already across the creek and thrusting herself up the other side. At my pace, it would be a quarter of an hour before I reached him, but doggedly I continued. The mare had to work twice as hard to avoid stepping on my feet as well as keeping track of her own, as she slipped and tripped down the mountain slope. Having finally reached the bottom I picked my way over the rocks in the trickling creek, trying to keep my boots dry. Rick watched our tedious progress with poorly disguised impatience.

'See? And no-one got hurt,' I proclaimed as we topped the gully's bank.

'Only because Miss Fox turned herself inside out to avoid landing on you.'

I had to admit it – even I could see we wouldn't get a lot of mustering done at this rate. I resolved to ride down the next gorge …

'The safest way to go down is to point the horse forward, straight down the hill.'

'We'll die!'

'You'll be right. She won't fall no matter how steep it is. She'll just slide down on her backside.'

I opted to try another safety technique, an Alice initiative, zigzagging along the bank to lessen the gradient.

'That will kill you!' Rick called out. 'She'll roll on you for sure.'

Miss Fox struggled with her left legs up the hill and the right pair down the hill. I felt her slipping, fighting to keep her weight upright. I got his point, but it was too late – to say I was worried was an understatement: there was no way it was not going to hurt when 600 kilos of horse rolled on me. I prayed she could get us out of the trouble I'd so effectively got us into.

'Give 'er her head!' Rick yelled from the base of the gully, the panic in his voice bouncing off the gorge walls.

There was just one way left to do it: Rick's way.

'Just lean back, give her plenty of rein and she'll do the rest.'

I let the reins loosen and allowed the mare to take over. She righted herself, headed straight down the hill and within seconds had nimbly navigated down the gully to the other waiting horse.

'Good job, Alice.'

I didn't know who was more relieved – me, Rick, or the horse.

Rick was my constant teacher: how to close a gate safely; where to stand to avoid being kicked; how not to get your arm smashed when vaccinating in the crush; how to be invisible behind fence posts; and how to move deftly to dodge cattle or direct them into a yard. With daily lessons and on-the-job experience, my confidence and competence grew, until I could yard up a fresh mob of cows on my own. But no matter how good the teacher, you can't skip the initiation process. You have to learn the lessons for yourself one buck, one blister and one faceful of dirt at a time. Rick's 'Don't worry, she's bluffing' reverberated in my head as a cow snorted at me while heading for the gate, then trotted straight over the top of me, knocking me flat to the ground. That day I began to make up some of my own lessons. The first being: until I can tell a bluffing cow from a bloody serious one, I would give the cow the benefit of the doubt.

How I loved it all. How we wished it could continue. We ignored the fact that this wasn't a relationship; it wasn't even a whiff of one. We took it one day at a time, trying not to guess the next step. But all too soon I'd be back at university and Rick would be off to take up the position he'd postponed on Moola Bulla Station in the Kimberleys.

A semi reprieve came when I was offered a place to study agricultural science at the University of Queensland's Brisbane campus. With my relocation to Brisbane, I would be a mere four-hour drive from Rosevale. Rick and I could scratch a few weekends together before his imminent departure.

I returned to Melbourne to pack up my life and three weeks later I was cramming the boot of my Beetle with the essentials to start my life in Queensland: one frypan, one egg cup, one plate, one bowl, one portable stereo, one large cushion, a few clothes and numerous textbooks. My bike (essential, as fuel and parking fees would be luxuries out of my reach) was strapped on the roof rack – ropes extending in every direction with the truckies' hitches that Rick had taught me. I heard Jeremy's voice in my head, proudly sizing up my load: 'It's like tying a cat's arse up with a snig chain. It ain't pretty. But it's strong.'

With my load securely attached and barely a backward glance I drove the 2000 kilometres to Queensland. I didn't give any thought to how it was going to come together: the move, making ends meet for the next four years on student rations, finding accommodation, finding work, the cowboy. They'd sort themselves out. It was 1992 and I was nineteen and invincible.

Thirteen

Within a week of reaching Brisbane I'd rented a grubby, dilapidated studio unit for $70 a week in a rough inner-city suburb – a bike and ferry ride away from the university. It had a tiny kitchen and bathroom and was simply furnished with a red laminate table, two chairs and a 1950s refrigerator. But it did have polished floors and a balcony with large glass doors opening onto a private back garden. An ancient macadamia tree hung over the balcony. To someone else it might have screamed of poverty, but to me it sang of freedom. I scrubbed it from top to bottom and moved into 'the Tree House', as I dubbed it, with my cushion, egg cup, saucepan and frypan. I was home.

As a housewarming present Rick gave me a vintage Green River butchering knife he'd picked up at a second-hand store, having put new rivets into the handle and sharpened it before presenting it to me.

'These old knives, they're beauties,' he mused, gliding it along his forearm, slicing the wiry black hairs off at their roots. 'Now you have a decent knife I can use when I come and visit.' Lovingly he pointed out its other features while I feigned interest.

'See how balanced it is? The handle fits well in your hand. Great steel, this. It'll hold its edge for a long time. And plenty left on it, too.'

Uninspired, I just nodded. *Get a grip; it's just a knife.*

'You know, we'll have to stay together now, 'cos one day I want this knife back. It's a bloody good knife.'

It's a wonderful knife!

I found two jobs within an easy bike ride, one waitressing and the other as a barmaid. The local op shops completed my range of homewares, providing a second plate and bowl, two aluminium saucepans and a fold-out bed/couch. I indulged one step further, purchasing two jars of jam which would provide excellent glasses once the contents had been eaten.

Just as I was settling in, Rick got the call he'd been waiting for to say the Northern Territory highways had opened after the wet season and he could leave any time. As well versed as we were in the art of long-distance love, the year ahead would inflict a new strain on our scant communications. Rick had told me what to expect. He would be out in a stock camp, camping in his swag for weeks at a time and only coming into the station for supplies every four to six weeks. At least there was a weekly mail and supplies run, although letters would take up to three weeks to arrive. Our weekly phone calls would stop altogether.

I put on a brave face for our last weekend together, which coincided with Rick's twenty-first birthday. We savoured each moment, pretending that it was not our last time together for the rest of the year. But despite our plucky nonchalance our pillow talk was strained, in anticipation of the long separation. It was pointless starting any long-winded meaningful conversations.

This was the mother of all goodbyes. I felt leaden as I watched him put his bag in the back of the ute the next morning, helping to strap down the tonneau cover, dawdling over each elastic hook, simulating efficiency.

We kissed. We hugged. Another kiss, another hug, trying to fill the void that was opening up inside us, but they made it worse, each one more inadequate, falling short of what was needed and craved.

'Just get going,' I said at last.

My first letter postmarked Halls Creek, Western Australia, arrived two weeks later. Rick sounded as happy as a pig in mud – in his element working gruelling hours in primitive conditions and even finding some rodeos to ride in on the occasional weekend off.

Three weeks later another batch of letters arrived, describing the waddy mates he'd made; the paddocks that had no fences, just cliffs to mark their boundaries; and the mustering of mobs of cattle from single paddocks in numbers that eclipsed his family's entire herd. With each page I read, something splintered inside me. I was losing him to cowboy utopia.

As the academic year progressed, the impact of my decision to move to Brisbane began to weigh me down. Despite my two casual jobs, money was tight and a constant concern. The other major concern was my grades: working so much, I just wasn't putting enough time into study. I struggled to stay awake in lectures, and turned in rushed and scantily researched assignments. My grades slipped and so did my self-esteem.

I had no phone at the Tree House and didn't own a mobile, so communicating by anything other than letter required a prearranged call at the local phone box. Loneliness crept in. I adopted a grey cat I named Kimberley – Kim for short. Mum came up for Easter, which got me through another five days.

I kept in touch with Rick's family, taking Sally out of boarding school for weekend visits. Peggy invited me to join them at the Gold Coast while they were visiting Peter at his boarding school at Southport. She also dropped in with pot plants grown from cuttings from her own garden, as well as a cream blouse and camel-coloured skirt she'd made. 'I thought the plants might make the place feel more homely and the clothes might come in handy,' she told me kindly.

I visited Rosevale on a couple of occasions, even joining David and Grahame in the yards for some cattle work, where they continued to be patient and generous with their time and knowledge, furthering my education, answering my questions, welcoming me despite the obvious missing link.

Waiting for Rick's return I'd put life on hold, just going through the motions of working and studying. I was so lonely. Lonely in a way that I'd never known before, as if I were no longer a part of a community. The guys I worked with at the pub took me under their wing like brothers and introduced me to Brisbane's nightlife after the pub closed at night. These friendships, however, had none of the depth of those I'd left behind in Melbourne.

Then Andrew started working at the pub and the flirting began. My fading memories of Rick and our lightweight communications were taking their toll on my commitment. I was close to letting it all go, hoping, as each small rectangle arrived with his neat script, that there would be something, anything, inside to fortify me.

Then one day in June a letter arrived that obliterated my last shred of faith, extinguishing what small flame of commitment still glowed. The stockmen were to be given a mid-season break – two weeks holiday in August. I expected he'd fly back to see me, to rekindle the embers. But he wanted to do the rodeo circuit in the Territory instead: *It's a once in a lifetime opportunity, Alice, while I'm up here*, he wrote.

Fuck him, I thought, dropping the letter in the bin. I felt like I'd dropped off his radar. *Why did I promise to wait for a bloke I barely knew? I'm an idiot.*

Then it was the end of June and my twentieth birthday. Flowers arrived from Rick. Carnations. He'd asked his mother to organise them. The card said little; I felt little. It seemed I'd been relegated to 'she's nothing special' status. Why was I staying faithful to a man who would prefer to ride a bull than be with me? It was time I got back in the game, time I felt the intoxicating pulse of life in my body once more. It was my birthday, dammit, and I wasn't going to mope around a second longer. *This girl is going dancing.*

Dusting off the black patent stilettos that had been buried in the bottom of the cupboard, my skin trembled with anticipation as I fished out my good black dress – after all, it was my birthday, why shouldn't I glam it up a bit, I told myself, stroking mascara onto my eyelashes. But I knew what I was up to, I knew where he'd be. He always let me know where I could find him: 'In case you change your mind,' he'd say, as he left the pub where we worked.

I scanned the throbbing nightclub. Over two metres tall, Andrew stood out above the bobbing heads, his black cowlick swept back with sweat from dancing. I stepped on to the dance floor and made a beeline for him, weaving through the bodies. Previously I'd pretended not to notice his strong back and tight arse, muscular from a lifetime of surfing and rugby – now I let myself take it all in, every inch of those long legs and broad back, as he moved to the dance music. I tapped him on the shoulder and he turned. His stunned expression was quickly supplanted by a wicked smile. 'What brings you here?'

'It's my birthday and I want a birthday kiss.'

Wrapping his long arms around me he lifted me up effortlessly, bending his head to meet mine, kissing me with gentle confidence. Blood soared through my veins, awakening forgotten extremities.

'What took you so long?' he whispered into the nape of my neck.

'I really don't know,' I answered truthfully.

The Brisbane River peacefully meandered towards the sea in the early dawn light as we walked home along her banks, shoes in one hand, hotdogs dripping with mustard and onions in the other. I'd crossed the line I'd drawn for myself since meeting Rick eighteen months before and wondered why I hadn't done this before. I felt great.

For the next few months, Andrew and I spent most evenings together. His reckless, larrikin, rugby-boy manner amused me. He was a tonic to my spirit after a long-distance relationship that had been fraught with constraints and reserved emotions and appropriate conduct. He brought me roses for no reason. I felt like the centre of his world.

Andrew wasn't concerned about the ringer in the Kimberleys. 'I'm here and he's not,' he said simply.

I wrote to Rick less often. The fervour was gone, but I would wait until we were face to face to tell him I'd moved on. A letter in late August was the only indication that he sensed things between us were falling apart.

Dear Alice,
Work seems to be hard to get back into after our time off. Everyone is really tired at the moment. I was expecting you to call on Saturday night, but you must have been busy. If you are keen to set a date for the next phone call, you can try on 19 September. Missing you heaps. Please <u>hang on</u> for another two months.
Love, Rick

I wanted to crumple up the letter and throw it away. I should've. But I couldn't. I put it away in the box in my cupboard with the others. Guiltily I called at the arranged time. There was little either of us could say that was of interest to the other. And the real truth, the words that needed to be said but remained unspoken, hung between us.

By late October Andrew was planning for us to spend the Christmas holidays with his family on the north coast of New South Wales. I couldn't commit to going, but I couldn't say why either. I was tiring of Andrew's loose work ethic and the larrikin antics that I now found childish instead of charming. I wanted him to grow up and act like an adult.

With a commitment, however tenuous it had become, lingering between us, I needed to see Rick and cut all ties before I could move on. And the truth was curiosity burnt within me. I wanted to see him, this man whose face and smell were erased memories, yet who held enough power over me that I would promise to wait for him while he played cowboy. How could I know how I felt about this ringer on the other side of Australia until I saw him again in the flesh? Resigned, Andrew gave me the space I needed to sort through my feelings. I didn't understand my own conflicting thoughts and emotions, so how could I expect Andrew to?

The jacarandas were blooming along the river bordering the university. Out west the purple blooms herald the birth of a new crop of calves, but in Brisbane they mean end-of-year exams, and I needed to study. I had more on my mind than botany and biochemistry, however. Rick was back. He'd arrived at Rosevale the previous night and was now on his way to Brisbane.

The biochemistry notes were a blur of Krebs cycles and formulas as I sat at the table ostensibly studying, ears pricked to the note of every passing car. The Tree House shook as someone bounded up the stairs. My hands tingled as I opened the door. A box of fruit he'd picked up at a roadside stall was tucked under Rick's arm. He was taller and more muscular. A hint of anxiousness flickered across his hazel eyes. The quick, unsure peck 'hello' on the lips and an awkward embrace mirrored nothing of the lovers who stood on those steps ten months before. Rick put the box on the bench, grabbing a white peach to munch on while I made us a cup of tea.

'God, I've missed fresh fruit. Do you want some?'

This is never going to work. He brought me bloody fruit – to eat himself! You'd think he'd know it'd take more than a box of

*fruit to make up for a year's separation and choosing bulls over
me. Hasn't he heard of flowers?*

We took our mugs of tea into the lounge room. He looked like
a trespasser sitting in Andrew's chair. We chatted about the things
that didn't fit into letters, and he told me how the other ringers had
asked him for help with spelling in their own letters home.

'But you spell "can't" with an "r"!'

'I know, it's a worry. But I'm telling you, in comparison I was
like a professor.'

It was so good to have a proper shave, he said. Even though the
men would be covered in dirt, sweat and blood, Rick was the only
one who had a bogey at the end of each day and washed his clothes
every week, because with no actual showers out at camp, a bogey
was often a wash in a trough or a water tank. For his crime of
washing daily and brushing his teeth morning and night, the other
ringers made fun of him, calling him the 'flash ringer'.

He got out his photos. 'These two guys out on the station –
they were on the run and had aliases.'

We laughed and a familiar feeling washed through me as I let
go of some of my resentment and hurt and began to relax and enjoy
his presence. The conversation wove towards confessions, and we
shared the significant things that had remained unspoken between
us all year. It was awkward, really awkward – and quite shocking –
as he confessed to having some one-night stands. Stunned that he
had managed to find a girl up there, yet strangely relieved, I told
him about Andrew.

Maybe we should have called it quits at the start of the year
and given each other the freedom to meet other people, rather than
put ourselves through the loneliness and guilt all year. But here we
were, talking and laughing thanks to our naive promises.

We spent the next two days hanging out and catching up. His
effect on me was unsettling. He didn't fit my image of a prospective
suitor. His dating technique was wanting by anyone's standards –

I suspect he approached courting like the Wranglers he wore in Melbourne: without apology; take it or leave it. Rick was not about to dance around to impress anyone – but that intangible energy that drew me in and captivated me was still there. I was reluctant to fall for him again, as there could only be more of the same to come: more distance, more constant craving, more heartache.

It wasn't logical. Logic pleaded for a simpler way. Logic begged for a boyfriend who would be by my side in the evening, a boyfriend whose world and interests resembled mine, a boyfriend who would do things and say things to woo me and make me feel like the centre of his world. But poor ol' logic, outmanoeuvred once again, packed up her bags and left the building.

I lay cradled in his arm, my head resting on his chest.

'You do realise we nearly didn't make it?' I murmured.

'But we did.'

'I hope it was worth it.'

'It was.'

'Even the rodeos?'

'Especially the rodeos.'

Goddamn, I wish he'd just lie to make me feel better!

'But I'm sorry that you weren't a part of it. You should've come over, Alice. You would have loved it.'

'You didn't ask.'

'I didn't think you would've wanted to. Anyway, you needed to do your thing.'

'I didn't think you wanted me; that you thought I'd cramp your style.' I paused for a moment. 'But it would have been nice if you'd asked.'

The truth was that while, yes, I would've liked to have been asked, I was relieved he hadn't. It would have been too tempting to lose myself in his adventure.

After my last exam, I resigned from my jobs and ended the lease on my beloved Tree House. I felt a wrench mixed with relief as I shut the door for the last time and left the memories of Andrew behind. The new year, 1993, would be a clean start.

With my belongings and books in storage and Kim on my lap, the VW Beetle and I returned home to Melbourne for Christmas, promising to be back at Rosevale in time for our third New Year's Eve together. Rick promised to have Miss Fox shod, ready for Benroy.

And so 1992 drew to a close. It had been tougher than we'd anticipated.

Fourteen

While branding at Benroy that summer was as exciting as ever, it was also work, and after a year apart I felt the relationship needed a shot in the arm with some time together to reconnect, refamiliarise and revitalise our feelings. I'd hoped that once I was back at uni in Brisbane to begin my second year of the degree, we would settle into some type of routine and do the things that couples do: travel on weekends; go out to dinner; dance; picnic; lie in bed late on Sundays, eating croissants and reading the paper. But the drought across Queensland and New South Wales raged unrelenting through late summer and into autumn, and the needs of Rosevale had to take precedence. Cattle had been sent away on agistment, but there was still not enough grass for those remaining. Tempers were frayed throughout the countryside.

Rick was sometimes curt on the phone and often distracted and impatient. He cancelled consecutive trips to Brisbane – droughts don't care if it's the Sabbath: water had to be carted seven days a week; the cattle needed to be fed molasses and cottonseed to be kept alive. So, inevitably, like Mohammed, I went to my mountain – to be with Rick, on his land, by his side, and spend another weekend putting out feed for the cattle and watching Rick buck out bulls at the occasional Saturday night rodeo. The four-hour trek from Brisbane to Rosevale and then back again to Brisbane forty-eight hours later became monotonous. The vast quilted plains of the Darling Downs lost their appeal for me as they droned past endlessly. There was plenty of time to think.

My roller-coaster of feelings about Rick continued. *Was I with him because I didn't know any better? Was this relationship just a bad habit I couldn't break? Was I too lazy to end it? Or were we soulmates and that's why we were drawn to each other?*

The genie couldn't wait to get on board – this was her kind of ride. She anticipated imminent victory: *You'll be happier without him. Trust me*, she cooed.

On the trips home, I would imagine how much easier it would be to go out to the pub with other students and nurse a hangover on a Sunday instead of shovelling cottonseed. I missed dancing at nightclubs. I wanted to be more than just a 'good mate' who was getting 'half handy' to have around. I began to wonder if I was delusional. Maybe I was just a pleasant distraction until the real thing came along. I didn't want to wake up one day and find myself to be the fool.

After another bad phone call, I could tell Rick's heart was not in it – I felt I was just another spoke in his endless cycle of things to do. I realised I was breaking my own cardinal rule: to choose happiness as my compass. If becoming happy meant I had to sever a limb to preserve the body then I was prepared to do it. He had called to cancel yet another a visit to Brisbane. 'Fine,' I said as I hung up. You never can tell what a woman means when she says 'Fine', and he'd blown it – it was the last straw. I'd had a gutful and decided to break up on the weekend face to face. Rick deserved that. I called back and told him I would come to Rosevale.

The logistics of breaking up in person were complicated, I realised, as once more I drove alongside the incoherent line of marching electricity poles skewed by the unstable cracking clay soils of the Downs. I couldn't break up as soon as I arrived and then leave straight away, in the middle of the night. That would be rude to the rest of the family – not to mention hugely awkward. I decided to do it Sunday morning, then go.

In hindsight, the plan had some flaws; it's actually quite difficult to stay pissed off while being pleasant. And, unaware that our fate was balancing on a knife edge, Rick offered solace.

'Listen, Alice, I'm sorry for being short on the phone last week and I really am grateful for your patience, everything you put up with, and all your help during the year. I know I haven't made it to Brisbane much. It's just so hard to get away with this bloody drought. I was hoping, if you're still keen, that I could come to Melbourne with you in June, for your twenty-first.'

'I'd love that!'

And, just like that, he'd pulled us back from the brink. As a couple, we were a long way off a perfect score, but we'd regained a fifty–fifty chance of success. I drove home that Sunday perplexed that this torturous liaison would continue; confounded that my ironclad resolve to end this affair had somehow wavered. The genie was beside herself at the last-minute reprieve.

Four weeks later and we were packed for our first holiday together since Rick's visit to Melbourne nearly two years before. We'd decided to drive his ute. He was crestfallen at the sight of the cat, who was equally disgusted as she was loaded onto the immaculate front seat.

'She's not coming, is she?'

'Of course. What else would I do? Love me, love my cat!'

Rick let it drop. We both knew there was more at stake and in unspoken agreement we pretended not to see the grey fur accumulating on his black dash mats.

On my twenty-first birthday he handed me a small parcel, crudely wrapped, delivered with a kiss. My heart quickened as I opened the intriguing package and my eyes widened as the paper revealed its secret: it wasn't quite a diamond ring, but something to which I could ascribe equivalent significance – a pocketknife, my very first Old Timer. He handed me another, larger, parcel containing a knife pouch and a matching leather work belt that he'd made – impractical gifts for a city chick, but essential for someone living on the land. A pocketknife is as much a part of the outback work uniform as Wranglers, boots and hat.

As only a girl can, I imbued the gift with all sorts of symbolism – it was a talisman, a display of affection for the world to see, a token of his commitment, a sign of our future. With my fingers wrapped tightly around the pocketknife, I concluded that his feelings matched mine and the two and a half years of strained loneliness, endless travel and piercing goodbyes had not been in vain.

The 4000-kilometre-return road trip – great bonding time with family, friends and each other – reinvigorated us. We kissed each other goodbye at the end of the trip with a renewed passion and considerably less tension. The world felt lighter, manageable. I was eager to get into the fourth semester of my degree.

In no time, it seemed, the university drive was purple again with the fallen petals of the jacarandas, signalling the end of exams and the end of my second year of living in Queensland. At Rosevale, the passing of a year was marked by the laying of new carpet in a soft cream colour that Peggy, Sal and I'd chosen, in feigned consultation with Grahame, and the addition of a breadmaker to replace the vat of kombucha tea brewing on Peggy's kitchen bench.

As usual, I returned to Melbourne for Christmas and was back at Rosevale in time to welcome in 1994 with Rick and join the branding team at Benroy.

On the third morning of mustering, a stone bruise rendered Miss Fox lame. Her understudy was my nemesis, Ambassador, the bucking bronc of my second branding season. It was ride him or stay behind in the kitchen. And as I'd take a bruised backside before domesticity any day I decided to put our colourful (no reference to my purple arse) history behind us.

I unsaddled Miss Fox and removed her bridle, lengthening the cheek straps before putting it on Ambassador. As I pulled up the girth, I wondered if horses really could smell fear. With my reins gathered, I swung up into the saddle and sat still for a moment, breathing the nerves away, as Rick offered advice.

'If he tries to bolt or buck or feels out of control, don't pull on both reins at once – that could make him rear up. Use one lead and pull him into a tight circle.'

'Is that supposed to make me feel better?'

'You'll be right.'

The pounding in my ears settled to a quiet thrum, as something inside me shifted. *C'mon, you old brute. Try me. I'm ready for your tricks.*

Do you think he tried anything? Not a flicker. He was the perfect gentleman. He'd got the memo – I'd got a promotion and had a pocketknife to prove it.

The branding at Benroy was the least painful and most enjoyable to date for all concerned, with everyone completing the week with flesh and bones intact.

The evenings had a heightened atmosphere that was full of anticipation for the imminent wedding between Rick's brother David and his high-school sweetheart, Sonya, at the end of the month. Sonya and I had become good friends during 1993. She worked and lived in Brisbane, so we'd driven the round trip to Rosevale together many times to visit our cowboys. Rick and I were both in the bridal party.

Weddings are a great excuse for a gathering in the country. People may not see each other for years unless there is a marriage or a funeral, and then friendships that have spanned generations and share a multitude of links are revived and lubricated. This wedding would be no exception.

Sonya looked lovely in a traditional white lace, sequinned bridal gown. The groom and his groomsmen, unfamiliar without their stock-in-trade Wranglers and Akubras, were dashing in black tuxedos, as were the 200 or so guests in black tie and full-length evening gowns.

Impassioned by the event, Rick's Uncle Phil took us aside later in the evening. 'So when are you two getting hitched?' I braced myself for Rick's reply.

'No plans, Phil. Just having fun.'

I wanted to boast to Phil of my pocketknife, but thought better of it.

'Well, the next wedding I go to, it better be yours. But I'm tellin' you, don't come and ask me to be a babysitter when you two have kids. This bugger was a shit of a kid' – he pointed to Rick – 'and you've got a bit of a wild streak' – pointing at me – 'so I figure, anything by him and outta you is sure to be trouble.' The backhanded approval felt good.

Whether I, and marriage, were in the equation or not, Rick was definitely focused on his future. He'd been saving and investing his jackaroo wages since leaving high school and had built up a healthy nest egg, and was chucking his unbridled energy into two rental properties. The first was a three-bedroom brick home in Toowoomba. The second was a more hands-on project – a derelict old farmhouse that he moved onto a block of land bought for $3000 on the outskirts of the town of Jandowae. The house was the size of a large public toilet block without a vestige of exterior paint left. To call it a 'renovator's delight' was an overstatement. My ideas and experience with renovating had some traction in this shack, and Rick brought me in as second-in-command. I don't think he regretted it, even though I nearly brought an untimely end to us both one morning, as I set to work painting the steep pitched roof, perhaps not thinking the task through to its conclusion ...

Splish, splat went the brush, back and forth, back and forth, as I merrily worked my way around the roof. To complete the final square metre I stepped sideways – onto wet paint. I had completely painted myself in. My legs flew out from under me and I fell onto my stomach, skidding towards the sheer drop – spreadeagled I slid, praying for friction to override gravity. Mercifully, my descent gradually slowed to a stop, so I could catch my breath and scream pathetically for Rick to rescue me. The slightest movement sent me slipping towards the gutter again. I could hear Rick clambering up the ladder on the other side and across the roof. My hero appeared on the pitch. I breathed a sigh of relief. Then I realised what I'd done.

Rick, presuming I possessed some common sense and had left an exit for myself, leapt onto the rippled steel canvas of fresh silver paint and succumbed to the lethal, glass-like, slippery surface. From my prone position I could do nothing except witness my rescue party fall victim to my stupidity. Horrified, picturing his crumpled body lifeless on the ground below while the roof dried with me permanently adhered, I watched Rick surf past me bolt upright – unblinking, skidding smoothly, even with a degree of poise, and at the approach of the five-metre drop calmly extend his right leg, brace himself on the gutter, and with a final heart-stopping totter, brake to a stop. Erect. One foot on the gutter, the other on the roof.

'Bloody hell, Alice, what were you thinking?'

In shock and feeling a bit precious, I responded the best I could: I cried.

Monkeylike, he swung down the gutter and jumped off the roof to the ground, wandering off to fetch a ladder. After easing me down and getting me onto firm ground, he considered it safe to laugh at me. The front half of me was covered in silver paint – hair, face, shirt, jeans and boots. Unamused, I suggested with conviction and some well-chosen expletives that he could complete his roof unaided and I would stick to ground-level improvements.

We knocked out some walls and added on a big new family room and a double garage. The apple-green laminate kitchen came together with a tub of Gumption, elbow grease, and a couple of new shelves and hinges for the cupboards. And, finally, with a coat of paint outside and inside, a tidy three-bedroom cottage with a shining silver roof stood ready to rent out where once a sad humpy had been.

Fifteen

I wished a coat of paint could freshen me up that easily. I felt as weathered as that old cottage before the TLC. Since leaving high school, I'd adventured around Australia, acquired a university debt large enough to make a small European country feel nervous, endured an aching loneliness that had become my constant companion, pulled countless beers, cleaned innumerable toilets and houses, survived on a poverty-line budget and developed a rampaging fear of failure and a severe case of anxiety about my grades. As I started the second semester for 1994 and another batch of poor grades was all I had to show for the slog, I doubted my path.

Quitting would have been easy. The option beckoned like a seductive mistress, suggesting herself as a quick fix to my woes. But I looked away from those temptress eyelashes promising pleasures and comfort and plodded on, remaining loyal to my chosen path that once seemed so right – maybe it would again. So I persevered, putting one lecture, one day, one term in front of another, gradually moving closer to my destination. My grades gradually improved as I progressed through third year into my chosen field of animal science. I was invigorated by sticking my hand up a cow's bum in practicals that alternated with lectures on physiology and biochemistry, moving away from subjects like biometrics and botany that had given me pathological narcolepsy. Casual work in the chicken broiler industry fitted around my lectures and increased to full-time work during holidays. A promising career in the chicken industry awaited me at graduation, if I wanted it.

As the months went by we fell into a sort of routine. Rick did his thing while I did mine. Together we created some overlap. Sometimes he'd come to Brisbane, but usually I would join him at Rosevale or accompany him to a campdraft or rodeo. At the campdrafts he'd ride his horses and socialise during the day while I sat in the front of the truck studying. I was reminded of my outsider status when Rick and his friends talked horses, saddles, pedigrees, rules, scores and the way the cattle ran. Unable to fathom my lack of participation, they tried to recruit me. 'You'll have to have a go to know how it feels, Alice. You know what they say: campdrafting is like masturbation – plenty of fun to do, but pretty boring to watch after a while.'

If only! My legs still chafed if I rode for longer than three hours. I filed the invitation away, but ride in front of these people? The nerves alone would kill me even if chasing a beast at full gallop didn't.

Campdrafts and rodeos proved to be perfect incubators for my genie. Like long-lost friends she'd roll out insecurities, doubts, and scathing self-reviews. Even after three and a half years, the old questions resurfaced. The women at the campdrafts were born in the saddle; Wranglers melted onto their tiny sculpted frames and weeny waists, and when they talked cattle you could hear that it ran in their veins. Looking at them, I still wondered why Rick was with me, why he was persevering. He could have shortcut all this nonsense, all the long-distance strain, all the hassle, all the lessons and got himself a ready-made handy girlfriend to ride by his side.

At the rodeos I hung out the back of the chutes, staying close to Rick. I'd say 'g'day' to regular faces on the circuit as I weaved through the yards towards Rick's posse of mates, dodging the black slimy spittle shooting out the sides of the mouths of the tobacco-chewing bull riders. I preferred being out the back to being in the audience. Out back the action was more intense and the excitement in the air was palpable. Even now, if I close my eyes, it feels more like twenty seconds than twenty years since I last trod those dusty back yards ...

With Rick's ride only two bulls away, I climb up the rails next to the chutes to get a bird's-eye view and allow myself to be intoxicated by the smell of the bull hides, the fear in the riders' eyes, their sweat-soaked shirts, the adrenaline pulsating through the raised veins straining on their necks, the intense expressions as they see nothing except their bound hand and the back of the bull's head. My pulse quickens as Rick climbs into the chute with the 900 kilos of bull, the expanse of black mottled hide dwarfing my cowboy.

Strapped in, Rick thumps the rope one last time to ensure the tight grip will hold. He raises his free hand and yells, 'Outside!' The chute is flung open, the bull thunders out, the crowd roars and the clown steps in front of the bull to bait him away from bucking back into the chute. The bull's head is low as he kicks his hindquarters high, twisting his mammoth carcass in tight concentric circles to evict his rider. Rick stays in the centre of the beast, sitting pretty, 'mind in the middle – leg either side'. The old bull whips sideways, trying to pull him in, but Rick swings his weight outwards and manages to stay out of the well. The horn blows, signalling the eight seconds are up. He drops his hand, frees the ropes, casually swings a leg over as if he's dismounting from a kids' merry-go-round, and runs back to the chutes as the clown coaxes the bull up the arena out of the way.

I'd scramble down from my vantage point, eager to spend a few moments together before he started preparing again for his next ride. The moments together were slim pickings indeed.

It was exhausting, projecting every spare thought onto a man 300 kilometres away, a man who thought commitment = marriage = children = dependent wife = handbrake = life over. Rick would attempt to reassure me: 'You're my best mate. We're happy. Why do you need me to say more? Why can't we just keep going like this? Having fun, being mates?'

I wanted to be mates. I wanted him. But I didn't want *this* – this perpetual state of limbo, like the endless plains of the Darling Downs with a horizon that kept its fixed distance despite every step I took towards it.

I had to make decisions about my career direction, which would dictate my speciality subjects in the final eighteen months of study. Professional jobs in the beef industry were few and far between and hotly contested. My prospects in the broiler chicken industry, while maybe not suited to my romantic ideas of working in agriculture, were solid. It would be sensible to consider specialising in my feathered friends. But the job with chickens was based in Brisbane and would set us up for another round of long-distance love, and I knew I didn't have another round in me. But at least, I thought resentfully, a future with chickens would be a sure bet compared to Rick and his carefully meted out hints of a future life together.

I wanted to know what Rick thought behind the reticence – I needed solid reassurance that this long-distance thing was worth it, not hints and symbolic pocketknives. I waited until he came to Brisbane next and stuck it on him, point blank.

'Do you think we'll ever be more, Rick? I mean, really more?'

'Why can't we just take it one day at a time? It's worked until now.'

But his stock response was no longer enough. 'It's working for you, Rick. It's not working for me. It's *never* worked for me. You know where your life is heading – it's the same, with or without me. I have decisions to make about my future and most of them depend on you and us. I want to know where I'm heading. Where are we heading? For Christ's sake, throw me a friggin' bone here, Rick!'

I wasn't looking for a proposal – just a clue of what was on the horizon. But it was more than he could give, and I'd had enough. I needed to stop waiting and start living; to set my compass to a new north; to get my life back – with or without him.

I let it out, all the genie's scripts rattling through my head: the frustrations, the lack of direction, the crushing feeling in my heart when we said goodbye. Like a tortoise under attack he retreated into his shell. I knew I was pushing him away, but I couldn't help myself.

'Rick, it doesn't matter how much you like something and want it to work, sometimes you have to know when to stop throwing good money after bad.'

'I'm sick of listening to this shit!' He stormed off, as I knew he would.

The genie smiled to herself; she found the anger in his voice strangely soothing. She just had to push a little further and he'd walk for good.

'That's right, leave. You've never cared!'

But even as I punched the words out, I realised that it wasn't Rick I was yelling at. Plain as day, I saw her: the genie was exposed as light flooded her dark chamber and her true motives, that she'd glazed with noble intention, were exposed. She'd been so arrogant, so sure that the divorce and abuse hadn't affected her, so confident that she'd dodged the psycho bullet. Looks like she was fucked up after all.

I heaved with long overdue sobs. The deep pit of fear; fear of it all going pear-shaped, for him to leave, was uncovered. There would never be enough words to fill that pit, never enough reassurance.

Finally the anger melted into an eerie calmness. The fear was not gone, but the truth of it had been revealed. I could move on. I wanted to move on together. He wanted things to remain as they were.

We'd arrived at an impasse. There was nothing said between us when he came home and slipped into bed beside me. For once I'd run out of words. The two people who used to sleep entwined in a single jackaroo's swag were long gone. There was a chasm between us; a chasm I thought was now too wide for either of us to cross. Mutual frustration and unspoken disappointment hung between us the next morning. Our eyes struggled to meet as he got in his ute to go home. It would be over as soon as one of us had the guts to pull the trigger. I wondered who it would be.

Sixteen

With a barrage of mid-semester exams launching themselves upon me, breaking up would have to wait until I had the strength to deal with the havoc it would wreak on my emotions. For the next few weeks I tried to focus on one day at a time, until the last exam was finished.

A dragging sense of surrender and inevitability had left me sombre. My classmates had been celebrating for hours, but I had to work. Rick had said he'd join me afterwards. At the last minute my evening shift at the restaurant was cancelled, leaving me standing in my bedroom dressed in my emerald green batik Malaysian uniform, deciding what to wear to the pub. My fingers sifted through my hair, undoing the braid, as I stared blankly at a pile of clothes, mesmerised by the decisions I had to make to get my life in order and hopefully, in the process, my joie de vivre.

Rapid footsteps bounding up the old timber stairs made the old workers' cottage I was renting tremble. I was pleased he'd arrived earlier than we'd arranged so we could get to the pub with my classmates, have a few drinks and be in a crowd. I wasn't ready to be alone with him. It would be the first time we'd seen each other since the fight. I didn't know what I wanted to say to him any more, having commenced the process of shutting down emotions, like tying off each vein in succession to protect the blood supply to major organs before a surgical amputation.

I caught him off-guard when I opened the front door and his face lit up at the unexpected sight of me. After the way we'd left things, seeing him smile so wonderfully at me I almost forgot the ravine I'd carved between us.

'This is a nice surprise. Aren't you meant to be at work?'

'Well, there weren't many bookings, so my shift was—'

Cutting off my explanation, Rick kissed me excitedly, bundling me backwards into my bedroom and shutting the door behind us. 'Whatever. I'm glad you're here.' The gleam in his eye and the crooked grin on his face made me think for a moment that it was he who'd just finished exams. 'I've got something to say, Alice.'

He stood facing me with his hands resting on my forearms, his eyes locked onto mine, his smile quivering and his voice serious.

'From Boroondara to Newry, from Newry to Rosevale, from Rosevale to Melbourne, from Brisbane to the Kimberleys and from Jandowae to Brisbane; our relationship has survived distance and time and lasted when many others would have faltered. And I've been thinking, I want to be the groom at a wedding and I want my best friend by my side.'

As my mind slowly processed what I was hearing, a proposal plain as day – no equivocation, no guarded sentiment – he continued: 'I'm so lucky to have found you, Alice. I've been a fool. Will you marry me?'

I wrapped my arms around his neck. 'Richard, I would love to marry you! What happened to taking it one day at a time?'

'We still can. We can just do it together. I thought I wouldn't be able to do my own thing once we got married, but then I figured, what's my problem? What am I waiting for? I have the perfect girl, I should be with her.'

'Have I ever stopped you doing your own thing?'

'Never. You are always there backing me up. That's why I know I would be a very lucky ringer if you married me.'

'Rick, I don't want to be a handbrake. I'm your mate.'

'I know, that's why I love you.'

Rick was quick to make sure his sub-clauses were heard up front. 'I thought we'd have a long engagement. After all, you've got eighteen months of uni left, we should wait until that's over and give ourselves a bit of time.'

'That's fine, Rick.'

'And I don't want to have kids for a while either. I've got stuff I want to do first.'

'Relax, Rick. I'm not spending all these years at uni only to not use my degree. Let's not get ahead of ourselves. I'm blown away that we're going to get married one day.'

'Well, I have to marry you if I want to get that Green River knife back.'

'Thanks for that.'

Rick called Mum and the squeals of delight over the phone could've been heard down the street. 'I guess Jill's okay with it,' Rick said, rubbing his ear.

Dad was out of the country and would get the news on his return. We drove out to Rosevale to tell Rick's family, arriving after they'd gone to bed. The next morning everyone was in the kitchen preparing roast beef sandwiches for lunch boxes. Peggy's breadmaker, relegated to the bottom of the cupboard alongside the decommissioned sprouting trays, had been supplanted on the kitchen bench by a juicer and the comforting sizzle of Grahame's rissoles was now lost among Peggy and Sally's frenetic chopping and whizzing.

A continuous stream of high-pitched babble was my attempt to cover up my nerves. We had planned to tell everyone our news that evening over dinner, but after ten minutes of this Rick let out a huge sigh. 'Jesus, Alice! There's no way I can listen to this all day or it's going to be a bloody long day fencing. I'm telling them now.' He stood up. 'Mum, Dad, we've got something to tell you.'

Everyone stopped and looked up.

'Yesterday I asked Alice to marry me and she said "Yes".'

Peggy's eyes filled with tears (that I'm fairly confident were of joy). Even Grahame looked animated, maybe even thrilled. The kitchen was filled with kisses and hugs.

Rick sat back down quite pleased with himself. 'At least we can get on and get some work done and I won't have to listen to you pretending to be "normal" all day.'

Later Rick took me to the stables to see the young horses he was breaking in. He pointed to a large amber-coloured chestnut with a long white blaze and a gentle eye. 'See this one? His name is Skittles. I broke him in last year. With a bit more work, I think he'll be good for you.'

I reached out and let Skittles sniff my hand. The world I would become a part of came into focus. And I knew that one day soon, the last few years would become memories of a courtship that taxed our reserves, but was worth it, as we ride off into the sunset together.

While the announcement of our marriage was welcomed by both sets of parents, for Rick's family, there was a due process to follow. Marriage first. Living together second.

Even a few years earlier, the idea of marriage without living together beforehand would've been unthinkable to me. And before that, as a teenager, the idea of marriage was an enigma in itself. How things change and people adapt.

With sticky questions emerging such as 'What to do with Alice after she graduates?' and 'Where will she live until the wedding?', not to mention 'They can't get married in summer, because that's when we're branding', Rick decided to fast-track his timetable and we planned to marry the following spring, on 30 September 1995. Even though I would still have a couple of months before I finished my degree it would mean we'd be settled in by the all-important branding.

But not everyone was happy for us. Rick's grandfather, Gaffer, had his doubts. However, nearly twelve months would pass before he deemed it suitable to share them with us.

For so many momentous occasions in life, the triggers are often innocuous and unremarkable. One day, about five months before the wedding, Rick asked me to collect the key to the fuel tank from Gaffer's laundry. Gaffer's house was down the hill from Grahame and Peg, near the main yards and sheds. Coiled like an expectant spring, he appeared at the top of the laundry steps, seizing the opportunity to speak to me alone and let the thoughts that had been brewing spill over. The amiability I'd known for the previous four years was gone. I was no longer his grandson's novel amusement, I was the wife-to-be. The prospective daughter-in-law, a potential dropped stitch that could cause the unravelling of his precious legacy, woven together by generations of hard work.

'Alice, have you thought about this? You're not from the country. You can't do what country girls do. You think you can. You think you like it. But that's now, when you come out for weekends and holidays. How will you feel when it goes on and on, never changing, always the same? It's a tough life. City girls don't last out here, Alice. I've seen it before. Most of them spend a couple of years out here then want to go back to the city. Then what will you do? What will Rick do? What would that do to Rick? What would that do to us?'

'I'm sorry you feel that way, Gaffer.' Unable to say more for the burning behind my eyes, I walked out. There was no way I was going to cry in front of him.

Maybe if he'd got to me earlier he would have stood a chance of scaring me off, but he'd left his run too late – the invitations were as good as in the mail. But the blindsiding derailed my emotions and threw my innocent bliss into disarray.

Too often during our courtship I'd been told with equal measure of truth and jest that other women could bring land, cattle or useful contacts to a marriage. What did I bring? A cat (albeit a very nice one), a university debt and a VW Beetle. Love was not the issue. This was business. And I had nothing on my balance sheet.

Gaffer's words fell right into the fallow soil of my insecurities, germinating dormant seeds of self-doubt: *Why has Rick chosen to marry me? I bring nothing to this marriage. I wonder if he's made the right choice. I love Rick. I want what's best for him. Am I what's best for him or will I be a millstone around his neck and forever an outsider?*

I put the sprouting doubts to the back of my mind and hoped they would wither – after all, I had little mental space for self-flagellation: my mind was filled with study for my final semester – and all things ivory and lace.

Once married we would live at Cardowan, the 3700-hectare breeder block (for breeding cows, not humans) adjoining Benroy, a half-hour drive from Rosevale. We were thrilled. Cardowan was nestled in the country and the hills that we loved and felt drawn to. And it would be a comfortable distance from eyes that were watching our every move.

A month out from the wedding, our neighbours-to-be – Grahame's cousin, John O'Shanesy, and his wife, Joan – invited us to a dinner party to meet some of the locals. With nothing to wear that was suitable for a formal dinner party, Peggy altered a cream 1960s woollen lace cocktail dress for me. I felt like I'd arrived on a movie set as we drove into the sweeping white gravel driveway and saw ahead of us a magnificent homestead – the original Greenup home, Wylarah.

A deep 'Howdy, neighbours!' boomed through the crisp twilight air as we walked up the sandstone stairs, worn from a century of use, onto the wide wooden verandah. Determined that we would be strangers no more, but rather friends for life, John gave me an enveloping hug, wrapping me in his long, lanky arms before pumping Rick's hand enthusiastically and drawing us through into the living room. Then Joan bustled in, dousing us generously with hugs and kisses.

'How wonderful to have neighbours again,' she said, as she presented me with a glass of champagne.

Eagerly I accepted her offer of a tour of Wylarah and received a condensed version of the Greenup family history and an introduction to each generation of the family tree through the cascade of portraits on the dining room walls. Joan referred to each ancestor on a first-name basis, colouring in their sketchy outlines with familiarity and anecdotes gleaned from reading one hundred years of diaries preserved at Wylarah. Rick listened with attention: Joan's knowledge of his family heritage was far greater than his.

'Wylarah was settled in the 1880s by Alfred Greenup – he'd be your ... great-great-grandfather, Rick. Alfred designed the house himself, which was completed in 1891.'

'So why do the Greenups live at Rosevale?' I asked.

'Rosevale was George's mother's property,' Joan replied.

'Whose?'

'Gaffer,' Rick explained. 'Gaffer's name is George.'

'George was born here and moved to Rosevale when he grew up. But he kept the breeding country next door to here, you know, the block called Benroy. Here's a picture of George's mother, Ruby.'

Joan pointed to a faded, sepia-toned photograph on the wall. 'Ruby was a Bassingthwaighte. She married Harold Greenup, George's father, and moved to Wylarah.'

Joan continued at a hundred miles an hour while I struggled to keep up. 'George's sister Francis, John's mother, remained at

Wylarah and married a man from Sydney, Gordon O'Shanesy. Gaffer never had much time for Gordon, didn't think he was much of a cattle man or farmer – you know, coming from the city.'

I wondered briefly whether this explained Gaffer's concerns with me.

'Rosevale was a half-day horse ride south of Wylarah. Each year Gaffer walked the cattle from the breeding country at Benroy to Rosevale for fattening.'

Rick's eyes got the faraway look I recognised from Benroy. He was drawn to vestiges of forgotten times; it was what lured him across the continent to work in remote areas where bronco branding with ropes instead of cradles was still an everyday practice. He would've loved to have lived before electricity, motorised vehicles, hydraulics and other industrial advancements that made his world noisy and put mobs of cattle on trucks instead of on the stock routes. A pioneer at heart, he'd often told me he was born a century late. New frontiers were all but gone for Rick – hence the need to create his own.

'Much of the original land adjoining Wylarah that was run under pastoral lease was resumed by the government for soldier settlement after the First World War. Wylarah was reduced to less than a thousand hectares – hardly any cattle country. John's more of a ploughman than a cowman.' Joan laughed at her own joke then continued, 'Cardowan was one of those blocks of land. It was settled by a Robert McLaughlin, who built the house at Cardowan. And Harold, your great-grandfather, helped Robert mill the timber. It was the neighbourly thing to do.'

I was taken aback by the barrage of history linked to Rick. Joan's soliloquy reminded me that I was marrying not just a man, but a dynasty – a far cry from my family, whose shallow roots and penchant for migration after escaping a war-ravaged Europe made it difficult to keep track of our heritage and relatives.

Joan showed us round the great central hall of dark-panelled timber enclosed by a double gabled roof, telling us tales of her predecessors, Rick's ancestors, and bringing them to life, as if they'd just stepped out the door. '... quite the scandal it was at the time, when the Greenup girls trotted into town riding astride like men.'

From the hall a series of gracious rooms led out via French doors onto the wide verandah that spanned three sides. 'It's amazing, Joan. I've never seen anything like it.'

'Ah, you should see her at her best. Wylarah is wonderful for balls. Which we are very overdue for – we must organise one soon. Now, let's have a top-up before we continue.' She scurried off in search of the champagne bottle, leaving me to absorb my surroundings.

I marvelled at the grandeur of this home so saturated in family history. Its very existence seemed an architectural feat, given the remoteness from civilisation, tradespeople and building materials during its gestation. With drinks replenished we resumed our tour, this time keeping the bottle with us in case of another emergency refill. At the northern end of the house, a small spire housed a bell. Joan indicated the improvised horseshoe handle attached to a skyward-bound wire. 'Go on, ring it,' she insisted.

I strained to pull the iron shoe down and displace the huge brass bell from its reverie, before picking up the rhythm, moving in time to the bell's swinging arc to release it, allowing a haunting, rich chime to resonate through the cavernous building and echo across the fields, heralding our presence to no-one.

The other guests arrived as the bell hushed and our tour concluded, and the conversation took on a broader scope as we were seated at the mahogany table laid for ten, set with heirloom silver and crystal. With understated ease, Joan served a memorable three-course meal that had been made from scratch on her wood-fired stove – French onion soup followed by beef wellington, with lashings of lemon delicious pudding and whipped cream for dessert.

There was a wood-fired stove at Cardowan and I was terrified of it, but this evening and this dinner party with Joan gave me hope.

Later in the kitchen, as we prepared coffee, she explained the nuances of the different timbers required to generate different heats and temperatures, depending on the desired outcome. 'Alice, I've found that a large log of ironbark, after about three hours, is wonderful for pavlovas. But if I need a high vigorous heat, say for pork crackling, then I would use smaller pieces of spotted gum and stoke it right up. It's just a matter of practise – you'll get the hang of it, and you'll have plenty of failures too, but that's all part of the fun.'

I looked around the kitchen and the remnants of the feast, feeling dwarfed by her capacity to cook and entertain. 'Oh, Joan, I don't think I could ever hold a dinner party like this.'

'You don't have to, Alice. You do your thing. Entertain your own way. Be your own person.'

We carried the tray of coffee and Royal Doulton cups and saucers back to the dining table, where the conversation and wine flowed. Even though the company was delightful and we'd discovered kindred spirits, that night we were to stay at the Cardowan homestead for the first time and the intense urge to see our future home up close induced us to depart at an uncharacteristically respectable hour – in truth, that may have been the last time we ever left Wylarah so early. I won't revisit all the occasions (and non-occasions) that served as feeble excuses to break out the poetry, flip the lid on the piano, grab jars of lentils as makeshift maracas, bash out some John Denver tunes or climb on the roof to watch the stars – instead, let's just say that was to be the first of many memorable evenings together with John and Joan.

Buoyed by the knowledge that I'd found friendly waters and could put my anchor down safely, I laughed and prattled incessantly for the ten-kilometre drive to Cardowan, although with no other houses between Wylarah and Cardowan, I made a mental note to never break down out there.

Cardowan was built on one of the highest elevations of the Great Dividing Range at the headwaters of the northern Burnett catchment, whereas Rosevale was on the southern side, and part of the Great Murray–Darling Basin. There was an invisible demarcation between these watersheds; the southern side socialised with the southern side and northern side likewise. So even though Cardowan was only half an hour from Rosevale, it was part of an entirely different community from the one Rick had grown up with.

I had glimpsed the corrugated tin roof of Cardowan glinting in the sunlight while mustering at Benroy, but I'd never seen the house up close. Old Jack and his wife, Mrs Hughes, had lived at Cardowan until our engagement, so Rick had not been inside since his parents bought the property from old Mr McLaughlin, more than ten years before. We would move into Cardowan with no sense of what was in store for us. There would be no poring through the real-estate pages and endless weekends of house inspections followed by the bitter disappointment of missing out on a house that we'd fallen in love with. Cardowan would be our home and the wee town of Kumbia would be our postcode – like it or lump it!

The 1920s weatherboard Queenslander stood quietly in the moonlight with lazy self-assurance as Rick's ute bumped up the driveway. Remnants of peeling white paint reflected in the ute's headlights. A picket fence, built too close to the house, smiled hopefully at us, reminding me of neglected teeth that were once perfect, white and shiny, now chipped, grey and dull – a loose one here and there leaning forward at an awkward angle.

The timber balustrade wobbled under my hand as we slowly walked up the seven steps and opened the solid timber door at the rear of the house. My heart pounded as we fumbled for a light switch. The bulb illuminated a dark timbered laundry that led into a west-facing breezeway of beige-painted fibro with a linoleum floor. The breezeway adjoined the kitchen, complete with the dreaded wood-fired oven and a plug-in electric stove that was little more than a camping appliance. Both would be hopeless for stir-fries, I thought with a hint of frustration. A small empty room adjacent to the kitchen, which I presumed would have been a bedroom, completed the original part of the homestead, a modest four-room cottage.

The original verandah had been converted into a large corridor leading to the newer wing of the homestead, comprising four bedrooms, an office, formal dining and living rooms and two built-in verandahs facing north and south. The rooms in the newer part were huge. My studio Tree House would have fitted inside the main bedroom with space left over. A large set of bay windows in the main bedroom faced east – perfect for early risers (I made a mental to-do note: *black-out curtains for bedroom*). A single bathroom adjoined the corridor, and instantly failed to inspire me with its mauve laminate wall panelling and dark-brown checked linoleum, although redeeming itself slightly thanks to the matching pale-blue pedestal basin and bath of desirable wallowing proportions.

Rick joined me on the first exploration circuit, but soon tired. Accustomed to my nocturnal behaviour, he sensibly chose to let my enthusiasm exhaust itself of its own accord and climbed into the swag he'd rolled out on the floor of one of the bedrooms.

While he snored I removed the dark dusty curtains in each of the bedrooms, discovering behind them ten-pane French doors opening onto the verandahs. With my curiosity well and truly in the driver's seat I pulled back the brittle linoleum in one bedroom to reveal sound hardwood floorboards. And the next. And just one little peek in the third. Around 2 a.m. in a frenzy of discovery, I started removing the first layer of the worn grey carpet adjoining the kitchen – just to get a glimpse at what was underneath – and discovered two more layers of lino, a layer of newspaper and, within each crack in the floorboards, twists of newspaper tightly stuffed. Sadly without my pocketknife to scrape and lever up the twists of paper, I was thwarted, and headed for bed suddenly exhausted. Like a spraying tomcat, I'd left my mark on every room.

I nestled next to Rick in the swag, swaddled with gratitude that this rambling old home and I had found each other, and mentally sorted through what was needed to reawaken her. As I lay in the darkness, it dawned on me: this was not playing house, or another weekend adventure. This would be our home.

I'm home.

Seventeen

Loud footsteps pounding through the house with confident familiarity woke us at 4 a.m. I knew immediately there was more than one set. The hairs on the back of my neck prickled and my hands tingled as the flight mechanism kicked in and blood left them for more vital tasks. Rick leapt out of the swag, grabbing the only thing in the house that could be used in self-defence – his five-centimetre-long Old Timer pocketknife – and crept up to the doorway.

There was no way I was going to be left alone in the bedroom, so reluctantly I joined Rick to track down our intruders. Unfamiliar with the house's layout we edged along the walls and slid around each corner. I was behind Rick, clipping his heels, ears straining to ascertain where the footsteps came from and where the intruders were hiding. It was obvious they knew the terrain and had the upper hand. We had only our stealth and, hopefully, the element of surprise – that is, if they didn't already know we were there. I wondered if confrontation was the best idea. We could escape out one of the side doors and run into the paddock – I figured we could walk to Wylarah in under three hours. But what if there were more of them hiding outside in the trees? I'd be useless in a skirmish: I could never remember the self-defence karate manoeuvres my brother Doug taught me – I always ended up on the ground in a headlock, whatever kung-fu trick I tried. I reckoned Rick could take his chances wielding the Old Timer if he wanted, but I'd try negotiation.

The heavy footsteps circled back around us. 'They must be on the verandah,' Rick whispered, altering our course. The footsteps got louder. Closer. We froze.

The footsteps resumed behind us.

It's not possible!

Suddenly Rick straightened and sauntered arrogantly back the way we'd come. I wanted to scream at him to stop but couldn't for fear of revealing our position. Finding the nearest light, he flicked it on, causing me to shrink into a corner wishing for a piece of furniture to hide behind.

'What are you doing?' I hissed, trying to sound as angry as I could at .01 decibels.

'We're hunting *possums*, Alice.'

'For christ sake, Rick, they had me scared shitless!'

'Me too. Wanna call it a night?'

'Gladly.'

We went back to bed, but with my heart still racing from the possum ambush I struggled to fall asleep, and lay wondering what other wildlife we would be sharing the house with. For now, however, the possums could have Cardowan. My plans for sprucing her up would have to go on the back burner until we were married and I'd finished my final exams.

With only a month to go the wedding was coming together little by little, despite the distance between the organising committee, spread as it was between Rosevale, Brisbane and Melbourne. Invitations were made and sent out by Mum from Melbourne. Peggy made

*Newlyweds Mum and Dad at Dad's graduation
ceremony: Bachelor of Science, Mathematics.
University of Adelaide, 1966.*

Don't put me in a cage ... Eighteen and invincible: posing on the Yamaha at the Uluru camping ground in central Australia, 1990.

A cowboy stole my heart. Rick's eight-second ride on High as a Kite at the Bell Rodeo while some annoying girl in background hogs the rails taking photos — doesn't she own a hat? And what's with the brown jeans, haven't you heard of Wranglers? 1993.

*The Greenup family in 1992 [clockwise from top left] : Rick,
Grahame, Sally, David, Peggy and Peter. I took this shot in the
front yard at Rosevale before Rick left for the Kimberleys. Given his
track record of injuries and the minor issue of him missing the self-
preservation gene, I suspect Peggy wanted a family portrait while
Rick was in one piece.*

Just hitched.
September 30 1995,
The Southport School
(TSS) Chapel. Babes
at 23 and 24, giddy
with the moment
and exhausted from
partying with friends
and family from as
far afield as Adelaide,
Melbourne and
western Queensland.

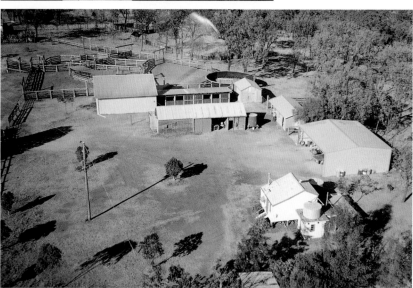

Aerial shot of Cardowan, taken when Rick was shooting wild dogs
from a chopper around 2001. Our homestead is just out of the picture,
but why would you take a shot of that? The yards and sheds — now
that's interesting! Note new yards, sheds, stables, horse training yard
and arena in background. Most of the silver-leafed ironbark trees in the
background subsequently died as the drought stretched out until 2010.

Best wedding gift ever. December 1995. Sally and I, ecstatic at Jumma Creek as it runs a banker after big rain — the best rain since meeting Rick five years before. Now we could wash in the creek instead of with a bucket after a day's branding at Benroy.

2007: excavating in the dry, sandy riverbeds to get clean, fresh water to keep stock alive. Trees were dying in their thousands across the landscape, pastures were turning to dust.

Dinner anyone? First bush kill at Boroondarra skillfully done by Brett, Willy and Rick.

Rick wins Maiden Campdraft at Bell in 2003, a couple of months after the accident that made me rethink my life. I removed my eye patch for the photo so I didn't look like such a idiot, but ... 'I've got one eye on you, and the other one on your mate.'

Photo shoot for the Australian Womens' Weekly *Search for Australia's Most Inspiring Rural Women, 2006. James is seven days old. Rick holds a 22-month-old Ruby in the background.* (Photo: Melissa McCord)

Rory, James and Ruby watch the branding intently from outside the yards, standing on a large round bale of hay as the sun sets and the men brand the last calves at the end of a long day.

A handful of our Santa Gertrudis bulls — the end result of years of breeding and annual cycles of mustering, branding, farming and the plethora of other jobs on a cattle station. At the end of the day, this is why we do it: the inescapable love of the cattle and horses, the land, and the rural community whose heart beats with passion and honour. (Photo: Kent Ward)

Sally's bridesmaid's dress and my wedding dress – a simple design in ivory silk georgette with a lace bodice and short organza sleeves. Mum and I bought the silk together on a visit to Melbourne, then we scoured the fabric shops for remnants of antique cotton lace for the bodice. In her horde of material, Peggy found leftover lace from Rick's christening gown, which we added to the mix. I dyed the white lace in diluted coffee to match the silk georgette and hand-stitched the lace pieces onto the bodice. A remnant bolt of delicate ivory organza provided just enough for a veil.

In the days preceding the wedding, which was to be held at The Southport School, Rick's old school, a large contingent of friends and family from all over Australia descended on the Gold Coast for a week-long party. Our evenings were filled with dinners, cocktails, nightclubs and a series of pre-wedding barbecues, while the days were spent making final arrangements.

Two silver urns filled with cream and white flowers flanked the bridal table and behind them stood two 1.5-metre-high freestanding candelabras that Rick made himself, blacksmithing old twisted iron he'd scavenged and painted a glossy black. Maroon tablecloths complemented the rich timbers of the old school hall.

On the morning of the wedding, Joan arrived at the hotel with masses of crimson and champagne roses for the bridal party, as she'd promised the month before. 'You can't possibly buy your own flowers,' she'd insisted. 'They should be a gift. It's good luck.'

With preparations completed, my confidence and self-assurance evaporated until I was unrecognisable to myself by the time the vintage 1960s Chevrolets arrived to take us to the chapel. My legs were weak and strangely numb as Dad escorted me down the aisle to Rick. His strong frame and rigid muscular arm, showing no signs of the tumour that had so nearly stolen him, kept me steady as the lack of sleep from a week of partying with friends, nervous energy and giddiness from the roaring emotions threatened to destabilise me.

Rick and I exchanged our stilted vows in front of his friends and family and my friends and family – and there, front and centre, were our first mutual friends, Jeremy and Robyn, the agar in which the delicate first cells of our relationship multiplied and grew.

After the ceremony three generations of TSS old boys, including Gaffer, stood outside the chapel and chanted the school war cry with spine-tingling fervour.

By dessert we'd made our first compromise as a married couple. Rick wanted his favourite ding-a-ling country love song as a wedding song. I wanted a traditional wedding song, a slow cuddling waltz. The solution? 'Unchained Melody' for me; 'Two of a Kind' by Garth Brooks for him. (Don't know it? Imagine an upbeat, heel-clicking, knee-slapping number and you've got it.)

We honeymooned in Bali, indulging in pampering massages and Malibu cocktails by the pool. My cowboy took to the scene like a frog to a swamp, haggling enthusiastically with the street sellers, never tiring of the harassment. We ate noodle and rice delights and grilled corn on the cob from the local street stalls at night and during the day wandered far afield in our hired SUV. Rick revelled in the challenge of Bali-style driving, adopting the horn-hooting, rally-driving techniques of the locals with relish, while I stuck to the passenger side, leaving fingernail imprints on the black vinyl dashboard. With final exams awaiting my return, I used quiet undistracted moments when Rick was sleeping to study parasitology and endocrinology.

Returning to Australia we moved into Cardowan – with the cat, the egg cup, the cushion, the divan and my futon. I made a bookshelf from besser bricks and dressed it up by creating a curtain and pelmet effect with a remnant of green satin brocade that I found in a cupboard. We scrounged some hand-me-down furniture from the family, but the house still looked vast and empty with our scant furnishings.

Our first purchase as a married couple was a second-hand two-metre-long freezer. It was for the beef. With a freezer to stock, a 'killer' was taken into the town butcher for slaughter and carcass breakdown. Four days later, we went to Rosevale to 'do the meat'.

The sight of 300-odd kilos of meat to be packaged for freezing is enough to send the sanest person loopy. A mountain of mince must be bagged; a hummock of sausages divided; mammoth roasts cut; rib fillets, corned briskets, T-bones, Y-bones, blade, the tail, the tongue – all need sorting and dividing into manageable parcels. It is a strained, delicate affair. Rick's presence always brings solace to both his parents on this dreaded day of days, keeping the task of Doing the Meat as efficient and pleasant as possible for all concerned. For Peggy, his rapid assistance, 'Yes ma'am!' attitude and sharp butchering knives are balm on raw nerves, and for Grahame, Rick is a welcome decoy providing an escape route to fix a mill in the top paddock that has become conveniently urgent.

After my initiation into Doing the Meat, we lugged five large eskies of meat and two 22-gallon tubs of bones (for the dogs) home in the ute and unloaded them into the freezer. Now we had a little something to eat – half a cow.

While we were away Cardowan had received some early rain, which was followed up with the best rain in years, raining in torrents and destroying two dams in its fury. Their fragile walls, dried and cracked from years of drought, were no match for the force of the water that inundated them.

'So does that mean the drought is over?' I asked Rick.

'You're getting a bit ahead of yourself, Alice. It's rained. But it will take a lot more before this land, the creeks and rivers recover from what they've been through. This has only wet the topsoil. Water used to seep from these hills down the rock faces for weeks after rain in a good season. Geez, it'd be good to see that again.'

In spite of losing two dams and the precious stock water that they would have stored, and even though we had a long way to go to recover from the ravages of the drought that had persisted for five years, the rain was the best wedding gift imaginable.

I returned to Brisbane for my remaining four weeks of lectures, coming back to Cardowan for a week to study for final exams in November. While rewriting my biochemistry notes, engrossed in the transformation of muscle into meat, the phone rang, its bell loud enough to be heard at the cattle yards, slicing through the sound of pen scratching on paper. The voice of one of my closest schoolfriends, Merran, was on the other end. She'd just been up for the week of the wedding and it was a treat to hear from her so soon, but as soon as she spoke I knew something was wrong.

She told me that one of our best friends had drowned in a terrible accident. Shocked, I was even more devastated to discover that the funeral would coincide with my last exam. I was torn: I desperately wanted to be with his family and my friends, but a week later I sat my final exam, while my friends sat side by side at the funeral of one of our dearest.

I aced the exams but there was little pleasure in the results. The death of one of my inner circle brought my choices into stark focus, highlighting the permanence of my decisions – to study in Queensland, to marry Rick, to move to the outback. A vast gulf now separated me from my friends. They'd been my family long before Rick, and now I'd chosen a path separating me from them. Before I'd said 'I do' I'd had options, exit strategies, freedom. Now I was trapped. Just one path lay before me. I should know; I built it. It led to Cardowan and it was called marriage – for better, for worse.

The genie's patience had paid off, now she was going to release the doubts she'd been cultivating in the dark while I'd been distracted with wedding trinkets and bovine reproduction. It served me right for not listening to her, to Mum and Dad, to

Gaffer – they'd all warned me, saying I couldn't hack it out here, it was too isolated, I had no friends. *Now you're bloody well stuck here!* the genie hissed into my ear. *What are you going to do now?*

I didn't know what I was going to do, but I knew one thing: I'd make sure I never proved Gaffer right.

Eighteen

I needed to regain my independence, my sense of self; to have something more in my world than Rick. Getting busy was the best way to silence the genie and pack her menacing doubts away. The 'to do' list was straightforward: I needed to get a job.

My choice to work baffled Gaffer – or more accurately, it offended him – and having already crossed that barrier of telling me what he thought of me, he was not about to retreat.

'What are you doing, getting a job? You already have one! At home, looking after Rick and entertaining bull clients. If you did that properly, you wouldn't need to get a job.'

I was dumbfounded – I'd been told *not* to get a job. This went against every fibre of my being – against every universal law that I held and still hold dear, not to mention against my razor-sharp need to be independent and self-reliant. I was hardly going to rely on Rick's pay packet or the company cheque book to provide me with soft furnishings or a new dress. I'd heard the family mantra too many times: 'Buy the bull first and the carpet comes later.' Rick's Nana, Gaffer's wife, had said it in the fifties and it was as legendary as she was.

Anyway, I wanted to work. I wanted to learn. I wanted to find my purpose, my place in this new land I intended to make my home. Correction: I *needed* to. Surely Rick can make his own lunch, I guiltily contemplated. Would I really be such a bad wife if he didn't have freshly baked lamingtons, still moist from their dunking in hot chocolate and lightly tossed in desiccated coconut, waiting to greet him at smoko? I tried to grasp the lifelong implications of making Rick endure such neglect and the possibility that I might occasionally resort to the heinous crime of buying ready-made baked goods.

Grahame and Peggy actually seemed relieved that I'd chosen to get a job; it meant one fewer mouth for the business to feed. They knew times had changed. The persevering drought, increased costs and reduced prices for cattle were at the root of this change. By the mid-nineties, extra off-farm income was needed to underpin many farms across Queensland and put food on the table, while the farms that produced the food that is trucked into the cities day after day often ran at a loss, devouring precious equity, eroding livelihoods and straining relationships.

My options for work were not abundant. Resolved to put the long-distance aspect of our relationship behind us, I hoped to get something close to Cardowan in Kingaroy, fifty kilometres to the north-east. Kingaroy is a large town by country standards, with 10,000 people in the encompassing shire. I was prepared to do anything, but my scorching desire was to use my degree in agriculture, ideally in the beef industry. However, I knew beef jobs in this district were as rare as a bull with tits, so I would gratefully do anything agriculture-related.

The major crops grown in the region were summer crops such as maize, peanuts, navy beans and sorghum, however the unrelenting dry seasons and rising costs of production had generated an interest in alternative crops and more water-use efficient farming systems. Programs to support the development and implementation of more environmentally friendly farming strategies were commencing, creating new jobs. Hallelujah! I secured a job in one such program, with the Department of Primary Industries, based in Kingaroy. My main roles were in adult education, facilitation, cropping and soil conservation, working across a region that extended from Kumbia to a few hundred kilometres north of Kingaroy. Even though the tractors didn't moo, I was working with rural people and was thrilled to get the job.

The position was based at a sprawling research station with an emphasis on grain research. The station teemed with scientists, economists, entomologists, agronomists, technical assistants and farmhands, with a clutch of stock inspectors, one vet and one beef extension officer (the dream position I secretly coveted) to support the regional agricultural industry. I was given a small wooden desk in an open-plan office and a laptop computer of my own. I felt important and grown-up with my first computer. I thought I looked so professional putting my laptop in its case and carrying it around to meetings and home to work on – important people work at home in the evenings, in case you didn't know!

As a young female graduate, city bred and with scant technical knowledge of the subject matter, I trod carefully to stay on the right side of the local farmers. Like wary dogs that had been kicked in the guts too many times, these farmers had in-built wanker radars and were not in the business of humouring government employees. They'd met too many self-professed agricultural messiahs offering salvation while not depending themselves on the implications of their own advice. And the farmers were time poor, so you'd better deliver or get out of their face, off their farm and let them get back to their real work.

I knew nothing, so I admitted it, and built relationships on the presumption that people don't care how much you know until they know how much you care. My new surname also proved to be a passport to get me beyond the flyscreen door.

'Ah, you're a Greenup. You're on the land: you understand. C'mon in. Do you want a cuppa?'

'Actually, I was born in Melbourne and moved to Queensland only a few years ago, and to Kumbia a few months ago.'

'Well, you know now what it's like to have your livelihood depend on rain and the season and the markets – that makes you one of us.'

It wasn't true. Not then. Although I did know how it felt to wonder where my next meal was coming from and how far I could stretch the potato soup, seasoned with chicken bones – the only protein I would see for a week. However, compared with those hand-to-mouth student days, my pay cheques from the government now turned up in my bank account every fortnight. I didn't have to rely on the vagaries of the season or the fickle market to determine what groceries I could buy, or if I could reupholster the old couch, or whether I would be able to make the next school payments for my children.

I said nothing more to dissuade them of my credentials. The time would come when I too would dance at the beck of the seasons, and my fortune would depend on the climate, tempered by fate and human interference.

Over the months I fostered a great working relationship with my farmers. Grateful to be heard, they let me in on the inner workings of their family businesses. I listened to their concerns and areas of interest and arranged field days, study tours, small on-farm research trials and industry experts to address their issues. The meetings were attended mainly by men and the practicalities of spending hours in paddocks far from amenities were constant considerations. While the rest of the tour group was comfortable having 'watered Gusey's maize' I was forced to refrain from excessive water intake or discover new depths to my bladder to avoid squatting in Johno's peanuts – a small discomfort I was willing to endure to keep up with the blokes.

When I referred to a tractor and planter by colour, rather than manufacturer and type of press wheel, or mentioned 'angled cornery bits' instead of 'angle iron', and exclaimed, 'Wow, they're the biggest tyres I've ever seen!' rather than 'What sort of linkage does it have?', they forgave my shortcomings.

The job brought with it a welcome variation to my role as Rick's shadow and his 'better half', as I was often introduced on the southern side of the range. On the northern side, Rick was as much a newcomer as I and we were equals finding our way in a new community. By the year's close, it was not uncommon to hear 'Meet Rick, Alice's better half.' But no matter how immersed I became in my career, when I was out with Rick and his family on the Rosevale side of the range, my role was clear and singular. I was Rick's wife.

The reality of my dual identities hit me like a slap in the face when I attended a meeting of the United Graziers Association on the southern side of the range. With the national president in attendance to discuss the current political climate and the pressing issues affecting the beef industry, I was salivating in anticipation. I had met the president, Larry Acton, and attended some meetings with him – albeit as a trainee – while working part-time at the Queensland Farmers Federation during my last year at uni, gaining first-hand insights and a keen interest in agripolitics and policy.

After the formal part of the meeting was adjourned, the women retired to the kitchen to prepare refreshments while the men stayed outside to burrow down deeper into the issues. At first the gender division was not apparent to me – I'd presumed everyone had taken their places according to their areas of interest – and without question my preferred place was within earshot of Larry. This discourse was no idle gossip – issues such as market access, disease threats, the continuing drought, drought relief, exceptional circumstances finance, quarantine security, and the rates of depression and suicide scourging the outback were on the table.

Like a dog waiting for more scraps from the feast, I was oblivious to my right and proper place.

I nestled alongside Rick on an outer wing of the clutch of men, catching only a few sentences before my presence was registered by one of the older generation. He turned to me, his head inclined quizzically.

'Yes, Alice?'

'I'm, um, just listening,' my voice squeaked unnaturally, so unlike the voice of the professional agricultural scientist who worked on the other side of the range.

'Well, I think we're all in need of a cuppa. Who would like a cup of tea?' he asked, offering my services.

Frustrated as much with myself, that a few words and a glance was all it took to admonish me, I wandered off to begrudgingly assume my duties, ferrying cups of tea to the men. Rick looked at me, thankfully, apologetically. 'Do you want a hand?' he offered.

'No thanks. One of us may as well learn what's happening in the world.'

I was consoled that things were different at home. There we were a team. My work involved regular night meetings to fit in with the farmers' schedules as well as travelling long distances around the state. I was often home late after Rick or away for days at a time. Not one to baulk at any task at hand, Rick threw familial convention aside and took it upon himself to cook dinner when I worked late.

In March he started his repertoire with the standard steak and three veg, a recipe he'd cultivated in the stock camp. By April he'd progressed to more complex meals, such as spaghetti bolognaise and corned beef with white sauce, writing the recipe for a roux, the basis of a white sauce, into his work notebook alongside vital stock information. In May I summoned my most encouraging compliments when I came home to a 'mustard' instead of a 'curry', and in June I insisted emphatically that I couldn't smell the charcoal from the carport when he cooked pizzas on 250° C in fifteen minutes to save time. In July the tables were turned as he taught me about Burdekin ducks, aka brumbies in the sand hills, aka corned beef fritters. By August I had coaxed him into using the simmer function on the cook top, which improved his roux and white sauce immeasurably and ensured that innumerable heads of broccoli and innocent potatoes no longer died in vain. And by year's end, he was dazzling me and himself with a successful and diverse menu.

On weekends and after work we slowly began renovating Cardowan with the intention of displaying the house's original beauty, her great bones and ironbark skins. While many were forthcoming with suggestions of how to change the house, Joan had wisely suggested we 'do nothing except live in it for at least a year. Get to know the house and see what it reveals to you before changing anything.' She was right of course – all those draft plans made in the early days for major redesigns went by the wayside as we realised how the sun warmed the northern verandah through the winter – a perfect spot for a kids' playroom one day; and that a bedroom the size of a small apartment held a certain decadence of a bygone era that would be lost by dividing up the space into smaller rooms and an en suite. However, the lino and lamipanel lining the bathroom and kitchen walls remained first on the hit list.

Gradually we filled the rooms with hand-me-down furniture and cast iron beds that Rick restored from odds and ends he'd scavenged from the dump. A second-hand electric stove–oven was a steal at $200 – then we discovered the house needed another $1500 worth of rewiring to upgrade the mains power and install our 'bargain'. And eventually the crumbling white pickets made way for a post-and-rail fence built to outlive the next generation. There was always something happening at Cardowan and visiting friends soon learnt that a bed and a beer always came with a hammer, chainsaw or crowbar.

On the few occasions when we both finished work while it was still daylight we'd sit on the southern verandah in our squatters' chairs enjoying a cold one before cooking dinner together. Our conversations would be punctuated with the sound of gunshots. 'Got one!' Rick would cheer, having taken out one of the rabbits that were breeding up, taunting him, hopping around the sheds. Holding hands, we'd walk over to the crime scene. A pair of grey ears and a puff of fur would be all that remained, plastered to the weatherboards.

'Rick, do you think the .223 could be just a tad overkill?'

When we weren't renovating or popping off rogue bunnies, we loaded up our schedules with extra work to get ahead. During the week Rick worked long days for his parents, managing the surrounding 4000 hectares of aggregate country and often travelling to Rosevale to build yards and do stockwork. On the weekends we hosted paying guests who wanted to experience a working farm and, unable to be idle even for a moment, Rick also took in outside horses for breaking in and training.

With Cardowan built on a rocky plateau, there was nowhere suitable for training horses without rendering them lame within half an hour. Our first essential improvement was to build a horse arena – we hired a dozer to cut a flat pad out of the side of the hill, about the size of two tennis courts, which we fenced with a 1.8-metre-high post-and-rail fence, hanging black ex-mine conveyor belting from the top rail, as the arena walls. For two days Rick carted sand from the river to provide ten centimetres of soft training surface. With our arena complete, we got into our horse riding.

As another summer approached and the days lengthened, I would come home to a saddled horse waiting for me, and my teacher ready to give me another lesson. We began at the basics: the grip of my reins, the squeeze of my legs, sitting square, leaning back into my stops, smooth departures and smooth stops.

'The shortest distance between two points is a straight line, Alice. It's all about the stop and the turnaround, not motorbike whoops-a-daisy turns.'

Skittles and I were working better as a team, but when we progressed to roll backs and turnarounds, it seemed to fall apart. I'd confuse myself and the horse. The roll back felt awkward, strained, heavy – nothing like the effortless shift of weight and direction that Rick's horses achieved. Out the corner of my eye, I saw Rick wince. It looked so easy when he demonstrated; he just wasn't explaining himself right: 'You're contradicting what you said yesterday!' I yelled.

'That was yesterday! Today I'm saying something different!' he yelled back.

Frustrated, I yanked on the horse. Poor Skittles – caught in the middle of a domestic dispute. My guilt about taking it out on the innocent horse pulled my brain back into gear. I took a deep breath and stopped arguing: with Rick, with Skittles. I tried Rick's suggestion, even though I was sure it wouldn't work, and felt Skittles respond.

Shit, it worked. I looked up, grinning in spite of myself, and saw Rick smiling at me from the fence.

'Feels good, doesn't it? When it flows like that.'

'Wow.'

'And once you've had a go at campdrafting, you'll understand better what we're trying to achieve in the training process.'

I was encouraged that Rick thought I could have a go at campdrafting and not break my neck. 'Do you think I'd be ready by next year?'

'I think you should nominate for the draft next month.'

'Are you serious?'

'Too right. The only way you'll get ready, Alice, is to have a go.'

Nineteen

Leaning over the top rail of the camp I watch the mob of nine cattle. I have to choose one to take. It's my turn after this guy on the chestnut gelding. My heart is racing. I've emptied my bowels three times already this morning and am praying they'll stay intact for the duration of my run.

I ride into the yard. Skittles is agitated, sensing my nerves. I'm no longer concerned about diarrhoea; I think I will be sick instead. I cut out the beast chosen for me by Rick.

It wasn't so bad, much like cutting out the cows and calves at home. We'd decided on a foolproof strategy: get my beast and get outside. Most riders do fancy work cutting the beast, I'm happy with poking it to the front and getting the gates open straight away.

'Call the gate,' Rick instructs from the side as soon as my beast is separated from the mob.

'Gate!'

The gate opens. I move forward on the steer, it sees me coming and runs straight back to the mob. Skittles and I stand there flat-footed, wondering what happened. Now I've got to cut it out again. This time we scoot it off the side of the mob, sending it *straight towards the opening at the top of the pen. The beast looks up, seeing the gap in the fence. He runs out, pausing briefly to sniff at the ground as he leaps through the gateway, sensing his escape. The sweat saturating my palms is making the leather reins slippery. I'm terrified Skittles will bolt after the beast. I shorten my reins with a white-knuckled grip. I realise with astonishment that I'm in control; he isn't doing anything reckless. I click him forward into a canter. Precious seconds have passed while I've fumbled, taking my eyes off the beast, worrying about my reins. I try to catch the steer, but all I can see is its dust – it's gone. Game over.*

'Thirteen,' the judge calls out, obliged to score me. That is, thirteen out of a possible one hundred.

That first attempt at drafting seems as fresh as the day it happened. It was hideous, but my pride somehow survived. Now that the unofficial judges sitting on the fence knew I was pathetic, there was no need to worry about them next time, and I had a new goal – to beat my first score of thirteen.

My second attempt was worse: I couldn't even get out of the camp. The sound of the judge's stockwhip cracking through the air to cancel my ride sent the blood pulsing up my neck, reddening my face. It was a 'no score'.

I had nothing left to lose, but the third and fourth rides continued in this fashion, giving the judge's whip a work-out at my expense. This sport was not good for the ego. Unable to rally the ol' chutzpah again, my pride was in tatters. I was thoroughly embarrassed to be taking up the valuable time of these experienced competitors with my feeble amateurish attempts.

'You've paid your money, you've got every right to be here,' Rick reassured. 'Everyone starts out like that.'

I appreciated his words of comfort and what he was considerately omitting to say: everyone starts when they're three, not twenty-three!

With a marginally better idea of what I was trying to do when campdrafting, I practised riding with more focus and renewed diligence. My riding needed infinite attention but I couldn't neglect everything else. I divided my leisure hours between riding and gardening.

Cardowan's minimal garden was almost devoid of trees and shrubs. I appraised the blank canvas of sparse brown lawn and did a stocktake of the existing infrastructure I had to work with: five out-of-commission rainwater tanks dotted around the yard on broken stands, pretending to be garden features; two Hill's Hoists (who needs two?); one huge brown timber laundry within metres of the back door; and two straight-edged garden beds bordering the front verandah with old scented roses that looked like lonely crimson-and-peach watchmen. A cluster of red geraniums leaning on the corner of the laundry looked as if someone didn't finish the weeding, while two sprawling magenta bougainvillea and a clump of agapanthus provided more clues to what survives untended in a drought.

I laid out where I wanted to put new garden beds and took up my shovel ready to attack the landscape. Rick found me as I was heading off.

'What are you doing?'

'What do you think I'm doing? I'm building some new gardens.'

'Not with that shovel you're not.'

'What do you mean?'

'I mean you can't build a garden with a shovel.'

I was confused and frustrated with the cryptic interruption. I'd built plenty of gardens, both in Brisbane and in Brighton. Gardening in Brighton was the best – the sandy loamy soils made for easy digging and the gentle climate and regular rainfall meant that most things grew easily and vigorously. Where you wanted a garden bed, you put a garden bed. What you wanted to plant, you planted.

'I've built plenty of gardens. I think I know what I'm doing.'

'Not out here you haven't. And by the looks of that shovel, you won't get far.'

'What's wrong with my shovel?'

'Well, you'll need a crowbar to start with.'

'A *what*?'

Rick went and got me his crowbar, shaking his head at the size of the beds I'd planned. Every sod turned was an effort: thumping the crowbar into the puggy, sticky ground and levering the soil and rocks apart so the shovel could do its share. We took it in turns on the crowbar and shovel and by day's end had one garden bed and numerous blisters.

Obliging family and friends brought special specimens up from Victoria when they visited so I could re-create the gardens of my childhood, but cut-leaf silver birches, fuchsias and magnolias failed to establish and withered until I accepted defeat and called the time of death, throwing another twiggy corpse into the rubbish. Many of the plants I yearned to use in the garden didn't survive the first month; some struggled on, eking out my hope, but eventually they all moved to a higher plane, while my optimism and vision of an outback oasis sank lower and lower.

For lack of options I propagated the geraniums and divided the agapanthus, resignedly acknowledging the restrictions of the hot climate, summer rainfall and dry winter months, eventually scouring the drought-hardy gardens of Joan, Peggy, Aunt Shirley and my newest friend and avid gardener, Carolyn, for cuttings. I also got inspiration from their creations – each magnificent garden built under extreme conditions and each a gentle cool refuge from the soaring temperatures in the paddock. I learnt that if I couldn't dig down, I could build up my garden beds with newspaper and hay.

I developed a collection of hardy succulents and other drought-tolerant plants and scavenged self-sown poinciana and jacaranda seedlings from the roadside in Brisbane, which I planted alongside a fast-growing tipuana in a semicircle on the hot western side of the house. They would provide shade and eventually a foundation for a gentler microclimate on our barren rectangle. I needed to be patient and resourceful.

What Cardowan lacked in water and sandy loam soils it made up for in an abundance of logs and rocks for landscaping. Rick was enlisted as my off-sider. My man would help with gardening – not with pissy little gardening jobs like weeding, but big manly jobs that involved machinery. Everyday gardening implements like secateurs and wheelbarrows were sniffed at with disgust and cast aside for chainsaws, earth-moving equipment and tractors. Without question, the favourite toy of Rick and Grahame was the front-end loader – a veritable workhorse and every gardener's dream machine for moving dirt and rocks. Despite my misgiving about Rick's lack of romantic ways during our courtship, now we were married he got me rocks – and in my book, rocks trump flowers.

'You know what Dad says about women and gardens?' he grunted, levering a rock into place with a crowbar.

'No, Rick, tell me.'

'He says women are never happy when it comes to gardens. He says, "If you build a house on a good soil plain she'll bring in rocks and if you build a house on rocks she'll want soil brought in".'

I don't argue with truth.

Finished installing our first load of rocks, Rick and I headed back out, taking the flat-bed truck and the loader into a paddock that offered a wealth of large rocks. The loader is a precarious beast, with its narrow wheelbase and height, and should always be kept at right angles to the slope of the hill. Rick had been tempting fate all morning. He was working parallel to the slope in the loader, getting huge flat rocks that easily weighed half a tonne each to use as landings at the base of the stairs. His fearlessness had already meant some close calls, with the wheels lifting dangerously in protest at his manoeuvres. 'It's right,' he insisted, but I opted to stay on the solid stable ground, walking ahead of the loader to scout for rocks.

As Rick swung the bucket up the hill to grab a rock, the front tyre kicked up on a small boulder and the extra shift in the weight was enough to destabilise the big yellow beast. This time his gambling luck was exhausted and the loader began to roll, tilting its weight sideways down the hill. Rick leapt up from the seat and leant out the open doorway in starfish position – hanging on by one arm and standing on one leg, the other arm and leg outstretched. The redressing of weight slowed the momentum of the loader rolling sideways. As the balance point was shifted, the loader tottered precariously, perched on a knife edge, then stabilised and was still, with only a flea's fart tipping the scales in our favour.

We allowed ourselves a premature sigh of relief while Rick considered his options. Any normal person would jump clear while he could and save his own life, leaving the loader to its ruin. But Rick's not normal and there is that issue of him missing out on the self-preservation gene. Rick weighed up whether to adjust the bucket lower or sideways or drop the rippers – the wrong decision and it would be lights out for Grahame's favourite child – the loader, I mean. He needed to get his arm back inside the cab to adjust the controls. Already convinced of impending disaster, I formulated the words to break to Grahame what we'd done. However, never the quitter and ever the optimist, Rick slid his outer arm onto the doorjamb in order to free up the right one, so he could get hold of a lever to reposition the bucket. This indiscernible movement tipped the scales and the old girl resumed her roll.

'Jump on the wheel!' Rick shouted.

Fast wit is essential to avoid disaster in most situations, but in my case 'blind stupidity' is a better term to label my actions as I obeyed Rick's directions without hesitation. At rest, the tops of the wheels were level with my shoulders but as the front wheel lifted further off the ground, it towered above me. However, obediently I leapt up onto it, gripping the rim with white knuckles, feet on the bottom part of the rim, pushing my bottom out as far as I could and thinking heavy thoughts – as heavy as a sixty-kilogram counterweight on the left front wheel of a three-tonne loader could be. Humouring our tenacity, the loader stopped her roll, curious to see if we had any more tricks up our sleeves before she completed her arc.

With Rick swinging out as far as he could from the door and me attached to the front wheel, the loader was poised with two wheels on the ground and two wheels in the air, perfectly balanced. A good short-term result – but we were stuck; no-one could move. No-one could even fart.

'Now what, Houdini?' I yelled, then instantly regretted it, fearing that the exhalation would be enough to destabilise our circus trick and catapult us down the hill, legs, arms, rocks, yellow steel and all.

Our escape depended on Rick getting one arm back inside the cabin to adjust the levers controlling the bucket. *Think heavy, Alice.*

I concentrated on pushing my bum even further out. *Heavy, heavy, heeaavvyy.*

I watched, my body tense, as Rick eased one arm into the cabin with the speed of a slug. The loader swayed on her wheels, toying with her decision.

HEEAAVVYY. I urged every cell of my body to achieve its greatest mass potential, and planned my escape route to avoid going all the way over with the wheel. One wrong move …

The bucket dropped to the ground and the rippers dug in behind as Rick worked the two controls simultaneously with one hand, back and forth. With her needs heard and understood, the soothed leviathan rolled back onto four wheels. Blood resumed pulsing into my extremities.

Our shared energy to beautify Cardowan and build a life together was invigorating to say the least and our first year of marriage was filled with fresh experiences. A new job, new people, new community, new garden, new horse, new sport. Inevitably, however, somewhere along the line the novelty stopped being so shiny and new. The honeymoon was over and negative thoughts crept in again. Ever the opportunist, the genie awoke and set to work.

Twenty

People in the bush think anyone's fair game after 5.30 a.m. and considering there was a small window between five and six when they might have caught Rick before he went out to the paddock, it was common for the phone to ring before six – it was also equally common that they would've already missed him and that I would have to stumble out of bed clearing my voice before answering the phone so I could fake it, pretending that I too had caught the first worm. 'Hi, Rick's gone already. Can I take a message?'

Caught out, the voice on the other end would chastise my croaky, just-woken voice. 'Jeez, Alice, did you just wake up? The sun's been up for ages. Suzie's already milked two cows, got the kids and me breakfast and made our lunches while you've bin asleep.' Then the clincher would come as the caller did the maths: 'I s'pose Rick had to make his own lunch and breakfast? No wonder the poor bugger's so skinny.'

My dutiful laughter in reply would be tinny and hollow. And, in silent mental agreement, I'd resume questioning my suitability as a good country wife for Rick. I'd draw up a mental balance sheet of my pros and cons, filling the 'con' side of the ledger all too easily: wakes up at a tardy 7 a.m.; can't ride (and cranky when he tries to teach me); no truck licence; can't drive a tractor; constantly home late; travels for work, inconsiderately leaving him to look after himself – I'd even stopped ironing his jeans. In so many vital tasks, I fell short. I still habitually appraised his alternatives at each campdraft, always finding rich pickings of more qualified substitutes.

The second year of marriage droned on. It seemed that the only aberrations of the unchanging life stretching ahead of me were the emotions of the people around me that were inextricably linked to where the meniscus sat in the rain gauge. The homesickness and permanence of my situation felt like a suffocating blanket. I needed to link back to the things that I was passionate about before Rick became my passion. The ballet and theatre were a big part of my life in Melbourne, but I'd not been to the ballet since moving to Queensland. I bought season tickets.

I didn't have any friends living in Brisbane. I guess that's the downside of doing a degree in agriculture – people I'd known at uni had moved to every corner of rural Australia for their careers. Rick came to the ballet once to humour me, but neither of us could deny it: Rick was not interested and his stoic endurance in the theatre ruined the experience for me. So alone I made the trip to Brisbane each month and watched a dance company perform. The loneliness was worst after a moving, breathtaking contemporary performance, when I craved to share the experience and conduct a post-mortem of the dancers, the choreography, the music. I tried to convey what I saw and felt to Rick. He didn't get it at all.

I'd hoped resurrecting this neglected passion would help bridge the gap between old life and new; instead the gap widened. I withdrew in resentment that Rick would not become the man I wanted him to be, or substitute for the girlfriend – the confidante – I craved. I could see nothing before me but the cup half empty. I studied this man and this woman, this husband and wife, and I wondered what brought them together. I picked apart every action and every word. Conversations became strained, laced with disappointment. I wish I could tell you I behaved more maturely, but I was too busy wallowing in my disenchantment to grow up. So if you find my behaviour annoying, you have my sympathy – but my job here is to be honest, not infallible. Living with a brooding gloomster was no bundle of fun for Rick either. I didn't care. I wanted him to be brushed with my heavy black tar.

For the previous six years I'd kept homesickness at bay by spending a few weeks in Victoria each year, topping up my fix of friends. My salvation from my gloom was to be a trip I'd planned for us to take to Adelaide and Melbourne for the Christmas holidays. Spending time with friends and family who knew me, who shared my interests, who accepted me for who I was, would be a much needed tonic and a relief from loneliness, my fermenting mind and the foreboding sense that I would never measure up. With a swag of accumulated annual leave up my sleeve, I intended to spend three weeks away from Queensland, away from Cardowan and Rick's 5 a.m. starts. Three weeks for us to get back on the same page. Three weeks for us to rediscover our connection. Three weeks for me to remember that I was okay. Three weeks to find our laughter.

On a family farm, putting in an application for leave is not quite as simple as if you work for the government – it doesn't matter how much notice and how much leave accumulated or overtime done – that just goes into the bottomless pit called a farm. Rick's family didn't want him to be away longer than two weeks. In fact, they'd prefer one week. He needed to get back for branding; branding without Rick was an anomaly. 'Surely they could survive without you!' I bitched at him jealously. They held a meeting to discuss expectations. It was resolved that David and Rick would get two weeks' holiday per year, irrespective of public holidays – maybe three in a good year once the drought had broken. I was the lone rebel railing at the exploitation. Rick didn't care if he had no holidays at all. He loved working. I needed to escape.

My heart sank as I realised that Rick's constraints were now my own. When I married Rick, I became part of an established framework – a family structure, a family business and a life in agriculture with seasonal demands that would always take precedence over the individual.

My stint with the Queensland Farmers Federation during my last year at uni had left me with aspirations. Now I contemplated where else my career could have taken me if I'd got a job in the city among the George Street policymakers, the movers and the shakers that guide statewide strategies for agriculture. *You could have been so much more*, the genie goaded, playing on my desire to feel valued.

The full consequences of marrying a man on the land had finally dawned on me. My wings were clipped. I know, I know; there's nothing about this scenario that I shouldn't have seen coming. Gaffer told me, straight up. Mum and Dad had cautioned me. And I'd dismissed their concerns as symptoms of the rural–city divide. No-one could accuse me of not knowing what I signed up for. I'd spent six years coming in second to Rick's work, and his passion for his land and his family business. Maybe I'd been too impatient to merge my life with Rick's. I thought I knew what I was getting myself into, but knowing about it and living it with no more 'outs' are very different things. Despite my new career, my personal income and independence did not liberate me from the property. This was my life. I was no longer a backpacker, a student, changing course on whim, free to live, be and do as I pleased.

As I stewed about the situation, my gut would twist and I couldn't sleep. The pain in my stomach lingered, sometimes dull and niggling; sometimes a searing jab. Handing me a prescription, the doctor said, 'It's probably an ulcer – take this when it flares up, and we'll see if it settles down.'

With a strained compromise in place, we drove to Adelaide for Christmas, spending the first thousand kilometres arguing and the second thousand making up. Lazy days on the beach and in the hills with my maternal family whisked by – a mere splinter of the family tree and roots that I needed.

From Adelaide we went to Melbourne for a week. It was great to be home, but after some rushed get-togethers with friends, visits to childhood haunts and a quick camping trip to Wilson's Prom it was all over – rather like a horse race: just a blur of colour and just as it gets interesting it's finished. All too soon we were back on the Newell Highway and two days later we were driving up the gravel driveway towards Cardowan. But to me it didn't feel like coming home. It didn't even feel like a splendid holiday in the bush. It felt like a 3700-hectare prison. An unseen force like an invisible rope tied around my ankle was pulling me south, 2000 kilometres to Melbourne, back to my real home. I was shitty as we drove up to the house. Shitty enough to undo all the pleasantness of the trip. Shitty enough to take him down with me. *Why not ruin his mood too? After all, it's his fault I'm back here.*

Without unpacking we attended a party out of the district the following night. I'd know a couple of people at the party as acquaintances, the rest would be anonymous faces. I would have preferred to stay at home and sulk, missing my friends in Melbourne. The ute was silent with my brooding as we made the three-hour trip to the party. It was a hot midsummer night and I wore a long, white cotton dress with sandals. As we arrived I saw everyone, male and female, was wearing Wranglers and shirts. I stood out like dog's balls. I felt like a dickhead. It was 7 p.m. and I already wanted to go home.

Rick engaged in conversation effortlessly. I ran out of conversation openers and mated up with my wine bottle instead. It was just too hard. I drifted between groups trying to find someone or a conversation to connect to. Rick was elsewhere. As the night wore on a couple of the blokes got a skinful of rum. Tired of drifting, I found myself sitting next to them attempting a conversation. My attempts went over like a lead balloon, but I persevered, trying to build a bridge between our world views. I'm not sure how or why it deteriorated. Some disparaging remarks were made of my campdrafting efforts ... my attitude ... something about knowing my place, the impropriety of asking questions of people evidently too important to discuss trivialities with an amateur.

Maybe I was too forthright, maybe it was something I said or my diluted English accent or that I was out of 'uniform', or maybe I'd just eaten a shit sandwich for lunch, but whatever it was, I got a piece of someone's mind – a mind that had been marinating in rum. Bloodshot eyes seared through my flesh and thin lips curled back in disdain as they spat at me: 'Alice, you're just a bloody silvertail married to a Greenup, they're just a bunch of fuckin' silvertails too.'

'You don't even know me!'

'I know your type. You were born with a silver spoon. You talk like you've got a plum in your mouth. You dress all fancy – look at you – what's with that dress? You silvertails fuckin' stick together. I know that.'

I struggled to grasp what I was hearing. I'm *a silvertail? After all the houses and restaurants I've cleaned, wiping up vomit from the floors of restaurant bathrooms, cleaning men's urinals? All the beers I've pulled and the abuse I've copped in pubs to make ends meet – scrimping and scavenging second-hand outfits – one of which I'm wearing now – he thinks I was born with a silver spoon? Screw him. Screw them all.*

When you're in your twenties, the opinions of other people still matter even when they shouldn't – of course that's easy to say now, with a few more character lines embellishing my face. But right there, sitting on that hay bale, I wanted to set him straight, give him a piece of my mind, however I knew that if I'd opened my mouth I would have crumpled into a messy puddle of tears. I was drunk, desperately homesick and, overall, feeling quite fragile.

I removed myself and found Rick, pulling him aside into the darkness of the garden, telling him the tale amid a bad case of ugly hiccupping blubbering: '... and then he ... aheh, aheh ... said ... aheh ... that ... aheh ... I was ...' Rick could see I was in no state to rejoin the party. We drove home in virtual silence, my pitiful 'aheh, aheh's breaking the quiet thrum of the ute. He was angry. I was hurt. We were both bewildered and confused.

The wrench of farewelling Melbourne with a new sense of permanence and the constant strain of trying to fit in, coupled with the wretched blindsiding from the bloodshot eyes, knocked me off my feet and out for the count. I couldn't get back up. I didn't even feel like trying. My mind plunged into a dark place, taking up residence in the genie's chamber. *Who could I trust? Who could I talk to? Who was judging me? Scorning me? Laughing at me?* I avoided campdrafts or, if I went, stayed close to the horse trailer, avoiding the crowd. I wouldn't leave Rick's side at the bar, wary and scared I'd run into the bloodshot eyes or another of his kind, no longer feeling safe or adventurous or keen to meet new people.

I felt lonelier than I did in all the years I lived alone in Brisbane. I didn't want to leave Rick or my new world, but I felt adrift and lost. Thoughts built for self-sabotage and blame festered. *He never gave up anything to be with me. He didn't even try to live in Melbourne.* Once I'd got on that merry-go-round, I seemed unable to stop it. For weeks I continued in this manner: snivelling, precious, punishing Rick. I gave in to self-indulgent emotional spewing. I cried without a trigger. Night after night, I sat on the verandah and wept. Rick would sit with me, his downcast eyes showing confusion, fear and sorrow.

'Is there anything I can do?'

'No, it's not you. It's nothing you've done or haven't done. I don't even know why I'm crying, but I just can't stop.'

Even I was sick of my own company. In Melbourne I would have gone for long walks along the beach until clarity prevailed and the next step on my path would be revealed in the swish of the waves against the breakwater. At Cardowan, I walked up the dirt track and I walked back down the dirt track. I walked up. I walked down. Up. Down. No friggin' difference – different day, same trees, same shit.

The trees don't speak to me like the waves. At least that is what I thought. In truth, I hadn't taken the time to learn their language or hear the whispers of the landscape. I was like an immigrant who refuses to learn the native tongue of their new country, then bitches and moans that no-one takes the time to talk to them. Sadness found an ally in shame for putting Rick through this ordeal. I became leaden with guilt and self-loathing. Maybe that was better than blame.

I saw a psychologist. Obligingly he listened as I poured out my woes, blubbering, regurgitating my life struggles, my strained relationship with Dad, my self-pitying misery, my guilt for the way this was all impacting Rick. My soliloquy slowed and the tears dried as I cleared the contents of my baggage. Wiping my eyes I glanced up, perceiving that my psychologist was barely engaged with my riveting tale. Instead of commiserating I sensed a bored, almost yawning, response on the other side of the desk. 'Is that it?'

I considered rephrasing, reiterating, recolouring some of the more painful tragic episodes in my life – maybe he didn't catch those bits – but I sensed his response wouldn't change.

'Yes, that's about it,' I murmured as I blew my nose.

'Well, from what I can make of it, you've had some challenges in life. Who hasn't? And you've probably got a good dose of homesickness. So what?'

'I feel bad about how this is all impacting Rick.'

'Well, you *should* feel bad about putting Rick through all this. He's a nice guy from what I can see.'

'I want to be happy. For us to be happy.'

'Well, be happy.'

'It isn't that simple.'

'Yes it is. Decide to be happy. Now.'

'Can I do that?'

'Of course you can. I can see you're depressed, but you've gotta ask yourself: why? You're healthy and you're married to a great guy – there are people out there with real issues – life-threatening issues! Your depression is pure self-indulgence.'

He all but smacked me on the bottom, saying pull yourself together and get over it. I'd been told! His harsh, unsympathetic words pulled me back into line. He spoke truth. I did want to get my act together. He gave me a book on the psychology of positive thinking and some homework exercises and said I could come back if the homework didn't improve things.

I walked out his door and out of the genie's chamber, closing both doors behind me. I felt stronger this time. As if, for once, the cork in that genie's bottle might just hold.

Twenty-one

Over the next few months I worked hard at keeping my mind free of the crap that had taken residence there, working with my newfound and much cherished axiom from *Hamlet* that 'nothing is ever good or bad, only thinking makes it so'.

I took a secondment to Brisbane for three months, working in policy. It was a great eye-opener for me to see what I had missed out on while living at Cardowan – the career opportunities I'd craved; the corporate ladder I'd wanted to climb; the flash suits and high heels I wanted to wear; the intoxicating sense of importance fuelled by meetings and working to deadlines, developing vital strategic policies for primary industries. Then there was the food of city living – sushi, Indian, Thai – I got to live it all.

And I learnt that all along I'd been tilting at windmills, that the ego had been calling the shots and the world I'd coveted was a house of straw. I couldn't bear the ceilings, the high-rise living, the jostling for promotion, the disconnection from the grass-roots producers and the arrogant development of policy from the inner-city shadows of George Street. I began again to count down to the weekends.

And I missed my man. My patient man.

I looked at Rick across the kitchen table one Sunday morning. He was sipping his scalding black tea and reading *Queensland Country Life*, and my stomach flipped, as if I hadn't seen him for so long, even though he'd been there the whole time.

'I don't know what I was thinking, Rick. I'm sorry. Really sorry about what I've put you through this year.'

'It doesn't matter, Alice. I just want to see you get whatever it was out of your system and be happy. I've missed my little mate. It's good to have you back.' He stood up from the table and kissed me on the lips.

'How many eggs do you want?' he asked, grabbing the frying pan.

Cardowan took on a golden hue when the three months were up and I reimmersed myself in my outback world with renewed love. Having coming home just in time for New Year's and the 1997 branding season, I used some leave to join in the muster and for the first time gave my annual trip to Melbourne a miss. I shoved my suits to the back of the wardrobe in favour of checked shirts and Wranglers and, with Rick's guidance, got a new Akubra hat with my own bash that didn't make me look like an agent and that stayed on my head when I cantered. I was looking more the part, but it would be some time before I realised I'd swung the pendulum past the midpoint and had lost the balance between my old self and being like them.

Nevertheless, there were some practical benefits to the clothes, of course. My ears and neck no longer got sunburnt from wearing the cap that I'd substituted for the 'Agent's Akubra' and the Wranglers didn't ride up my legs when I rode, so no more chafing. My riding improved to a point where I could wear my own set of spurs that Rick had bought me without jabbing the poor animal unwittingly. I now had two horses that I rode daily: my dear Skittles and a new one,

Peppy's Fox – a 14.3-hand quarter horse gelding. A chestnut four year old with a quiet, compliant temperament, he also had what's called in the game 'natural cow sense'. Both horses were working better across the board: in training, at campdrafts and out in the paddock mustering. Still no complete score outside at a campdraft, but I held my head high – there was no disgrace in being a beginner.

We joined the Kumbia campdraft committee, throwing ourselves behind this two-day Easter event, donating cattle for the competition and our timber and labour for rebuilding the yards. Rick took on the management of a wild dog containment program for the district. I was getting to know a number of the local farmers and my work colleagues, and we also became active in a regional host farming group – others like us who took in paying guests in exchange for an outback experience on a family farm. Circles of friendship rippled outwards from each hub and we were beginning to feel we belonged.

Wylarah continued to be a favourite port of call. It was the sheltered bay where I could anchor and lower my sails when the seas were choppy and my mind felt like capsizing again. Joan taught me how to make the most of country living. 'You'll always be lonely, Alice, if you're looking for everything in one or two people. Living in the country is like crossing the Atlantic on an ocean liner: these are the people you're stuck with. Find something to enjoy in everyone and embrace the eccentricities and you'll have a wonderful voyage.'

John and Joan had us over for dinner regularly, whether both of us or Rick by himself when I was away for work. The conclusion of one dinner party usually served as a date claimer for the next.

'We've had dinner here four times this month,' I'd apologise.

'I enjoy it. I love having you over. And winter is the perfect season for dinner parties,' Joan would assure us.

'How can we ever repay you?'

'Nonsense. It's not about keeping tabs, Alice. It goes around. You'll do it for someone else one day.'

Rick, John and Joan conspired to hold a surprise dinner party for my birthday in June, inviting some of my friends from work to join us. Joan made asparagus soup for the entree, roast lamb with broccolini and baby carrots as a main and for dessert brandy snaps filled with cream and strawberries that had been marinated in Cointreau. She'd made four batches of the brandy snap batter trying to get the perfect consistency – the balance of ingredients and the old wood-fired stove working in harmony.

After dinner Joan presented me with a painting she'd done of Skittles and me cantering out of an abstract background; a delicious blend of purples and shades of magenta. Her depiction of his chestnut face, white blaze and kind eyes was perfect. As if that wasn't enough, she handed me a second watercolour she'd painted the summer before, a field of ripe sorghum, the fiery red-orange blazing across the page. Both pictures had been framed by John.

'But wait, there's something for you too, Rick! John's finished your wedding present. Better late than never,' Joan blurted, beside herself with excitement.

'The roses for our bouquets were our wedding present!' Rick and I protested, but John strode off grinning, returning with a long hall table that he'd made using an old cupboard door for the table top and legs he'd turned from timber cut aeons ago at Wylarah.

'Now you'll have some of Wylarah at Cardowan,' he said simply.

Not a man for all seasons, Rick rejoiced at the winter solstice and the lengthening days when he could get more work done outside, despite Joan coaxing Rick not to rail against the annual tides, but to yield with the seasons. 'Winter is a time for renewal and rest,' Joan would tell him. 'Be patient, Rick, you've got your whole life to work.'

I admit, I too was keen, as always, to see the arrival of spring. Cardowan had revealed herself to be a house more suited to the summer months, whisking away stale hot air with her well-designed casement windows that acted like spinnakers, capturing breezes effortlessly even when there seemed to be no breeze at all – a pleasant trait in the scorching summer but bloody horrendous when frosts turned the lawn white and sealed the fate on yet another batch of poorly chosen plants.

As our third summer of living at Cardowan approached and the days obligingly lengthened, I began to look forward to campdrafts without trepidation and no longer felt the need to hide out in our horse float. With our new friends we watched each other's rides, encouraging one another – the more experienced ones generously offering tips and ideas about how I could improve. Riding was about learning and having fun. Who cared if I never scored? I was enjoying myself.

And then, out of the blue, I got a full course: I'd got out of the camp and completed each stage of the clover leaf pattern outside. It was a score – a low score, but a score. Dazed, I pulled Skittles up to a stop and rubbed his neck. Rick cantered towards me across the arena, his grin radiant in the dusty haze. As my ears cleared from the rushing blood in my head, I could hear hooting and whistling from the perimeter of the arena. A row of familiar grinning faces was perched along the rail. I may have been the one sitting on the horse, but there were a dozen other people in the saddle with me. Joy overflowed in my world.

The news that Joan had bone cancer ripped that joy from the world. Joan had survived breast cancer seven years before. This time the cancer returned with a vengeance in her bones. She acted as if nothing had changed. I was young enough to still believe in immortality.

She lost her hair. I bought some fabulous silk headscarves for her. It was a pathetically insufficient gesture.

Cancer doesn't wait until the timing is better. It doesn't care if you're in the middle of a drought. It is impatient to ruin. And a farm makes no concession to illness: farming bills must still be paid despite the medical expenses piling up. John went away contract harvesting to earn some essential income. Their children, Andrew and Penny, were away at university, leaving Joan alone at Wylarah with her chemo symptoms for company. Rick went over and helped with the cattle if they got out, but she hated to ask. I'd drop around and we'd admire the crocuses bursting through the alyssum and discuss what to do with the vista at the end of her olive grove. We'd have her over for dinner as often as we could coax her. They were simple meals: stir-fries, curries, barbecues. I stopped apologising for the basics.

'Alice, I enjoy this type of meal. Truly. I don't do barbecues or stir-fries. Never have. But this is nice. You do your thing well.'

'You've never done a barbecue?'

'No, never. Oh, maybe once in the eighties. But it was a disaster. We were having so much fun, we forgot to light the fire for the barbecue and no-one got fed until close to midnight. It turned out to be a great night – you can get away with not feeding people as long as there's plenty of wine and champagne.'

Before dinner we'd stroll around the Cardowan garden, planning improvements and layouts of garden beds that would become, one day.

'You must plant some shade trees in the front,' she implored. 'There's nowhere shady for me to park my car.'

A few weeks later Joan arrived with a small box, with 'FRAGILE' printed on the outside. She was bubbling over with excitement.

'It's just arrived. I had them sent by post.'

Inside the parcel were two small seedlings wrapped loosely in damp newspaper.

'They're Burdekin plums. I had them sent down from a nursery in Townsville. They're fabulous shade trees. And they'll survive out here. We have one at Wylarah.'

'Oh, Joan, thank you!'

'Now plant them where I can park under their shade when I come to visit.'

I promised. The fragile, 25-centimetre-high seedlings seemed incapable of providing shade; it seemed such a long way off before they would be anything more than hare bait. I planted them out into pots so they could grow some more before tackling the hard black soil, rocks and vagaries of the seasons.

Weeks flowed by. John came and went with his contract harvesting. Joan's stoicism was convincing. She taught me how one can choose to feel in any given moment, whatever crap is thrown at you. She did this herself by keeping busy with her painting, phone calls around the countryside and focusing on life's pleasures and her holy trinity: good food, good wine and good friends.

Once I saw her looking defeated. Once was enough. I knew the party was nearly over, but as at every signature Wylarah dinner party, we played until stumps.

On 26 December 1997, John remained with Joan in the hospital while Andrew and Penny stayed with us at Cardowan. They left their mum and dad alone to say goodbye and cloister themselves with their unique love and mateship. We sat on the verandah making light conversation. We cried. We shared stories and laughed with outrageous denial as the clock ticked by. Unable to turn it back and undo the pain, unable to turn it forward and skip the pain still to come, we waited in limbo for the phone to ring, pretending not to notice each insufferable minute, each second.

A strange calmness settled over us when the phone call finally came, signalling the end; that John's wife, Andrew and Penny's mum, and my north star was dead.

While the family was preparing the eulogy, they came across a half-completed painting Joan had been working on. It was of Rick riding Genesis, the pair to the one she gave me for my birthday.

Joan O'Shanesy was buried on 30 December, surrounded by family and friends that travelled from around Australia to commemorate the gift of her vibrant life.

In the months prior to her passing we had planned a New Year's Eve party at Cardowan, knowing that it could be her last. After the funeral, someone asked if it would be inappropriate to still hold the party. John confirmed our thoughts.

'Inappropriate? It would be inappropriate *not* to hold the party!'

So the New Year's Eve party went ahead. We'd learnt Joan's lessons well.

With another crop of calves on the ground, I took some time off again in January to help with branding and, although it was great to be out in the paddocks, which had become familiar, and I no longer felt like a fifth leg now Rick could send me on my own around a paddock, it wasn't quite the same. The family had stopped camping at Benroy, instead driving their truck from Rosevale each day while Rick and I trotted down to the shack from Cardowan. Rick wished they still camped out. Showering in a bathroom is so sterile compared with having a bogey in a waterhole or under a bucket with holes punched in its base when the waterholes dried up. The job got done, but it just wasn't like the good ol' days. And just like that, something special – an eighty-year-old tradition that gave the family its annual synchronisation, its connected pulse – was no more. Times had changed.

With branding sorted, Rick took up the guitar, a favourite hobby of John's, and together they enrolled in weekly guitar lessons. Every Wednesday after their lesson we opened a bottle of wine, had dinner – usually roast beef followed by John's favourite, lemon delicious pudding – and played cards. We shared every Wednesday like this for more than a year.

I'd felt cheated that I would never repay Joan's generosity and the way she took me under her wing, nursing me through my turbulent years. But she had one final lesson for me, which she whispered in my ear as I beat the egg whites for John's lemon delicious pudding: 'See, Alice, I told you that you'd do it for someone else one day. You just had to be patient for your turn to give. Giving back doesn't happen in a straight line or on a set timetable, and you're not the one that gets to say how and when. It goes around, linking up in every direction like a spider web, concentrating where and when it is needed. You understand now – it all balances out.'

Twenty-two

Cardowan is hinged between Kumbia fifteen kilometres to its east – which boasts a pub, a petrol station, primary school, kindergarten, a couple of stores, a mechanic, a one-man police station, a racetrack that also functions as a golf course, a pony club and campdraft ground – and, fifteen kilometres to its west, Ironpot, an even smaller community. Ironpot features the Ironpot Creek, the Ironpot Hall and the Ironpot Fire Brigade, a motley band of volunteers of which Rick (as the newest sucker to the district) was quickly appointed secretary. Burrandowan, a further twenty kilometres west of Ironpot, is denoted by a racetrack where the famous Burrandowan picnic races are held each May, a campdraft ground and a hall hewn from the ironbark forest seventy years before. However, what is lacked in amenities in our district is more than made up for with intense community spirit.

But in 1998 even that spirit was flailing beneath the iron grip of the drought. Spring had been and gone and the long days of summer dragged on without rain, without our lifeblood being replenished. The resilience of the local community was at its lowest ebb. The rich fabric of our world had faded to a dusty, brittle landscape. Stock waters had receded into muddy puddles that gripped at the legs of cattle like flypaper sticks to flies, rendering them helpless, their only salvation being to be towed out and moved to a less treacherous paddock or the kind reprieve of a bullet if they'd already given up. The wilted stalks of crops – another failure; another load of cottonseed and molasses to keep the cows alive. Everyone's thoughts were the same: *maybe next week it will rain.*

Gadget, a mate from Ironpot, organised an impromptu drought breaker – also known as a piss-up. A crowd of locals gathered at the Burrandowan racetrack armed with eskies and steaks to throw on the open-pit barbecues. Faces that we hadn't seen for ages appeared out of utes; families that had been cocooned, unable or unwilling to entertain, arrived from miles around to commiserate and share their experiences.

Dismal tales of helplessness and futility were passed around and frustration and loss aired: bores going dry, cattle getting bogged and dying, the endless carting of water, weaning calves prematurely and feeding them by hand so the cows stood a chance to survive, costs blowing out, crops withering in the sun and another year's income gone, lines of credit exhausted and nowhere to turn. Some had given up planting crops, whether from lack of hope or lack of funds. Some had planted without fertiliser to save money, a decision that would punish them if it did rain, but they'd had little choice after three years of failed crops.

They were stoic people, proud of their ability to withstand seasonal variations. But this drought, unwavering, unrelenting, spreading its pervasive melancholy like the cracks opening up in the ground in its wake, threatened to unravel the strongest minds, the sturdiest businesses, the kindest people.

The bit of rain we'd had at Cardowan meant we still had some options, like dry standing feed, or fresh puddles of water in some paddocks, but others who'd missed out on that rain had no water, no grass and no options. But still they hung on, glaring back into the fierce, dark eyes of depression, refusing to succumb, knowing in their hearts if they could just hang on then one day, *one day*, it would rain again.

Hope is founded on tantalising traces of what has been. As the stars multiplied on the deepening blanket above, glimmering silent sentinels bearing witness to the resilience of the human spirit, the conversation shifted from recent events to memories of seasons past.

'We used to have to do creek crossings once a week during summer. No sooner had you put them up and they were washed away again,' Hook, the most local of the Ironpot locals, recalled. There was a concurring murmur.

Rick regaled us with his story of harvesting green panic grass seed merely by sitting on the bonnet of his father's ute with a hessian sack, as they drove through the paddock, the seed from the grass towering above them fell into their laps.

John reminded us of the years when there weren't enough silos in the district for all the grain being harvested: 'We had to pile it up on the ground.'

Like lancing an abscess, the sharing of woes released pressure. Without a cure, it would scab over again and fester, but the immediate strain was off as we remembered we were not alone; we had each other; we were a community caring for each other's souls. And we had hope.

Reinforced with shared pain and hope, the stilted exchanges of dusk metamorphosed into comfortable chatter. Laughter filled the tepid evening air and pushed back against the inner clouds. We would get through this drought, as farmers had always done, and one day we would be able to remember why we chose this life on the land.

Rick and I drove home refreshed, like a Queensland State of Origin team at half-time – behind, but not defeated, primed to return to the playing field. Forget the tired muscles, weary minds, tears of frustration. Just stick it out and the game can be won.

That was not to say that we couldn't see ways to improve. There were lessons that we'd learnt from the drought to better withstand the next one, provided we could last that long and get another opportunity. But that night we'd discovered that even the best land managers were doing it tough; that there is always someone worse off and that this natural event needed to be waited out with respect, prudent management and perseverance.

Like a professional athlete, Rick decided that he would get stuck into training harder than ever, so next drought we would be better prepared. He knew that his stock skills went only part of the way to running a beef business and was keen to learn more so he could better manage the property. He'd heard about an eight-day residential course, Grazing for Profit, focusing on pasture management, grazing and business principles. Gaffer thought going away to learn about grazing was a slap in the face to the practical education on offer at Rosevale. 'What are you gonna learn at school that you can't learn here? Spend more time with your father, that's where you'll learn something useful.' But Grahame thought it was great that Rick wanted to do a course in business and grazing and gave him and David the time off to attend with his blessing, in spite of the pressure that the drought was inflicting. The school was in Rockhampton, a five-hour drive away. They would be away nine days in total.

I think that was the first time I had been alone at Cardowan and with every passing night I slept less and less, until my emotional state became proportionally irrational. By the fourth night I was haunted by every sound and every creak of the corrugated iron roof as the house breathed and relaxed her joints. At 3 a.m. I was still lying alert in bed, planning my escape from a siege of hypothetical escaped prisoners. I couldn't settle until I had resolved on the best course of action; tossing a coin between attack, or run and hide –

but where? *Do I hide in the bush or do I take to the road and walk the ten kilometres to Wylarah?* I started going to bed in tracksuit pants and t-shirt, sneakers at the ready.

The irony that I had never felt scared living alone in the rough suburbs of Brisbane twinkled in the back of my mind. But there was a huge difference – in the city I had street smarts, and was always equipped with an escape plan. Out here I was exposed, vulnerable. No-one would hear my screams. We had one phone in the house and it was a long way from the bedroom. *Oh no, how will I get to the phone before the attacker?* By the end of the week I was a wreck from sleeplessness, my nerves raw and jittery.

Like all wonders of manifestation, my fearful musings were rewarded on the second-last night with footsteps on the verandah. The difference from those four-legged furry intruders of our first night was unmistakable – these were definitely human. Then a man's voice bellowed in the darkness, calling out unintelligibly as he roamed up and down.

I decided to run, stealthily slipping on my sneakers and tiptoeing to the back of the house, straining my ears and avoiding the floorboards that creaked.

'Rick! Alice! Anyone home?'

I peeked out through a crack in the door and vaguely recognised the face in the darkness. It was Jetlag, on his way home from the Kumbia pub, heading back to Ironpot. Tipsy, but harmless. I stepped out into full view. 'Jesus Christ, Jetlag, you scared the shit out of me. What brings you around at this time of the night?'

'I just dropped in for a drink. You got any rum?'

'No!'

'How about a port then?'

'Well, I guess I could find some port ...'

'Nah, I'm right – just havin' a go. Your horses are out on the road. You better get them in or some drunk bugger might hit them.'

He stayed with me until I'd caught and led the renegade horses back to the yards. It was 1 a.m. when I pulled the doona back over myself, my body still trembling. The false scare was all that was needed to convince myself that my life was in peril and my heart rate skyrocketed to a new high. Sleeplessly I quivered under the doona for the remainder of the night, calling Rick at 5 a.m., a thoroughly hysterical mess. With only one more night alone to get through, Rick asked John to come over and be my nursemaid for dinner and ensure I was inebriated enough to ward off the mental gremlins before going to bed.

The following day Rick walked through the door, his reassuring smile a blissful tonic. I sank into his arms and within half an hour had collapsed into bed for the best sleep ever, knowing my guardian and protector had returned.

In my exhaustion, I'd forgotten to dismantle my fortress. Rick found my Green River butcher's knife under his pillow and a shotgun under the mattress – minus the bullets.

'Got ourselves a little spooked, did we?'

'Shit, Rick, I was a mental case. If you're ever going to be away again we need a better plan.'

We resolved on three courses of action: we put a phone line into the bedroom; I learnt how to shoot, thinning out the population of feral cardboard boxes during my training; and I acquired a rottweiler–German shepherd cross called Hugo, who turned out to be rather clumsy and pathetically friendly.

In truth, in the event of a real intruder with evil intentions I suspect none of these would have made one iota of difference, considering I didn't even know where the bullets were kept, and unless Hugo actually fell onto the intruder or they tripped over his hump on the kitchen floor, they'd escape unharmed.

Nevertheless, I felt more secure and turned my attention back to the Cardowan facelift, which was proceeding in fits and starts. It was time for the kitchen of my dreams. The builders moved in, the ironbark walls were pulled down and recycled into bench tops and cupboards. And, yes, after much deliberation, the wood-fired stove was forsaken for the two square metres of floor space it occupied. The hulking beast and I had formed a good working relationship; it had proved perfect for crisping up toast triangles for homemade pâté, ideal for lemon meringue pies and in its element for slow-braised beef cheeks and roasts. But I gladly ditched it for a spanking new stainless steel double oven with gas cooktop.

I settled into my dream kitchen just as I was settling into the world beyond Cardowan. Everything was falling into place. There was only one thing left on my wish list and that wish was about to be granted.

Twenty-three

The coveted position of beef extension officer at my local Department of Primary Industries office became available in 1998 when the incumbent retired after forty-five years of service, and I got my dream job working in the beef cattle industry in the fields of breeding and genetics, nutrition, marketing, pasture and land management, communication and education.

Oh ... my ... God!

My manager pressured me to specialise in one area. To appease him I said I would be a 'beef business system integration specialist'. He was happy, thinking I was specialising, and I was content knowing I wasn't.

In light of my specialty in generalisation, the following year I organised my first beef industry forum, designed to expose beef producers to information on a dozen business topics in a day and shift their aspirations. The forum attracted around 150 beef producers. A buzz of energy filled the rooms as attendees discussed family succession and communication, emerging markets, industry trends, nutrition, genetics and meat quality.

In 2000 we organised a second forum, bringing in speakers from overseas, including a chef from Asia, to demonstrate how education was being used to increase beef consumption in our export markets and the use of non-premium cuts (such as blade and round) for value-adding the carcass. Leading business people from other industry sectors came to share their success stories and specialists tackled technical issues associated with running a beef business.

I stepped behind the podium to welcome the 200 beef producers in attendance and paused mid-sentence as I heard a voice coming through the PA system. The voice sounded familiar. I detected a twang. No plum.

My God, it's me!

The sound of my own voice caught me off guard. It was the voice of the girl who'd washed up at Grahame and Peggy's after a cyclone. My stomach twisted as I located Rick and Peggy's faces beaming back at me from the audience. Grahame was studying his proceedings intently, occasionally glancing up. I felt a bit fraudulent under their gaze. They knew me when I couldn't tell a bull from a cow or a steer from a bullock. Now I was providing training in live animal assessment and helping beef producers design breeding programs to meet their markets.

Peggy had helped me collect my pasture plants for my second-year assignments. Now I was involved with pasture research and training in pasture management.

Rick showed me my first bush kill. Now I was leading groups of producers to meatworks where we observed kills, interpreted feedback and related this back to the live animal, and discussed nutrition, handling and management strategies to improve eating quality and animal welfare.

It was a bit late for self-recrimination, so I stuffed my inhibitions to the back of my mind and focused on running a tight program designed to inspire and enable change. To my beef producers, I was their beef extension officer and as long as I was at their service, they didn't care how I came to be there.

That second forum was heralded a great success. And so was the third.

As my career forged ahead in the late nineties, Rick felt his was stagnating. His ideas for developing the breeder country, expansion and new ways of doing business seemed to be falling on barren ground. Rick started to feel he'd become a second-in-command to his elder brother by function of birthright and location. Both natural leaders and passionate about the same things, the size of the business began to feel too small for these ambitious souls. Change was imminent: the mood was like a ticking time bomb.

I knew the fuse had been lit the day Gaffer bailed Rick up as he was loading his ute to head home.

'You leaving already?'

'Yeah. I've got weaners in the yards and waters to check on the way home.'

'Seems like you've always got somewhere else to be.'

'What do you mean by that?'

'I mean, you haven't been around here much lately, Rick.'

'Well, I'm getting things done at Cardowan and Benroy.'

'That country's looked after itself for the last fifty years, why does it need so much attention now?'

'Well, probably because it's had nothing done to it for fifty years.'

'The real work's here at Rosevale.'

'Do you expect me to spend the rest of my life looking after the empire you've built, painting fences white for you, year after year? Don't you remember what it was like to be in your twenties and want to do something for yourself? Well that's what I want. Christ, Gaffer, I thought if anyone would understand, it would be you.'

Spent, furious, disappointed, Rick stormed off.

The sticky issue of succession and how the Greenup family business would be managed in the long term had become the elephant in the room. To preserve harmony, the cold reality of how matters of management, roles, responsibilities and assets would be divided needed resolution.

Rick talked it over with friends – business people with no ties to the land who could be objective. Their message was clear: 'Why are you sticking around, Rick?'

'I guess I never thought about leaving.'

'Well, trust me. You're better off with a fire in your belly and twenty cents in your pocket than hanging around for some inheritance and letting that fire go out.'

Rick understood. His fire became his compass.

Change in the country moves in cycles. Every year the trees shed their bark, heralding summer, calves are born, branded, weaned, crops are planted, cows are mated, the trees shed their bark again, and we have all grown a year older.

Succession requires change. It is forced change. Uncomfortable change.

The wheel of generational change is slow, almost indiscernible to the eye, but it is there, unrelenting. The mind of the older generation is still vital and sharp – the body less so, but the young are fit and strong and want to make their mark on the world, like their forefathers. One generation wants to conquer the world, the other wants to steady up; one is bulletproof and ready to take on risk, the other is feeling very mortal and risk-averse; one sees change as progress, the other sees change as criticism.

Succession is a veritable minefield and an ideal host to incubate tension. It can't be avoided – except of course by bankruptcy or selling up the farm – but many families try, leaving it un-discussed and unresolved, causing decades of tension, anguish and conflict to the detriment of family relations and business health. The tough phase of transition needs to address issues of intergenerational equity: the ability of the older generation to afford retirement while leaving enough assets in the farm to be able to support the younger generation and maintain viability; how to treat siblings – some live off-farm, some live on-farm, and whether the distribution of assets should be fair or equitable. In the end, 'equal' and 'fair' rarely sit side by side in the final contracts and often the burning desire for the legacy to be preserved negates both. There are no right answers.

A good familial relationship doesn't remove the awkward issues that arise from siblings working together: different opinions, different attitudes to spending money, holidays, wages, working with staff – the potential for unrest in farming families is enormous. And if working with family isn't hard enough, then there are the flies in the ointment, the in-laws. Daughters- and sons-in-law hold a special place in both types of succession conversations – the conversations held in front of them, and the conversations held behind closed doors.

'How do we involve them, without them stirring up trouble? How can we protect our farm assets accumulated over generations? What if they break up? What if they can't have children? What if he/she runs off with the neighbour? She's got such expensive tastes – she'll spend it all if we sign anything over into his name. Best keep him on a wage until they've been married thirty years and she's proved herself.' It's possibly one of the greatest dreads for families on the land: that they will lose decades or generations of accumulated hard work to a daughter- or son-in law who was just passing through.

Fortunately for their kids, Grahame and Peg had seen too many families torn apart by the wrangling over assets, the patriarch or matriarch wanting to wield control until their death, festering resentments, destroying passions, ruining marriages. They had resolved when they were just newlyweds themselves that they would offer their children a clean break when the time was right.

In 1998, with tension mounting daily and another generation already toddling around at Rosevale, Grahame and Peggy decided the time for change was drawing near and called us all to a meeting to discuss the future of the business. It was a tense, sickening wait for meeting day, wondering what would happen. With nerves to rival all my campdrafting runs combined, I spent the morning on the toilet with a cleansing bout of diarrhoea – a full-blown physiological response to being in lockdown flight mode – all over a goddamn meeting.

Like most things, the anticipation was worse than the event. There was unanimous consensus that it would be best for Rick to eventually go out on his own and for David, as the eldest, to continue on at Rosevale managing the family legacy in partnership with Gaffer, Grahame, Peggy, Peter and Sally. At six and eight years younger than David, and still at university, the long-term roles of Peter and Sally remained open-ended.

Once it was decided that Rick would leave the family business, the conversation shifted to the question of when. My heart raced at the enormity of the discussion. The conversation moved at lightning speed. Each decision flowed to the next. Rick and David pushed for a date, a sunset clause that could be worked towards. The family decided that in four years, in 2002, Rick would be out of the family business with a proportion of the family land, predominantly Cardowan, with equal proportions of cattle and debt, and until then he would continue to work full-time for his family.

I've made it sound much simpler than it really was. Months of planning, consultation and thought by Grahame and Peg went into this decision and the final division of assets. We were relieved. By no means had we walked away with only twenty cents in our pocket, but neither had Rick hung around wanting more at the expense of extinguishing his fire. He would soon be his own master and his fire glowed with renewed vitality.

While I didn't bring family wealth and experience to the partnership, I was getting more comfortable with my contribution, knowing I brought something else: my mother's belief that she'd impressed upon me from an early age, that anything can be achieved, it's just a matter of conviction and application – a gift far greater than anything material. And this I shared with Rick when doubts arose.

We hoped four years would allow a smooth transition and time to grasp all the aspects of running a business and cattle stud on our own. I would have to step up and become Rick's right-hand man – his only workman, for that matter. Apart from spending my annual leave branding at Cardowan and Benroy and cleaning the toilets for the annual bull sale at Rosevale, I'd had no involvement in the family business so had a lot to learn about the intricacies of running a cattle business.

While happy to help Rick, I loathed working in the decrepit Cardowan yards. 'Don't expect the same set-up as Rosevale, Alice,' Rick had warned me about them before we moved in. 'The Cardowan yards are DC.'

'Do you mean the type of electricity they're connected to?'

'I wish. No, DC means "drag and carry" – you have to drag or carry every gate.'

How I hated those yards and avoided them at all costs. They were exhausting and dangerous to work in. To me, DC started to mean Divorce Counselling. The front-end loader did its best work *ever* the day it razed those yards to dust. In their place the men installed stables and a new set of yards with five-way drafting, branding race and cradle, vet crush, cow race and weighing scales.

During the succession transition we took over the management of some stock, established our own stud name (known as a prefix), and became familiar with the administration and marketing of stud animals. After four years, all the duties that the family currently shared would become our sole responsibility on Cardowan:

mustering, checking waters, feeding stock and crop farming, not to mention the payment of bills, the bookkeeping, the insurance, the bank loans and the stud herd recording.

We ran projections on the scale of business we would have from the succession. The numbers told us a pretty clear story: we would both need to work off-farm indefinitely – maybe forever – to keep the wolf from the door. But we had time to make changes and decided to expand our fledgling business until it was big enough for us to work the property together and support our future family.

One thing we knew for sure, we couldn't afford to hire any help. For decades the Greenup family business had relied on labour for farming and stockwork – sometimes as many as eight stockmen mustered a large paddock, galloping after bolting cows and calves, the sound of stockwhips filling the tranquil bush with explosive cracks as the cattle tumbled down the hills towards the yards.

'Helluva rush and great fun! But those days are gone,' Rick would say to me. 'If we're going to be viable, we're going to have to work smarter, with lower costs. That means fewer hands and yards that can be worked by one or two men.'

Long before, Sid, their head stockman, and Ol' Jack had planted a seed in Rick's mind: that working dogs would make mustering safer, easier and less stressful for men and cattle, as well as saving on labour. Gaffer didn't like dogs around cattle – 'Idiot dogs stir up the cattle, there's nothing worse!' – so the idea had remained dormant, but the time for change had come.

Rick had been preparing for the future for years, thinking about how his cattle business would operate, and he knew that it would rely on dogs. He got a couple of kelpies and border collies, and attended dog-training schools on weekends. He'd practise when no-one was around, educating himself, his dogs and the cattle. The family remained doubtful about the dogs' ability to do the job of men. Rick didn't argue his case, but he knew they would be one of the keys to our potential viability. Patiently he trained and waited for the right opportunity to prove what his team of dogs could do. After months of frustration, he agreed to meet the rest of the stockmen at 7 a.m. for mustering but set his alarm clock for 3 a.m., heading out alone to muster the paddock with his dogs in the dim dawn light. When the rest of the men arrived Rick had the cattle waiting in the yards ready for trucking. A few more moonlight musters and eventually Grahame and David conceded and let Rick do his thing without help.

Saving costs was only part of the solution to fuelling Rick's dream cattle operation. He could see scale was needed to build a business that could support us and our future family and we wanted to hit the ground running when the succession day arrived. Rick and I made an inventory of our private assets and liabilities to see what we could use to transform his vision of owning a cattle business into reality. We had the VW Beetle, a reasonable share portfolio, two rental houses, a loan against the rental houses and two incomes. At least for now, we didn't have to worry about the big debt coming his way with the cattle and land. We had two years to turn our assets into a cattle property. It was a long stretch by any standards.

Not easily daunted and eager to get off the sidelines and into the game, we bought forty-five pregnant Santa Gertrudis heifers in March 2000, midway through the succession transition. They were the first cattle I'd ever owned and the first Rick could call his own. Even Gaffer telling Rick that buying our heifers was 'like bringing sand to the Arabs' couldn't burst our bubble. We thought they were brilliant.

Given the delicacy needed during a succession transition, Rick wasn't game to ask if we could rent a paddock at Cardowan. Instead, we decided to keep it simple and approached a neighbour who had some empty paddocks on the place next door, Jumma. We'd never met him but he was said to be a tough, no-nonsense businessman. Locals told us: 'Don't bother. He's a hard case.' We figured the worst that could happen was that he'd say no.

He invited us over for a beer to talk about our proposal. My heart pounded as he opened the door. The Hard Case had an unassuming stature and moderate frame. His sharp, focused eyes and a direct manner of speech were the only hints of the steel core within. We sat on the edge of a wide, screened verandah, sipping our beers and talking about the unrelenting season. We were taken aback by his warm, open nature and even more astounded by his quick response to our request for agistment. The Hard Case agreed straight away. His enthusiasm for our venture was heartening. 'It's good to see you young ones having a go. Get stuck into it.'

Not wanting to unravel our good fortune we finished our beers and drove home, alternating between ecstatic outbursts and stunned silence at how easily our first cattle venture had come together.

Five months later we got a phone call from the Hard Case's stock and station agent. 'G'day, Rick, Dick Boyd here. Just letting you know that Jumma is for sale. Thought you might be interested.'

We were using one tiny paddock on Jumma. The property was way beyond our price tag and way out of our league. It was a 6800-hectare property that Rick had coveted his whole life. It was the jewel in the crown. Ambition to own it ran through the veins of his grandfather down the family tree and had pooled in Rick's heart.

Rick bluffed: 'Well yes, we are interested,' gesturing madly for me to listen on the other phone. Dick told us that the Hard Case would be happy to consider some vendor finance if it would help us out. My legs were weak. Jumma was an answer to our long-term viability issues. This might change our lives – if we could just make the impossible possible.

We had enough money for a small deposit. The Hard Case offered us five years vendor finance on the cattle – allowing us to buy his herd of 700 high quality Santa Gertrudis females to add to the forty-five heifers we already owned. Jumma could carry at least 1500 breeders in a normal season – agistment cattle could be brought in to fully stock the property and generate cash flow.

Grahame was adamant that buying Jumma would be a quick road to ruin. The drought was getting him down to new depths of despair, he could see no silver lining. Hope had left his business plan and he spared none for ours. He was looking at the facts. Established businesses and more experienced owners with high equity were suffering. We would have pitifully low equity, little experience, no staff, no emergency funds – and the drought still raged, preying on weaknesses and swallowing struggling businesses.

Night after night after night we stayed up past midnight preparing our business plan, budgets, five-year projected cash flows and stock flows.

Mum and Peggy could see the potential. Mum had recently sold her house in Brighton and relocated to Kingaroy. The difference from the sale of her Brighton home and her newest renovation project in Kingaroy she generously, and with massive faith, lent to us. Peggy also loaned us some of her personal savings for our deposit. Despite his fears and concerns for our potential financial demise, Grahame decided to give Rick and David a bonus for their years of hard work – he knew we would put it straight into our deposit. And that was enough to get us over the edge. We had our down payment and the bank agreed to back us for the rest. We cashed in our shares and maxed out the loans on our houses. If the worst-case scenario should occur, we'd calculated we could sell up and pay everyone back.

We called the local blacksmiths and had a brand made up – a brand of our very own, the numeral 0 with wings above it. 'Wings over nought', it said on the brand registration papers. To me, it looked like a bird flying into the setting sun. To Rick, it looked like it would sit well on the hide and make a clean brand on our cattle and horses. For both of us, it symbolised our hopes and dreams taking off on nothing but our belief in ourselves. We signed the contract in August 2000 and settlement would be in December.

Most of the dams and creeks on Jumma were dry. Trees were dying in their thousands on the Jumma hills and the cattle were in light to poor condition. We worked on weekends doing cattle work: mustering, getting final numbers for the sale contract. Rick bought me my own set of pliers, which he attached to my saddle, at the ready for any broken fence wire that dared to take me on. With my pocketknife on my belt, my pliers on my saddle and a man who relied on me in the paddock, I felt great. Terrified at what we'd undertaken, but great.

Jumma was run-down but the Hard Case let us have access to the property to get things in order prior to settlement. In the evenings after our jobs, we worked late into the night, repairing fences, fixing troughs, rehanging broken gates and putting out split posts for new fences that would improve stock access to water and make the paddocks stock-proof. We rebuilt a loading ramp for when we sold our first load of cattle.

The Beetle was not suited to the tasks of checking waters, fencing or carting hay. So, with the last of our savings, two more purchases were made – a quad bike for $2000 and a trailer for $300 to go behind, which formed the basis of our operation.

Now we were skint. There was no margin for error; no reserve to carry us through a rough patch. If only it would rain.

Twenty-four

After years of waiting, watching blue skies and tormenting clouds build then dissipate after a feeble attempt at a storm, a promising system built up in the west in October. We didn't get our hopes up. Good systems offering the potential of respite from the drought had come and gone too many times for us to get excited. We tried to stay unmoved, reserving our emotion, but tuned into ABC Radio at 6 a.m. and 12 p.m. every day to listen to the Rural Report's weather forecast, and watched the nightly weather report on television.

It was a strong solid system. Rain fell in Queensland's furthest reaches, 1600 kilometres to our west. Country that had received less than twenty-five millimetres of rain for the last three years copped a deluge.

C'mon. We urged it towards us. The system was now filling dams and blocking highways around Roma, 300 kilometres west of us.

C'mon, keep comin'. We began to allow ourselves to contemplate the possibility that it might rain, as the system edged its way towards us.

I went to bed and tried to sleep, but my legs were jittery with anticipation. The heat built up even though the sun had gone down hours before. The atmosphere was oppressive, muggy and stagnant. I threw back the thin cotton sheet and lay there. My ears pricked to an unfamiliar sound. It was the first drop of rain. It resonated like a small pebble thrown onto the corrugated iron roof. Then a cascade – a handful of pebbles; a tantalising prelude to the thunderous crashing that soon engulfed the sturdy weatherboard house. The stillness erupted into a blur of wind and rain as the storm exploded. We leapt out of bed and raced through the rooms closing windows and doors as the horizontal rain forced its way in.

I climbed onto the windowsill alongside the tank and leant out and up, stretching to clean out the accumulated leaves from the inlet sieve, ensuring all the rain streaming off the roof would be captured. I got drenched: it was wonderful. At last we would have rainwater in our tanks and could stop buying the tasteless bore water that had to be trucked out from town. My nostrils filled with the smell of fresh rain as it moistened the dry dirt. We watched the rain for another hour from every vantage point on our three verandahs. Finally we climbed back into bed, smiles embedded on our faces as we closed our eyes.

The next morning the yards glistened with a sheet of water. We pulled on our gumboots having first shaken out the Daddy-long-leg spiders that had taken up residence within them and padded out through the sodden yards, sploshing in the black mud, squashing the last remaining stumps of dead couch grass that had given up the fight. The rest had turned to dust and blown away months before. The cracks in the ground that had been wide enough to put your leg in up to the knee had closed with the swelling black clay soil.

The rain gauge attached to the fence post bore the good news. Seventy-five millimetres of rain had fallen overnight. Anxious to see the water going into the dams and creeks, we jumped in the ute and sped down the one-kilometre driveway, the familiar dust transformed into mud. Water fanned in every direction down the landscape, streams running into one another, building momentum as they merged in the gullies, forming metre-high torrents flowing towards dams, creeks and rivers. An offering of renewal and promise. Jumma Creek, which had been a chain of stagnant receding waterholes, was running a banker – eight metres wide and one metre deep over the bridge. Mere hours before, the creek bed was cracked and dusty and we were pumping water from streams hidden metres beneath the sandy creek beds.

We reversed the ute and headed in the opposite direction. The Boyne River and Manneum Creek were both running water and would pump life back into the paddocks on Jumma. We drove the ten kilometres down into the heart of Jumma. Jumma Creek wasn't running there yet. We pulled up alongside the dry creek bed, turning off the engine to listen and wait. The shooshing gurgle of water could be heard in the distance. After an interminably long time, the brown water snaked around the bend, not as a wall of water as I thought it might be, but a trickle, filling each hole and gully in its turn. Rick strolled alongside the flowing creek, easily keeping pace with the headwater. Gradually the flow gathered momentum, pushing debris – limbs of dead trees and long forgotten carcasses – ahead of it. Briefly the smell of death filled our nostrils and then cleared as the murky, laden water flushed out the river bed, giving sustenance to the bottlebrush trees, their branches weeping low into the creek bed, on their last breath. The roughly graded creek crossing below us, which had been dry minutes before, became impassable.

The next day it rained again. It was enough to plant a crop. More suited to a day in the saddle than the tractor, Rick put his preferences aside and embraced the challenges of farming. We still had a month before settlement, but the Hard Case lent us his tractor to plant the first crop and get our business underway. 'But I want it back on Thursday, Rick.' This gave us four days to plant a crop that would take at least two days. No problem, right? Wrong! Rick still worked for his parents on weekdays, so this gave him just the nights to plant our crop. The first night we worked until midnight checking and fixing the equipment. John was generous with his time and knowledge, explaining to Rick planting depths, seeding rates and other technical aspects of farming that we had no idea about.

For the next two days Rick farmed Jumma at night, planting a sorghum crop, and worked for his parents during the day. He put in a 45-hour shift with brief breaks for meals and catnaps, completing the planting with only hours to spare, the low loader arriving to take the tractor back as Rick was washing the last of the dirt off.

It rained twice more in November. The creeks and rivers ran again, every dam on the property overflowed; some twice. The grass was green, lush and abundant. The crop got a textbook start, growing well and evenly.

After settlement, Rick would continue working with his family full-time for another eighteen months, but there was more to do than we could manage on weekends, so I went part-time at the Department and looked after Jumma on the other days of the week. We closed the doors on our after-hours enterprises, which meant no more horse breaking and no more paying guests on weekends. We needed to focus on where are future lay: with Jumma.

I felt welcome there. Jumma, in the midst of the Great Dividing Range. Steep mountains. Deep gullies. Dense forests of spotted gums. Caves harbouring dingoes. Wide open plains. Fertile sandy loams. Black soil creek flats. Barren granite outcrops.

No longer an interloper in the wrong place, I belonged. Jumma became my land. I became her steward.

Twenty-five

With the widespread summer rain, cattle prices soared when the markets opened in January 2001 and land prices rocketed after a decade of doldrums. Our sorghum crop was a success and put some much-needed cash into our empty coffers.

There was comfort in knowing the water seeping out of the saturated hills would keep the pasture and creeks fresh for a couple of months, that the calves would be strong and sappy, and the cows stood a good chance to get back in calf, having regained much of their body condition. Their red coats gleamed – some were even fat – and all were unrecognisable as the 700 weak withered beasts that we'd bought three months before.

Ten years had passed since Rick taught me how to brand my first calf. Now we would brand our first calves with our very own brand, wings over nought. The cows were in mobs of fifty to 150, so including calves at foot we had up to 300 head in some paddocks. With no money for labour, the stock team would be Rick and me, for better or for worse. There was no-one to cover my arse now. I tried to emulate Rick's confidence.

To beat the heat, we mustered our first mob on the Australia Day long weekend starting around 4 a.m. on the Saturday. By 9 a.m. we were back at the yards drafting.

The Jumma yards were built in the early 1900s out of ironbark timber that had been felled on the property with crosscut saws then shaped with an adze and broadaxe with posts so wide you couldn't put your arms around them. They were designed and built in the days when labour was cheap and the cattle would have been handled with a minimum of six staff – efficiency was not part of the design brief. Nearly a hundred years later, with a workforce of two, yarding up involved a minor marathon as we worked through the long funnel design, drafting the cattle and bringing the calves up to the cradle.

Labour resources were not the only change the past century had brought – the breed and style of cattle had also undergone a renaissance. The yards were built for old-style Herefords – a smaller style of animal than their red tropical cousins, our Santa Gertrudis. The old timber race was not designed for the muscle and size of our bulls and they got stuck halfway along. Rick had to cut down four panels of our precious race with a chainsaw to get them out. And for some inane reason there was no smaller holding pen around the branding cradle, so if a calf got out of the cradle before being branded it was a mad dash to catch it in the massive fifty-by thirty-metre holding yard, sprinting after the escapee on foot, eventually catching and shouldering it back to the branding cradle, one of us swinging off the head and the other the tail.

It was slow going with just the two of us: drafting, yarding up, catching the calves in the cradle, dehorning, vaccinating and branding. The ambient temperature soared and the branding fire added to the scorching heat. The sweat dripped off us in sheets. My jeans stuck to my legs like heavy wet canvas. My arms and legs were weak with fatigue. As we tired and our reflexes slowed, more calves bounced through the cradle before we'd caught them properly. Chasing and wrestling them back expended precious energy from reserves that had already been drained, but we dug deeper and somehow found new reserves.

We stopped for lunch, too weary to talk. The guzzling of the water bottle was the only sound as we caught our breath. We were exhausted, and only halfway through the mob. We grinned at each other, no words needed. A small part of me thought how nice it would be to have some help but mainly I was so happy that it was just the two of us, just Rick and me, at the Jumma yards – yards that may have been falling down, but they were our yards – putting our new brand on each calf.

The next day, Rick and I, with our newest recruit, my ever willing and supportive mother riding Peppy's Fox, set out from the Jumma yards to return the cows to their paddock, having branded a hundred-odd calves the previous day.

Jumma is dissected by two creeks and one river that weave their way through the landscape, providing natural watering points in normal seasons. After rain, moving cattle to and from the yards challenges the stockman's skill, as the cattle must be taken through flowing creeks and deep waterholes – a task that is magnified with calves at foot. Calves are erratic, unpredictable and, if out of position, can tangle underneath the horse's legs. Calves must be handled without hesitation, yet with a delicate combination of assertiveness and coaxing. It is critical to keep the cattle moving forward, otherwise they turn back on themselves.

The first creek crossing is one hundred metres from the yards. We brought the mob down into the creek and pushed them up onto the other side. Things ran amuck pretty early on when the cows and calves lost sight of each other along the creek banks and turned back to look for each other. Confused cows and calves headed off in a myriad of directions, some out to the paddock where the calf used to be, some back to the yards where they'd seen each other last, some just off on their own doing a random escape, while others just stood there and bellowed. We were within a breath of losing the whole mob as they scattered everywhere.

Rick and the dogs were up the top of the gully, bending the cattle back onto the flats and struggling to keep the mob under control. Fast work and a calm demeanour were needed to pull the mob back together or we were rooted.

Skittles and I were in the creek bed urging the cows and calves out of the creek and up the bank, riding back and forth along the shallower edge. The water was halfway up his belly and would be above our heads if we were in the middle. I lifted my legs but the water still lapped at my stirrups.

Skittles had grown into a strong sixteen-hand horse that could almost throw you out of the saddle from the sheer power of his hindquarters when he thrust his body forward climbing out of steep gullies. He was a natural working with cattle and would regularly follow them of his own accord, often knowing better than I what was required of the job at hand.

With all the calves clambering out of the water, Skittles decided he should tail them up the bank. I suggested we retrace, pulling the reins to the left, urging him with my hands and legs to continue down the creek where we could find an easier gradient. But Skittles had made up his mind. He wanted to get out of the water and he wanted to stay with the calves in the thick of the action. He was going up the steep, slippery, muddy clay wall that had been gouged into the creek bank from the recent storms and he was going *now*.

Pulling on his face any more at that point would have just caused him to stumble and lose balance. We were committed. I grabbed the reins and leant forward to support his momentum. He thrust upward trying to climb the one-metre high vertical drop at the bottom of the seven-metre high slope, lost his footing on the greasy mud wall and fell backwards, with me underneath.

My feet slid easily out of my stirrups. The water was deepest in the centre of the creek where we landed and I was able to fall far enough away that, although he fell on top of me, I could duck under the water and swim away from his thrashing legs. Skittles righted himself and swam to the edge of the creek, waiting there for me to drag myself out. I collected the reins, led Skittles back into the shallows, and swung back on, dripping from head to foot. My precious saddle was soaked. My brain didn't even get a chance to register what just happened: the calves were scattering; there was no time for giving thanks and signing the cross. We galloped downstream to find a slope with a gradient we could handle then careered up the gully to catch the dispersing mob, cantering backwards and forwards, urging the cattle into a semblance of a cohesive herd.

Up higher on the bank the cattle were giving Rick a hard time, turning back, bellowing and dispersing through the trees. I could hear Rick yelling and cursing. I wondered what was wrong. Then I realised he was yelling at me as I cantered past towards the last of the runaways.

'Bloody hell, Alice, what've you been doing? I've been trying to hold them on my own. The cattle are going fuckin' everywhere! Get a move on or we'll blow the lot of them.'

He hadn't noticed that I was dripping, and that my hair, clothes and horse were saturated. I clenched my teeth. The time it would take to argue was time we didn't have. Every moment I was out of position was precious time wasted. If we lost the mob it could take another day to get them back together – with jobs to go to on Monday morning our schedule was tight and allowed for no error. The other real threat of scattering the mob was that if the cows and their calves got separated they might never 'mother up' again, a sure death sentence for a calf in this country, leaving it to the mercy of the dingoes without the protection of its mother. Cows and calves, one by one we got the mob together and by lunchtime had returned them to their paddock without much more incident. My clothes and saddle had dried, my pride was restored and the choice words I'd composed for Rick were forgotten in the euphoria of achievement. It was a close call, but we'd made it.

It had become obvious, however, that I couldn't pull my weight sufficiently in the paddock without dogs. At first I tried taking Rick's dogs out to work one at a time. Carp refused to recognise me out in the paddock, Split wouldn't hear his name when I called and Maverick worked for me like a reluctant long-haired teen. Old Luke and a young dog called Mac actually did as I asked – or, more correctly, they stayed with me and my horse with an understanding that they would hang around and be useful if I kept out of their way. So the two shorthair collies – Luke, a black-and-tan, and creamy Mac – became my right-hand men, so to speak, and I became immeasurably handier.

Rick got two UHF radios and made leather harnesses so we could wear them mustering. Within six months, with us each equipped with radios and a team of working dogs, we'd halved the time it took to muster a paddock.

The initial euphoria of buying Jumma soon wore off, as the temporary reprieve from the drought ran its course, and the countryside returned to its fragile state while the winter frosts stripped pastures of their nutrition. The full dams gave us about two years of stock water, but the tight timetables and unrealistic goals to run the property on weekends, not to mention our shoestring budget, left us a legacy of exhaustion and stress. There was a fair bit of yelling and cursing at each other during the cattle work as the pressure and responsibility took its toll. A fair few 'What the fuck did you think you were doing?''s were tossed around from both sides, as Rick lamented the absence of his old telepathic stockhands and I resented being treated like a first-year jillaroo. We were both exhausted and to make things worse I'd developed an opinion on most matters – and as anyone can tell you, there isn't room for two bosses in the paddock, particularly when one of them is vastly less experienced, but I was yet to learn that lesson.

After five years of marriage matters between us ebbed to a tense low. Old fears resurfaced since I equated arguments with separation and divorce. Like a religious fanatic, I stalked Rick around the house, trying to *resolve* the squabble, offering *enlightened* direction, insisting that each argument was a step further on the slippery slope of marital demise. Inevitably making it worse and, in doing so, proving my case to myself: that marriage is a tenuous affair and must be guarded and cultivated every moment. Rick felt as if he was living in a pressure cooker.

'For Christ's sake, it's just an argument. People have them, Alice; it doesn't mean they'll divorce. Get over it.'

I wondered if it was true. Rick did have more insight into this than I – most people Rick knew were married; he didn't know many divorced people. Conversely, most people I knew were divorced. I wondered: did Peggy and Grahame argue? I knew John and Joan had argued but that was about politics and music for fun, and I suspect more as foreplay than as an avenue for political enlightenment. Our arguing was never foreplay. It wasn't fun at all and definitely not a turn-on.

After some months of squabbling we did agree on one thing: that the yelling and screaming didn't get anything done faster or better, usually the opposite. We talked about it and decided to give away the bitching and have fun with our business. Just like that, we resolved to be nicer. I know it sounds simplistic and Pollyanna-ish, but it worked. We became less like squabbling siblings and more like mates with benefits again. We released the pressure valve when we worked together at Jumma and gave up trying to force the cattle to move in set ways and unrealistic timeframes; stopped rushing them, upsetting them and upsetting each other. Instead we learnt to watch and listen as Jumma taught us where the cattle preferred to water, where they chased the sweetest pick and how they liked to run in a paddock.

Month by month we became more comfortable with our mammoth undertaking, as our skills and knowledge in bookkeeping, business and property management grew with experience acquired by throwing ourselves in the deep end. And, according to plan, month after month we paid our bills and paid off our debt to the Hard Case despite the dry skies that had returned with a vengeance.

That year, I reached a personal high point when I mustered a paddock of fifty cows on my own with my dogs while Rick mustered the adjoining paddock. I think we were both stunned when I met him at the fence with my mob, all accounted for.

I was twenty-eight, living the dream, and bulletproof.

Twenty-six

8 February 2001

Dear Mrs Greenup,

Our records show you are overdue for your bi-annual pap smear examination …

Bloody letters keep arriving. I don't have time to go to the doctor for a pointless test. I'm young and in a monogamous relationship. It's hardly necessary.

I booked and kept an appointment just to stop the Big Brother bombardment. Job done. I could get on with life.

Not so easy! The doctor called a week later. 'Alice, there appear to be some abnormal cells in your test. I want you to see a specialist in Brisbane.'

Not one for fearing the worst, assuming the irregular test would be nothing, I booked into a gynaecologist with a nonchalance that only the immortal and bulletproof possess. Rick burrowed into the issue.

'So why do you have to go to Brisbane?'

'It's nothing. Just some abnormal cells.'

'What does that mean?'

'Well, in a worst-case scenario it could mean cervical cancer. But it's probably nothing.'

At the word 'cancer' Rick insisted on coming with me. It seemed unnecessary. There was so much work to do at home, he couldn't afford the eight hours stuck in a car for the return trip to Brisbane. It was out of character.

As we flicked through flimsy, tired back issues of the *Australian Women's Weekly* in the specialist's waiting room, I was self-conscious that he was with me – aware of the imposition I'd caused by him taking a day off work. Pictures of babies beamed down from every wall: twins, triplets, the odd single. 'Looks like we've come to the right place if we want to do IVF,' I whispered to Rick giggling.

'Mrs Greenup? Doctor will see you now.'

The softly spoken doctor greeted us – he was a bit too silky smooth for my taste.

'Okay. Right now, what your test shows is a very advanced stage of cancer cells in the cervix. This is an aggressive type of cell so we will do a biopsy today, followed by surgery next week to remove the part of your cervix that has the cancer.'

Christ, he doesn't beat around the bush!

Rick's hand reached out and grabbed mine, squeezing hard. It hurt. I wanted to pull away. But there was reassuring comfort in the pain, its presence. My hand was motionless.

Thank God he came. I couldn't have borne retelling what I'd just heard.

I asked if surgery was absolutely necessary. 'Could we run more tests?'

He turned to Rick, ignoring my question and avoiding my eyes. 'If this were my wife, I would be doing everything in my power to stop it immediately. This is an aggressive cancer. Every week we delay is putting her more at risk. Do you want to take a chance with your wife?'

If I wasn't still in shock my blood would be boiling. I reined in my offence and came back to the issues swirling through my head.

'Will you get it if you operate?'

'*When* we operate, we will remove part of your cervix, so we hope to get it all. And if we don't get it all the first time then we will need to cut out more.'

'Will this affect our ability to have children?'

'Yes, well, this surgery will reduce your ability to conceive, but we can look at our options such as IVF then. Our first priority is keeping you alive.'

He babbled on, describing the cascade of procedures, operations and treatments, but I only absorbed his last few words: '... and if we still don't have it all then we would look at a hysterectomy.'

Shit! Shit! Shit. Why haven't we had children? Why did I wait?

I pulled back from the rabbit hole I was tumbling down into. *Let's take stock*, I told myself. I would be alive; that would be better than dead. And we could adopt. I took a deep breath – if the worst-case scenario was infertility then I could find my way back from the hole of despair.

'So what you're saying is, if I have a hysterectomy will that get all the cancer?'

'Well, we can't be sure of that either. There are no guarantees that the cancer won't recur somewhere else.'

I began to remove myself from my body – this was a conversation that other people have. Not me. I couldn't comprehend his words. How can you still have cervical cancer when they've taken out your cervix? I was healthy, fit, young. Infertility or mortality was out of the question.

'But I'm too young to have this type of cancer!'

'No, Alice, cervical cancer develops mostly in women in your age group.'

Since when? I'd been so blasé about my pap smears for years – I thought that was old women's business.

Rick left the room for the biopsy. He didn't want to see me like that. I didn't want to be seen like that. We'd shared so much. We didn't want to share the invasion of my neglected cervix.

As I looked at the stainless steel lamp, shining into parts I'd never seen – parts Doctor seemed quite familiar with, my legs strung skywards, the instrument, with teeth like a miniature alligator tearing at my cervix, stealing flesh for the preliminary biopsy, I answered questions that failed to soothe, such as, 'So how did a Melbourne girl come to be living in the country?' And listened to such manly wisdom as, 'You shouldn't be feeling anything; there aren't any nerves there,' as I gasped in pain. And withheld words like, 'And how the fuck would you know?', as I thought better of offending Doctor.

I cleaned myself off – 'There might be some bleeding for a couple of days and slight discomfort,' he offered, as if he were telling me my bread might not rise due to the cool weather we'd been having. I sucked back everything. This was not the place to lose it – that was clear. This was straightforward clinical business. Not a sign of a tissue in his well-appointed suite for a wet eye. I adopted the persona I felt was required of me. Apparently we'd both forgotten that a life-threatening tumour was growing inside my reproductive tract, the purpose for my visit and his messing with my insides. We could have been discussing the seasonal rainfall by the time Rick rejoined us for all the intensity (or lack thereof) of the moment.

Silencing my doubts – 'It's common to disbelieve, dear, but this really is the best thing' – I booked the surgery for the following week, when we'd also get the biopsy results.

Afterwards, Rick and I sat in the cafe downstairs from the specialists' rooms, still trembling with the onslaught of information we'd been given, trying to sound normal as we ordered coffee and cake.

Under the doctor's gaze, a resigned fog had descended on my mind. Outside, however, something that had been latent stirred.

Maybe it was denial, maybe everyone thinks, 'It can't be me', but my body was telling me something different from what my ears were hearing.

I don't feel sick. I'm sure I would know if there was something wrong with my body. I can't believe this is what cancer feels like. Nothing is different. Wouldn't I know if I were sick?

I had unwelcome insight into what Dad and Joan had felt when diagnosed with the Big C – the sinking of spirit, the leaden heart, the empty lungs, the loss of control, trying to summon trust in someone you've just met who wants to cut away part of your body, rendering your life path forever altered – or even ending it.

Then there was the regret. The wracking regret. Lives unborn. Laughter of littlies. First steps. First ponies. Trips to Europe never taken, passports never used – waiting for the drought to end, for times to get better, when things would be less hectic. There was so much I still expected would unfold on my life path as I moved busily along it. Never enough time.

Even now, I feel unable to convey how I felt in that moment, and know my words are insufficient to describe my fluctuating emotions in the days that followed – holding on to the positive course, trembling, hoping, then stumbling and plummeting – thumping a pillow with rage at the injustice. I would be calm for a couple of days then the swell of emotions and panic would overcome me late at night when I was trying to sleep. One minute I'd be planning the following evening's meal, the next I would succumb to the sense that my life was like a plane locked on autopilot spiralling into the ocean while I so desperately wanted to take back the controls and steer myself to safety. Mostly I carried on with life as normal as the days ticked by towards the surgery.

We had a wedding in Sydney to attend and another the following week in Dubbo, so we'd delayed the operation to spend this precious time with Rick's schoolmates. In true Aussie style we put the best foot forward, hopped in the VW Beetle, shoved our feelings deep, deep down inside and puttered south to Sydney, where friends and frivolity waited.

The fears proved irrepressible with a power of their own, and champagne brought them bubbling to the surface. So like a good drunk on a bad day, I was in bed by 10 p.m. with a tearstained face and a husband who felt completely at a loss.

It was strange to be on this side of the fence; in the yard with the beast, instead of outside looking in on a friend or a father. But one thing is the same: you feel helpless. So helpless.

On our return to Cardowan a week later, I called to enquire about the biopsy and discovered that the biopsy had returned a negative result – no abnormal cells. Doctor insisted that the result changed nothing; it was just an aberration – the cancer would still be there and 'We will proceed with the operation'.

'But if the biopsy didn't detect any cancerous cells, how do you know where to cut – how will you know the bit you take out will get the cancer?'

Doctor assured me he would remove a bigger area of my cervix to ensure we got it all. This 'we' was beginning to feel less like a team kicking for the same goals and more like an 'us and them'.

'You have a very aggressive stage three cancer, Alice – this is no time to play games.'

You're damn right it isn't – not with my body.

Alarm bells went off inside me. Reluctantly, he agreed to extra tests and postponed the operation for another week.

As I was packing for my trip to Brisbane, the second lot of tests came back – also negative. Doctor (who we'd come to refer to as Dr Twin Baby Maker) grudgingly cancelled the operation again, conceding that there may have been an error with the original diagnosis. I consented to drive the eight-hour return trip to Brisbane each month for the next twelve months for check-ups.

As I hung up the phone my body shuddered at how easily and needlessly the joy of conceiving and bearing a child was nearly stolen from me. My emotions were a jumble of relief and horror that I'd almost compromised my body, my fertility and our unborn children.

The experience of being told I had cancer was a precious wake-up call, laying the truth at my feet for me to see: that a husband, a career and a cattle property were not enough and were not going to fulfil me as much as having children would. Some people have to wait until the very end – and I mean the *very* end – to have a life review but now for a few pensive weeks I reflected on my values and priorities.

The brush with the Big C should have been enough of a catalyst to instigate change, but the time for reflection was too short. Another Beef Forum was in the intense final stage of development and promotion, and tight schedules, urgent deadlines and a consuming sense of self-importance ensured regular doses of adrenaline coursed through my body. There was familiarity and solid ground in all this activity, so at twenty-nine, consumed with ego, a job, a debt, a drought and a property to run, I soon forgot about my wake-up call and resumed life – it was business as usual.

Twenty-seven

Like many, I was no stranger to cancer, having lived alongside it for the previous seven years. Before Joan's cancer claimed her, Dad's Big C had returned in 1995 after five years of remission. His brand was multiple myeloma. Fighting cancer had become an art to him, something to which he could apply his genius-like intellect, exercising his scientific mind and mathematical muscle researching the disease and emerging treatments.

He'd undergone regular radiotherapy. The repeated exposure to radiation gave him leukaemia. He underwent chemotherapy. The chemo did its job – it obliterated his immune system and everything else in its wake. (His solitary complaint during all the years of medical onslaught was that the chemo made 'beer taste like shit'.) In the process, the assault on his body left him with diabetes. As well as the medication he was on for multiple myeloma and leukaemia, he was injecting himself with insulin daily and playing a deadly balancing act managing the cocktail of drugs and diet. The barrage of treatments caused his heart to become enlarged, and pulmonary complaints joined the battery – just another tricky manoeuvre to be overcome in the drawn-out game of chess that he'd played with his cancer for over a decade. A cardiologist was added to his armoury of specialists. 'Alice, he's fighting three life-threatening illnesses at once,' his wife, Maxine, wailed into the phone and, just as I was succumbing to the fear, Dad's bombastic voice broadcasted in the background: 'AND LOVIN' IT!', sowing an unlikely seed of inspiration, rendering me smiling and proud.

I had become used to his fight as a background noise that simmered in our life. Dad was not concerned with the inevitable; he'd planned for it and had even held his own wake: 'Can't have those buggers drinking all that beer without me!' Once diagnosed he didn't budget on living past his mid-sixties – literally – and spent all his savings and retirement funds on good living and travelling around the world. 'I'd better hurry up and die soon – I'm nearly broke!' he'd say. It appeared his mathematical calculations hadn't factored in his own fighting spirit.

Another unbudgeted success: he recovered from the leukaemia. Against all odds, he survived whatever was thrown at him. With his track record and a healthy dose of denial, I began to accept that with the new treatments and constant vigilance for new outbreaks in his body that he would continue to hold the Big C at bay indefinitely.

Having received an 'all clear' from the cardiologist to recommence gentle exercise, Dad resumed walking on the treadmill in the garage. It was 1 March 2002. Half an hour later, Maxine found him collapsed, dead on the treadmill. Doug went over and helped move Dad's body into the bed.

'I swear, Alice, he had this smirk, like the Mona Lisa smile, on his lips.'

I think about that smile. Was it because the battle was over, or that his calculation of expenditure versus lifespan proved accurate, or that eleven years after his first near-death experience he was happy to meet his maker to finish that interrupted conversation about the meaning of life, and have all his questions about the complexities of the universe, string theory and quantum physics revealed to him? Maybe it meant nothing.

Rick and I went to Melbourne for the week before the funeral. By her own admission, Maxine was not in a state to handle his affairs, so I sorted out Dad's papers and necessary documents, discovering he had kept letters and cards that I had sent him over the years. I had kept the inverse set, written with his ballpoint pens in his strong angular script. I wept with a mix of frustration and happiness for a love I discovered that existed beneath the surface – and with sadness for our mutual stupidity and the relationship that would never be.

I pored over his writings, reflections, mathematical studies, his notes on Maralinga and atomic testing in Australia, and newspaper features about the expeditions he'd run with Mum in the seventies to discover the lost Mahogany Ship off the Warrnambool coast – revealing the life he'd lived, the one I never shared. I took the book he was reading, and fingered the bookmark denoting the last page he ever turned. It was Les Carlyon's *Gallipoli*, I'd given it to him at Christmas. Maxine was going to throw out the silly little things. No-one else wanted them. I took them. All of them. Connections to him, insights into his character and interests: the fossils, an unidentifiable piece of timber – a shipwreck relic from the expeditions, rocks, souvenir mugs, and the shell of a long deceased pet oyster, he'd found washed up on Port Phillip Bay and kept alive on a diet of fresh seawater and gravox.

Doug and his wife, Natasha, had given birth to their second child, a baby girl called Jessica, in February. Their first child, Nelson, was four. Nelson had some cherished memories of picking cherry tomatoes with Poppa Ian from his vegie patch. It gave Doug and Tash comfort that Dad met his grandchildren before his death and that Nelson had at least got to know him. I felt a familiar wrench, as part of me wished that we had had children earlier, and ours could have met their Poppa Ian.

The last time I saw my father was the previous September in Queensland, swimming in the pool of a lifelong friend, enjoying a cold one and a couple of prawns and oysters. I'm sure he knew that would be our last time together. I wish I'd stayed longer, taken the Monday off work. I never did that, and now that Monday I spent at work seems so pointless and unremarkable.

Dad was buried on 8 March 2002, Rick's thirty-first birthday. Rick left minutes after the funeral in time to catch a flight so he could return to work – heavens above, we had already been away for a week. At the wake (the one without Dad in attendance) I sat alone, surrounded by rollicking strangers who had known Dad, telling stories of his antics, devilry and the good ol' navy days. Doug and Tash had gone home to be with their newborn child and young son. Everyone was laughing and singing old navy songs, celebrating his gargantuan life as they knew it. For me, however, there was little to celebrate. It was the end of nearly thirty enigmatic years, and the death of our potential as a father and daughter. Tears of painful regret and loneliness for my father coursed down my cheeks, as the microphone passed from reveller to reveller. By the next morning the tears had dried but regret still sat heavy on my shoulders.

A few days later I returned to Cardowan and resumed an all-consuming hectic pace in our business and at work. I was turning thirty at the end of June and had buried my plans for a big party with Dad. I had a three-week trip to Vietnam planned in June, and there was a lot to do before then. Rick had decided to stay home and hold the fort.

I'd remained so busy since Dad's funeral that I'd barely allowed time to pack. After a stopover in Hong Kong with friends, I arrived in Hanoi to stay with an old schoolfriend for a few days before arranging a solo trip to Halong Bay.

In Halong Bay I felt freer than I had in years. I had no-one to confer with, no-one else's opinion or body clock to determine when I should have lunch or what activity to do, no phone, no computer, no accounts to do, no Rick, no Jumma, no waters to check, no clients, no horses to train, no dogs to feed, no fences to repair, no hay to put out. I was my own master and servant. At a guess, I'd say the last time I'd felt so free and unencumbered was hitchhiking in the Northern Territory. It was unsettling. I woke at 5 a.m. without an alarm clock and for no reason, with no cattle to muster or brand – just because it felt good.

The streets were deserted and the air was still cool as I walked the couple of kilometres around the peninsula to a small, secluded bay. I dived into the ocean, swimming up and down the bay, rolling in the warm gentle waves. I wondered: do I want to stay in the water or do I want to get out? Such a simple question and so perplexing. I had nowhere else to be and no-one to tell me what they wanted. It had been so long since I was not entwined with something, or someone – directing me, pulling me through each day, each hour, and each moment. I'd forgotten how to make a decision without a compelling reason; I was used to rushing, needing to be somewhere, doing the next thing, doing something, always something. I had forgotten how to just *be*.

The air was mild, a pleasant contrast to the draining, stifling humidity that the rising sun would bring. I swam some more. And floated. Unknowing, unresolved, I stayed. At one with the lolling rippling waves. The world was quiet. I was quiet. It had been so long since I'd listened to the whispers of the ocean.

Something will compel me in some direction; until then I will stay out here in the ocean.

So I stayed, and swam, and floated.

And wept.

I never saw it coming.

Tears rolled gently down my cheeks. For the first time since Dad died, I wasn't afraid of the emotion. I didn't have to be scared that if I started I'd never stop. No-one could walk in on me. Time was not an issue.

I had cried in small anguished bursts since Dad's funeral, but mostly I'd been white-knuckling through the days. I'd been afraid of the depth of my emotions. I was like the little boy with his finger in the dyke to hold back the water, terrified that if I took my finger out, the dyke would collapse. So three months after Dad's death, there I was in Vietnam, floating and crying, caressed and hel by the warm embrace of the ocean.

It wasn't just the grief for his death that consumed me, it was a greater grief, one that came with regret and the 'if's: If I had taken more time and made more trips to Melbourne; If I'd spent more time with him trying to break through the tough exterior; If I'd learnt more about his life journey, maybe I could have known him better. Well, I didn't. I moved to Queensland, I moved onto a cattle property. To Dad's way of thinking, Cardowan had been a landbound, withering destination; an awkward stopover on the way to his beloved coast. I got a job and I got busy. I couldn't go back. It was too late.

All 'ifs' are futile, and mine were no different. All we can do is use them as wake-up calls. So twelve months after my last life review, I was thrown into another innings of reflection and self-assessment, and the verdict was in – the balance was wanting. I chalked it up to inexperience and immaturity, gave myself absolution and vowed to allow more time for family and life beyond the barbed wire. I dived into the gentle waves and emerged calmer than I had been in months, maybe years.

Twenty-eight

But at thirty, consumed with a debt, a business and a job, life once again overtook my resolutions and my second wake-up call went unanswered. Our business, Greenup Santa Gertrudis and Quarter Horses, was launched on 1 July 2002, two days after my thirtieth birthday. From that day forward, Rick no longer worked for the family company – and no longer earned a wage. The family succession as it pertained to Rick was complete and something shifted inside him. It was a release, and his ambition and dreams ran free. We didn't have time to question our course. It was full steam ahead.

Keen to let someone else manage his cattle country so he could focus on cropping, John rented some paddocks to us where our first crop of bulls and steers could grow. Things were going well, until the phone rang one wintry Saturday afternoon.

'Alice, sorry, not a social call. Gotta be quick. What do you give cattle that are dehydrated?'

'Why?'

'Some of them ran out of water.'

'We're coming right over!' I slammed down the phone and ran outside yelling for Rick. We grabbed electrolytes and salt, and tore wildly along the twenty kilometres of dirt track to the paddock. John was responsible for keeping an eye on the water but had made a simple, but devastating, layman's error. He'd checked the tank for water but not the troughs. Somehow the pipe had been closed off and no water was feeding from the tank into the troughs in the paddock.

We were unprepared for the scene of annihilation that met us. It looked more like a battlefield than a paddock of lush sweet grass. Bodies of bulls and steers lay scattered across the field. Many were already dead and others were prostrate and helpless. As the dehydration wrought cruel havoc with their brains, those still standing charged me, knocking the water I held out in buckets from my arms. As I watched the precious water sink into the dry ground beneath, I felt sick, ripped apart inside; gut-wrenching grief mixed with anger and shame that animals that we cared for were in this predicament.

Rick called his family and Grahame and David arrived shortly after, their presence giving us some traction in the emotional quicksand.

We gathered every bucket and receptacle that could hold water. Rehydrating too quickly with pure water can cause further brain damage, so we mixed the water with salt and electrolytes, but the animals drank quickly, while others continued to charge at us, either in madness or desperation, spilling litres and litres of the precious fluid. Either way it was futile; they kept knocking over the buckets. We worked at a frantic pace late into the night, getting water to every animal that could drink and squirting electrolytes into the mouths of those too far gone to lift their heads, hoping that by some miracle we could save them.

It was dark. The side of the hill was silent except for the trudging of my footsteps as I lugged another bucket. The sound of Rick's rifle sporadically cracked through the air as individual battles were declared futile.

Rick and I were calm and focused with no visible emotion as we worked, without thought for our aching muscles, to revive or destroy our cattle. There came a point when there was nothing more we could do. Nothing anyone could do. I had no idea of the hour. We would be back at first light, but it was up to the cattle now. I climbed into the ute, covered my face with my blistered hands and wept, massive heavy sobs, unlike any I've ever known. There weren't enough tears to take away the haunting images of those beautiful animals whose heads I held in my arms as I pleaded with them to live, administering liquid, knowing they had given up as their sunken brown eyes became dull and lifeless.

Over the next week more died – even some that had looked robust. I wish now we had euthanased more – but we did not know what their chances for recovery were and – there's the catch – if we had euthanased them, then I would have wondered if we were premature in that decision.

Euthanasing animals is a ghastly job; you pray for the insight to make the right decision, and for forgiveness if you make the wrong one. Twenty animals died that day and another ten in the ensuing week. Rick pushed the carcasses into a heap and burnt them in a mass grave. We downgraded the surviving bulls to butcher grade, as the long-term damage to their bodies was unknown and we couldn't risk the integrity of our product.

Owning land and cattle is a great honour and responsibility, and sometimes we fail that which we care most about, in spite of our best intentions. I will be haunted by the experience until my own reckoning.

There's a saying in the bush: where you have livestock, you have dead stock. Cattle die from wild-dog attack, injury, birthing dystocia, snakebite, infection and disease, ingesting poisonous plants and numerous other causes that we are unable to diagnose. It's all about odds when you have thousands of animals in your care. Our goal is to minimise deaths, but shit happens. For most of the deaths, Rick is stoic; you have to be. But every now and then, a single animal dies that somehow represents all the others that died that year and I watch my tough man walk away from the dead beast with tears in his eyes and the release of frustration spilling from his mouth, wishing I could take away his pain.

Rick has stayed up all night with a colicky horse, then driven it at dawn to a vet two hours away for surgery only to see it die on the operating table. I saw him shoot his father's favourite old horse, Woollaroo, when he was injured galloping down a steep gorge at Benroy, the ankle tearing away from the hoof. I watched normally stoic stockmen weep that afternoon – all of them, from seventeen to seventy, grieving for Grahame's mate, the horse that wouldn't give up. I've seen Rick devastated when a cow gave up and died in a muddy waterhole, after only being stuck in there for a couple of hours, holding his head in his hands, saying to no-one: 'Why? Why? Why did she die?'

He rolls his eyes at me when I care for an orphaned calf, coaxing milk and electrolytes into its weakened body – 'You know the bloody thing is worth less than the milk you're giving it' – then he helps me feed that 'bloody thing' four times a day for the next month.

Even though our fledgling business could not afford any setbacks at such a precarious stage, we were determined that the cattle deaths were not going to send us under. To make up the lost income, Rick resumed training and breaking in horses and I took on some freelance work for consultants and wrote articles for industry magazines.

Rick's fervour and excitement about the business was infectious – rather like a funfair, where you can't help but be drawn in and before you know it you're lining up for a ticket on the roller-coaster ride, pursuing that combination of fear and exhilaration. As the season dragged on with barren skies, the grass fading with each passing week, we worked late into the nights putting out supplements to the cattle to maintain their condition, often getting home around midnight, pushing ourselves to new physical boundaries of endurance.

My freelance work was growing and on the back of securing a sizeable contract to organise a large industry forum, and another long-term contract under negotiation, I resigned from my government job. The contracts would tie in better with the property, making me available for the intensive parts of our program, such as branding and weaning.

I hadn't really thought about how babies would fit into the scheme of things, into that elusive work–life balance – all I knew was that I wanted them, and so did Rick. We let nature take her course, accepting that it might be a while before pad-slapping little feet trundled up and down our hallways, given my history of strange cycles. We figured one day I would throw up and that would be our cue to clear a room for a nursery. Until then I wasn't going to sit around waiting for the stork to arrive, so I immersed myself in work.

A new season of branding was upon us. Thirteen times the planet had circled the sun since I met Rick. Thirteen times the jacarandas had bloomed. And once again the sky burst with indigo clouds that offered nothing, the bark peeled away from the angophora trees and another crop of unmarked calves skipped alongside their mothers.

It was getting late for our summer rains, the rivers and dams were receding as the building summer heat scorched the ground day after day and we waited for a decent break in the season. The cows were slipping in condition as the calves, trusting all would be well, greedily drained the fat off their mothers' backs. We said farewell to 2002, and hoped for a better season and better times in 2003.

Twenty-nine

Branding signals a fresh start, new blood, new hope.

I had decided to take my new horse, Jem, when we mustered Jumma. The long days of gentle walking in paddocks and behind mobs of cattle would be great for his mind and development.

The sense of achievement when things fall into place between horse, rider, dogs and cattle is a natural high. I'd come to understand why Rick had always told me, 'Mustering is the most fun you can have with your clothes on'. To that I would add: mustering on a horse you have broken in and trained yourself is the ultimate in satisfaction.

I'd started training the unbroken two-year-old bay gelding the year before. Too wild to be loaded on the horse float, Rick borrowed a truck to transport the untamed horse and me to a four-day clinic where I would learn the art of horse breaking. My heart had raced as my breaker galloped down the ramp, unhaltered, unhandled, snorting at the imposition and distasteful presence of foul-smelling humans. I wondered what I had got myself into. Four days later Rick returned to collect us with the float and I showed off my saddled, bridled horse at a walk, a trot, and a canter.

Twelve months had passed since I'd broken in Jem. I'd worked him through the year and he felt sound and strong. I looked forward to taking his training to the next level and getting him started on cattle.

Our herd had grown and the bank balance was in good enough shape that we could hire some guys to help with the muster. They would camp at Cardowan with us for the two weeks it would take to muster and brand all our calves.

Lachlan Hornery and Shane Cullen arrived late Sunday evening, joining us for a roast dinner, to get a good night's sleep, ready for an early start that would be kicked off with a hearty stockman's breakfast.

I channelled Peggy's cooking prowess as I prepared the pantry, and was thankful that at least I didn't have to do it all on the wood-fired stove at Benroy. With me working in the paddock as well as cooking, it took army-style regimented planning and preparation to keep up to the hungry mouths three times a day. The benches were laden with fruitcakes I'd baked the previous week. I'd planned each day's meal for the next fortnight and had the menu pinned to the fridge. The fridge, freezers and cupboards bulged with food. In the morning, the kitchen was a frenzy of activity as endless rounds of corned-beef sandwiches were made and thrown into eskies, and the teapot brewed with black tea for the thermoses lined up on the bench. Sighing, I watched the pile of fruit disappear as it was tossed into the esky. It was day one and I already suspected I would have to make another hundred-kilometre round trip to the supermarket to replenish supplies.

We drove the fifteen-kilometre winding dirt road to Jumma where a dozen horses waited, having been trucked there over the weekend. Each person had two or three horses: one to ride in the morning and a fresh one for the afternoon. During a big muster there are usually be one or two minor injuries, such as staking a leg or hoof, and the inevitable loss of shoes, so spare horses are needed.

The landscape filled with the grey light of dawn as we saddled up and rode out to muster the first mob of cows. The horses were fresh, trying to jog-jog, anticipating the work ahead. By the time we'd walked an hour, the early sun and heavy humidity of a Queensland summer was drawing a lather of sweat from the horses' shoulders and they buckled down to a good walking pace.

Less than three hours later the paddock was mustered. We'd spread out across the 400-hectare paddock, bringing the herd together mob by mob from gullies and flats, out of heavy forest, and off rocky outcrops, gathering the 120 head of cows and their calves together with ease. It's always a welcome surprise when everything goes to plan, and a great start to the week. It was only mid-morning and Rick and I were already walking the mob back to the yards while the others started mustering another paddock, taking our two UHF radios to keep in touch with each other. We wouldn't need them.

The tinkling forest sounds of finches twittering and wind rustling in the she-oaks were swallowed up by the bleating of calves and their mothers' replies. The mob meandered down a track strewn through the ironbark saplings towards the yards.

Rick was riding Roxy, a three-year-old bay filly, on the wing, while the dogs controlled the lead and I held up the rear of the mob. My eyes were only partly on the cattle as I was consumed with my usual habit of scanning the pasture as I rode along, checking out which species of grass the cattle were selectively grazing and making mental notes of the pasture condition to discuss with Rick later. We ambled into a stand of blue gums, which prefer the loamy soils of the creek flats. I looked skywards, into the treetops, scanning for koalas. The first time I mustered Jumma I saw three within a hundred metres of each other. But they are elusive buggers and I hadn't spotted any since. I squinted, craning my neck. Some people say it is easier to discern the outline of a bump rather than the koala itself, as the koala's camouflaging grey fur blends inconspicuously with the mottled, light grey bark on the blue gums. Unrewarded, I looked back to my cattle, which had wandered off track while I was daydreaming.

I brought up the tail, urging the calves that were trailing behind to catch up to their mothers with a quiet 'Tch tch', and headed off the track to coax two wayward cows back to the mob. My gelding wove through a dense thicket of immature blue gums, picking his way over the sandy gravel and between granite rocks.

And then there was the blackness, sweet blackness.

Just like that, in a spilt second, your life can change.

Until that point, my world had been all about the physical: my body and the world around me that I could see, hear, touch, smell and taste. An instant later, I'd stopped thinking, evaluating, analysing. I left my physical world and teetered on the brink of another. I was no longer a body – the gravel and the ants that traversed the earth's surface were no longer separate from me. I just was. A composition of organic chemistry; a vibration of nature and all that is.

There was no pain and no fear in the blackness. It was peaceful and accepting. The pain and fear would come later, when I rejoined my body.

Part 2

We shall not cease from exploration, and the end of all our exploring will be to arrive where we started and know the place for the first time

T. S. ELIOT

Thirty

Hassled, bothered by humans to engage in the physical sensory world, I re-emerge from the sweet blackness. There is pain here. The other place is better. I come and go.

The sound of the chopper blades is deafening.

Rick shot some wild dogs out of a helicopter once; they had been giving our cows a cruelling that year, so he hired a chopper to hunt them down. From the vantage point of the chopper, he found them in a clearing as they lay waiting in a pack, stalking a calving cow. He shot three. Then the helicopter circled back around to get a bird's-eye look at Cardowan, our homestead. I was at work and missed the whole thing. I was envious: I'd always wanted to ride in a chopper and see Jumma and Cardowan from the air.

I won't see much today. I am strapped to a hard stretcher, every limb is pinned down. I can see the ceiling of the chopper and strain my eyes right and left to make out the outlines of the pilot and the three paramedics. I imagine what they can see out their windows as we rise up out of the mountains: towering ironbarks; dense spotted gum ridges stretching upward; granite boulders sitting atop each other; the canopy opening in places, offering glimpses of open native grassy woodlands; and the dark heavily foliaged ribbons denoting creeks and rivers that weave through the foothills.

I hear them on the radio, negotiating with the hospitals, trying to get me admitted to either the Princess Alexandra, which specialises in spinal injuries, or the Royal Brisbane Hospital, which specialises in neuro. It's a toss-up where I should go.

I try to drift off, craving the sweet blackness, the place where there is no pain and no separation between my body and spirit, but the pain in my head is consuming, excruciating and inescapable and keeps pulling me back into the world. The neck brace must be made of knife blades that are driving into my skull. The pain increases with every passing minute. I try telling the doctors. They can see I'm distressed and remove the oxygen mask so I can speak. 'Hurts. Head,' I mumble through clenched teeth. They make me more comfortable by putting a towel under my head, but there is little they can do. I close my eyes and will the flight to be over.

We arrive at the helipad of the Royal Brisbane Hospital. Neuro won. I wonder if this is a good or bad sign. From my prostrate position I glimpse the trauma staff racing out from the double doors adjoining the helipad, running to the helicopter, crouching low as the blades are still turning. It's overcast and raining lightly. I'm transferred onto another stretcher and taken to the trauma room. Another stretcher, more movement. *Just drift off, Alice, it will be over soon and you can be still again*, a calm voice inside my head instructs.

'Alice, we need to remove your jeans. Do you mind if we cut them off?'

Nurse number 2 pipes up: 'Do we have to cut them off? Why do we have to cut everything off around here? Why not just once, try to remove them in one piece? Do you know how much jeans cost?'

A trauma room debate rages around me. Nurse number 2 wins the argument, they concur that the bloody and torn red-checked shirt is beyond resurrection.

'Alice, we're going to try to remove your jeans without cutting them. If it hurts, please let us know and we'll cut them off.' The consideration is wasted on me.

I say nothing. The pain has wired my jaw shut with invisible sutures. A grunt escapes my constricted voice box. A grunt that means, 'I appreciate the courtesy, but you've mistaken me with someone who gives a shit. Just don't move my head.'

I surrender. I no longer care about my spiritual beliefs, my ambitions, my life's purpose, my work, my possessions, my modesty, my private ablutions. My body is in preservation and survival mode. I have reverted to a helpless dependent child and I don't care.

'Alice, we need to perform a CAT scan. Is there any possibility of you being pregnant?'

Suddenly I care. A spark awakens inside me. A flicker of light. My spirit remembers something greater. The question makes me recoil. I don't think I am pregnant, but we've been trying to fall pregnant for six months now, so it is possible. I feel a mix of relief and regret as the negative result is confirmed. Another layer of disappointment settles like sedimentary rock on top of last month's layer, although I know that if I were in the early stages of a pregnancy the chances of the foetus's survival would be slim after such a horrific trauma. My tests and treatment can go ahead unimpeded. I tell myself it's all for the best.

I am comforted by the arrival of Sally, who works in Brisbane near the hospital. She stays by my side as I am wheeled around for X-rays, CAT scans and blood tests. The tests reveal I have a couple of broken ribs, my liver is ruptured from the force of the kick, and my brain is bruised and swollen, bleeding in two spots in the occipital lobe and cerebellum at the rear of the brain, where it hit the ground, taking the full force.

There is little that can be done. A Plan A of 'Let's wait and see if the bleeding stops and the blood dissipates' is resolved upon.

Since Plan B is drilling into my brain to release the blood, I prefer Plan A. I'm considered stable and moved to the neuro ward for close monitoring and frequent CAT scans to assess the progress of the brain and liver contusions. 'Livers have a remarkable ability to rebuild,' the surgeon assures me. 'We'll know in a week or so whether yours will mend without surgery.' A gaping cut on my jaw is stitched up.

Five hours later Rick walks through the door with Mum. He shudders as he describes the accident to the doctors, shedding light on the cause of my injuries: 'Her horse bucked for no reason. He double-barrelled her with his rear legs while she was in the air. He kicked her in the neck and chest, slamming her to the ground. She landed on the back of her skull. She landed really hard.'

I vomit in regular violent waves, expelling the depths of my guts, racking my body with searing pain as the retching spasms take control of the muscles, moving my head and neck resentfully. I pray for the vomiting to stop so I can lie still. Rick and Mum try to help me, but I am immobile and can't escape my own vomit. It runs down my face and behind my neck. Through the long night my nurse repeatedly wipes me clean and changes my sheets, working tirelessly to restore my dignity.

Mum's presence is calm and soothing. She grounds Rick, countering his angst. The dark hours pass – snapshot images in between the inky blackness of my mind. In the dimly lit ward I see Rick sitting with his head in his hands, keening back and forth in the darkness. He thinks no-one can hear his pleas of 'Oh my God, oh my God'. I want to tell him I'm all right; that I will be back at Cardowan helping finish the muster in a couple of days. I don't know why he is so worried.

Morning dawns and before finishing her shift the nurse brings a washbasin to my bed and washes the caked blood from my hair. The warm water soothes my scalp and my spirit. She is attentive and considerate, paying careful attention to the first stage of my restoration, removing the dried, crusted blood and dirt and brushing my hair into a fan behind me to dry on the pillow.

Sometime in the afternoon, I am lucid enough to realise I have double vision. One nurse brings me an eye patch. Another brings me a hand mirror.

I am unprepared for the ghoulish sight before me. My face is swollen and bruised and I have a row of Frankenstein-like stitches along my jaw where the horse kicked me. The bruises are starting to show and like forensic evidence left at the scene of a crime they reveal hoof prints in the neck and ribs, explaining the excruciating pain of moving my head even a centimetre. My pulpy face is framed by my mass of light-brown hair, the black eye patch completing the effect. I look like I've been through eight rounds with Andrew Tyson or am an extra from the *Pirates of the Caribbean*. 'The stitches are well done. Nice and neat,' I offer reassuringly for Rick's benefit, trying to smile and catch his downcast eyes.

More CAT scans, more doctors; no better, no worse, more waiting. Mum returns to Kingaroy to work – there's nothing anyone can do. I fret about the men back at Cardowan. I have put them out, thrown out the work program. I should be at home looking after them, filling their stomachs with beef, vegetables and sticky date pudding. How will they cope without me? Removing the oxygen mask in bursts, I issue directions through my frozen jaw to Rick. 'There's a casserole in the fridge for dinner, another cake in the freezer that can be defrosted and the week's menu is on the fridge, all the supplies are there, ready to go.'

'Forget about Cardowan. The men'll be right, Alice.'

At my insistence he makes the call back to Cardowan and returns to my beside heartened – friends are rallying, turning up at Cardowan to continue the branding, and his schoolmates Mark and Lara are en route from the Gold Coast to cook and keep the show on the road. This comforts me slightly but Rick is still unsettled and distressed. He merely has to think about the accident and his eyes well up. His usual confidence is shattered. He seems vulnerable and haunted. I don't understand why. A close friend, James, is the first mate to visit. I watch them in the hallway hugging and wiping their eyes, their heads hung low. I can just make out Rick's whisper.

'Geez he drilled her. I can't believe she didn't die. I was so sure she'd died. Her eyes rolled back – you know, like when a cow dies … and the ants, they were all over her. We don't really know how she is, she's got some brain damage and her eyesight's no good. The kick in the guts pulverised her liver – we're waiting to see about that. The broken ribs are the least of our worries.'

I will later learn that in the hallway, Rick told James everything. Details he hadn't shared with anyone else, images and thoughts that haunted him. Images and thoughts that needed to be expunged. The full tale of what happened while I was in my sweet blackness, sinking into Jumma, I prised from Rick and others. Over the ensuing weeks I feel detached from the accident, even as I learn why Rick's eyes carry a darkness that hasn't been there before, and find myself giggling at the most ghastly images, unable to suppress my laughter in spite of the quizzical looks I get as the events of the missing day from my life are revealed. Slowly I piece together the minutes that congealed into a day that changed our lives.

Thirty-one

This is Rick's account of his experience of the day that changed our lives; the day I got a physical kick in the head and cosmic kick up the arse.

He looked back and saw her body suspended from the saddle. The horse spun, issuing a final kick with his back legs to her neck and chest, slamming her to the hard, dry ground, her head taking the full force of the landing. His heart stopped, his gut in his mouth.

Holy shit, she's finished, he thought, galloping over to the crumpled form on the ground. He flew off his horse and ran to her side, screaming, 'No!' But no-one could hear – he was alone, with no radio, surrounded by mountainous bushland. The nearest road was fifteen kilometres away, connected by rough steep tracks that wound their way through the forest.

All he thought was, *If I could just talk to her once more. Just once more.*

Blood flowed from her neck and mouth. He saw the whites as her eyes rolled back in her head and it reminded him of the many cows that he'd seen die – once those eyes rolled back it was all over.

There was nothing he could do to save her life. There seemed no point trying to get help. He decided to stay by her side, to be with her at the end.

The seconds seemed like minutes. Then she made some gurgling sounds. Maybe it wasn't hopeless? He was worried she would drown in her blood and wanted to roll her into the recovery position, but hesitated – his mind jostling between the likely injuries: a broken back or neck his first thought, followed by haemorrhaging, internal bleeding, brain damage.

'Alice, can you hear me?'

She groaned slightly in reply.

'I'm going to roll you onto your side. Tell me if it hurts.'

He tried to roll her but anywhere he touched her, she moaned with agony. She couldn't stand even the slightest movement, so he left her as she was, removing his shirt and placing it under her chin to stem the blood flowing from her neck.

He began to hope that maybe she would survive and that he should get some help. He wasn't confident about her state, she wasn't reviving and all he'd got from her was a grunt. But what if? His mind raced with the horrendous choice he had to make: *Should I leave her to die alone, or should I get help in case she survives?*

They were a long, long way away from a phone or people. He decided to get help and prayed that she would hold on until he got back.

She was lying out in the hot sun. He didn't like to leave her exposed, but what could he do? The horse stood twenty metres away watching, confused, as Rick tended to her. Her shirt was ripped and Rick could see a piece of the red-and-white gingham shirt stuck in the horse's shoe; he knew the horse had well and truly struck her hard.

'Alice, I've got to go and get help. Stay still. I'll be right back.'

He kissed her face tenderly, knowing it might be the last time he felt the warmth of her skin, and jumped on his horse, galloping towards the cattle yards. The dogs followed him, staying close to the horse's heels. The young filly galloped like a Melbourne Cup champion, for twice the distance – for five kilometres she gave him everything; up stony ridges, down gullies and across the first creek. She slowed before they came to the second creek. She had nothing left. They were straining forward coming up out of the creek when she collapsed on the bank, her legs stumbling then giving way beneath her. Spent. He knew he might have killed her. As he stepped off her heaving, gasping, prostrate body, he loosened the girth, pulling the saddle off in one swift move so she could get some air and praying she would be all right. The dogs stayed by the saddle.

His chest tight with dread, he continued on foot, drawing on every ounce of stamina he had, sprinting the last two kilometres of hills and gullies to the old abandoned house near the yards, giving thanks they had decided to keep an obsolete radio phone connected for emergencies.

Not wanting to spend unnecessary time away from his wife he rang his mother and asked her to call 000 and get an ambulance. Because it was impossible to give directions, he told her he'd meet the ambulance at the radio tower near the road in an hour.

Peg repeated the instructions and Rick hung up. He flew into the ute, hammering his way back at a death-defying speed – the ute sideways on each bend in the track, scratching dangerously for traction. It seemed to take an eternity as the coarsely graded track digressed through the paddocks, following contours, passing watering points and lick troughs while avoiding granite boulders and inaccessible gullies.

He returned to find the blood still running from her jaw and mouth and pooling on her chest and neck. The meat ants had sniffed out the scent of fresh blood and had made their way to the source, their brown red bodies scouring hungrily over her face and neck and into her moist dark mouth. He brushed the ants away in angry disgust, talking to her, hoping for signs of life as he picked off the last of the trespassers. A guttural moaning caused a new surge of hope.

He left her again, this time to meet the ambulance at the radio tower. Peg had called Wylarah and arranged for Penny and Caroline (John's daughter and sister) to meet Rick there too. The terrified look in Rick's eyes was seared into their memories. He asked them to wait for the ambulance and explained how to find Alice, then returned to her. Shirtless, he sat with her in the scorching sun, shading her face with his hands, trying to get a response. Half an hour later the ambulance arrived. Two hours had passed since the accident.

The paramedics inserted a drip, administered fluids and morphine and contacted the rescue helicopter – they told him there was no way they were going to try to move her in this country. An hour later the air was broken by the beating whisk of chopper blades. Everyone worked quickly and efficiently, but for him the whole process seemed to drag on forever. They carried her on a stretcher to the chopper and one doctor returned for a final briefing. When Rick asked how her neck and back were, he replied, 'Not good. It doesn't look good.'

The helicopter took off. Rick watched the black blob shrink then disappear behind the hills. There was nothing more to do.

All the while her horse Jem had stood calmly at a close distance, watching. Rick left him there and drove to the yards to give instructions to the men. When the stockmen returned that afternoon to collect the horses, Jem was wandering through the paddock, Roxy was standing not far from where she collapsed, and the dogs were sitting next to Rick's saddle.

Back at the house Rick feverishly packed two bags, one for him and one for Alice, not knowing if she'd ever need it, then drove the three hours to Brisbane to be by her side.

Thirty-two

The days that follow the accident are a blurry fog, punctuated with images and sounds.

Day 1

One of the helicopter paramedics drops by to check on my status. I have no image of his face in my mind, just a navy uniform and a sense of his care and concern. 'You're one lucky lady. We thought that neck was broken for sure.' I cannot turn or lift my head to look at the voice, but smile gratefully, inadequately.

Day 2

I am unable to leave my bed. I urinate in a bedpan and am washed by nurses. I vomit often and hope an obliging visitor is present to hold the bucket under my mouth, otherwise I can't move enough to get away from it and must lie in the vomit until a nurse can clean me and my sheets – again. The hospital pillow feels like a sledgehammer against my wounded skull. I crave to turn my head and get the weight off the back.

Day 3

A sense of modesty returns; a desire for self-reliance. With the aid of Rick and a nurse I am taken to the toilet. Note: If you ever have trouble seeing the brighter side of life then this is a good chance to pause for a moment and think about all the glorious times – the thousands of exquisite experiences – of performing bodily functions in privacy.

Day 4

Inspired by my progress, I aspire to another goal and take a shower in a chair. The gentle water cascading down my scalp awakens dulled follicles and capillaries, comforts the spirit and promises a normal life again, one day. My recovery takes gigantic leaps forward by these simple dignifying therapies.

Day 5

The bleeding in my brain stops and the coagulated blood in the brain begins to dissipate. There will be no need for brain surgery. The swelling is reducing, but the legacy of double vision remains. The liver is healing itself nicely. I commence physio and occupational therapy and see an ophthalmologist and countless neurosurgeons. I practise my physio, catching blue and red balloons and walking circuits of the ward as often as I can handle. I start on stairs. I have no sense of depth. I learn to use touch instead of sight to gauge distances and depth.

Day 6

Rick returns to Cardowan. The team of stockmen have reassembled to finish branding. Daily, before she goes to work, Sally brings me a juice of carrots, beetroot, orange, apple and ginger that she makes each morning, as well as a supply of fresh fruit – grapes, lychees and plump sweet nectarines – to tempt my appetite. The hospital food is a strong incentive to recover.

Day 7
There is little more that can be done with me – I am no longer critical and the other problems will or will not improve with time and therapy. There are some memory and recognition issues but I'm adamant that my recovery will be faster if I am away from sick people and in a normal house with fresh air and real food. I plead with the staff to let me out, promising to remain in Brisbane at the Greenup's family unit. I am released into Peggy's care with some strong pain relief.

The muscles in my neck are so weak that I can't sit in the car, and must resort to lying down on the back seat. My VW Beetle isn't big enough for me to lie down in and negotiating the coupé seating without incurring horrendous pain is impossible. Accepting the universe's prompting, Rick buys us a second-hand sedan. My accident has dragged us out of the sixties, giving us a car with four doors, a boot, air-conditioning, cassette deck and radio.

After three weeks my vision has not improved at all, but I am regaining some strength. Rick and I think I can look after myself during the days while he is out working. He drives to Brisbane to collect me and brings me home to Cardowan. I prepare myself for the sight of the house – after a houseful of jackaroos Cardowan is sure to be a war zone.

There are freshly picked flowers on the kitchen table. I look at Rick, dumbfounded. He tells me it wasn't him. Penny and another friend, Belinda, have cleaned Cardowan from top to bottom, making the beds, cleaning the bathroom and scrubbing the kitchen until no signs of the branding tribe remained. Relieved to back in the womb of our home, I shuffle tentatively through the vast, quiet house. Our home is immaculate and my bed is beautifully made, waiting for me.

Having been awake for over an hour I am exhausted. Rick draws the bedroom curtains closed and pulls back the doona. My soft pillow beckons, tantalising, offering a sublime sleep experience. I unfold myself into my bed slowly; thankfully, my head nestles into the soft pillow. I gather the crisp top sheet up close to my chin. It smells scrumptious. Only sheets that have been dried on the clothes line in fresh air smell like this. With half-mast lids, I declare my appreciation: 'I love the smell of fresh sheets—' Rick finishes my proclamation with me, '—there's nothing in the world like it.' Strangely, I feel sad for the first time since the accident.

Things have changed. Everything I thought I was, what I did, who I was – the world I had created – hinged on what I could do and how hard I worked. Now that is all gone.

Change scares a lot of people.

I am shit-scared.

Thirty-three

I creep through the grass and over logs. I stumble down an embankment, remembering too late that I can't read depth, as my feet slide down the greasy slope. What I thought was a ten-centimetre drop is closer to sixty centimetres. Flailing forward, I grasp for low-lying branches and tuffs of grass to brace myself.

This eyesight thing is giving me the shits. The ophthalmologists have given me no indication whatsoever about a recovery. It might be a year. It might be never. How will I function in the country unable to drive? There's no public transport, no taxis out here. I force the thought from my mind, back down with a few others that appear uninvited when my mind is left idle and alone to wander.

Rick has taken me out to the paddock where my hand-raised poddy calf, Brian, was released when I didn't come home from branding. Brian skips towards me when he hears me call. It's been over a month. His new friends join him, plummeting towards me, until they realise he is running to a dreaded human and turn on their heels to cavort off in the other direction. Brian halts, looking first at me, then to his mates, confused. He makes up his mind, running away with his new four-legged crowd. I am meant to be happy. All that powdered milk and wrestling to keep him hydrated and nourished have paid off. But I'm sad: my little mate is gone. I pretend not to be – who am I to be sad? I'm alive, aren't I? I wipe away the barely visible tears before getting back in the ute.

'Happy?'

'Disloyal little bugger!'

'I told you he'd forget you.'

In this sliver of a moment, this innocuous little incident, watching Brian skip away, the sensation that the accident has robbed me and violated my world grips me for the first time. Robbed of that moment when I let him go, robbed of my pet poddy, because in all truth and unbeknown to Rick, I think I was going to keep him around a bit longer.

The accident cheated me of so much: confidence, independence, driving, work, riding, walking briskly, physical abilities, absence of pain, peaceful painless sleep. Unable to drive and fulfil my work commitments, I resigned from my prized freelance contracts and I am now unemployed. I wonder how we will cope without the income. I wonder how I will cope without the work, the challenges and the professional network. With my body unable to do its dance, what will I do? What is my value? I need to contribute to this partnership. If I can't, then I am a burden.

I'd always thought it would be Rick in this situation, given his lack of regard for his own safety; never that it could me – after all, I was the one who picked her way carefully down the slopes. Some self-pity finds its way out. I'm fed up with saying how lucky I am; lucky to be alive. I want to complain. I'm tired of pretending that everything is all right, resisting the urge to lie down, moving through household tasks at a snail's pace, loath to burden Rick with any more than he is already juggling.

Afternoons slink into evenings. The rapid healing of the first fortnight plateaued weeks ago. I'm impatient with my lot. The pain in my neck is unbearable. Rick walks through the laundry door and finds me crying in the kitchen, standing over pumpkin and potato wedges. 'Leave it,' he implores, impatiently. 'I can do it. Lie down!' He takes the knife from me and finishes the job. I gingerley lay on the couch, sharing the leaden weight of my skull with the sofa's arm. We arrange for a cleaner to come and do the bigger household tasks. Rick helps prepare meals and do the washing, which I fold, agonisingly slowly. He does the shopping while I am at the physio twice a week.

I wonder how long he can go on carrying the load for us both.

By wearing an eye patch I can remove the double vision. This enables me to resume, in short bursts, some essential bookkeeping, one area that cannot be delegated to Rick, who is not computer literate. The bills and tax office wait for no-one.

Rick is working around the clock. He takes it in his stride, but even Rick with his boundless stamina and colossal capacity to work must be getting close to his limit. I study him and I watch him dig deeper. While it was me that was injured, I feel Rick's wounds are deeper and not healing as quickly. Years will pass before Rick can speak of that day without grief and horror haunting him.

I drop off the edge of my world into a void. My life consists of the walls of Cardowan and chauffeured trips to Kingaroy and Brisbane. I'm properly useless and for the first time I see my world with fresh eyes. I no longer need to think about what I can do ... do, do, do. None of that stuff ever did matter to Rick, just like he'd said so many times. I can see he loves me, Alice, the person I am inside – not the housemaid, the cook, the jillaroo or the account manager. I feel a fool. What a waste of energy all that worry was.

I thought I knew him, but I discover my husband anew. I see a raw tenderness. A love that is no longer hidden, but sits delicately on the surface, fragile, scared. I can no longer turn my head in bed to taste his kiss, but he holds me tenderly, bringing his face to mine, his lips brush across my lips, asking no more, filled with love and a cherishing that I'd never known, or never noticed.

For thirteen years, I had missed the signs that were right in front of me. I had even doubted his love. I had questioned my suitability; worried that I like to sleep in, stay up too late, that I didn't make his lunch or bake weekly batches of cakes for his morning tea, never ironed his jeans or picked up after him.

I'd wasted years looking at other women with envy, noting them as better candidates for Rick and more suited to his lifestyle. I'd been jealously frustrated that I would never ride with the skill of some and would always be branded as the city chick. I'd been deaf to his assurances.

The genie had hoped that my fears and guilt at being a burden to Rick would offer a fresh plot to cultivate another crop of self-doubt, but she's met her match. Instead, seedlings of faith, trust and a new type of love and confidence grow in their place.

My stamina and strength regain a portion of their former capacity, and the extrovert in me gets impatient to be dusted off and taken out – and the perfect stage for a resurrection is upon us. After five months of a hermit-like existence, in May we attend Beef 2003, a week-long international expo held in Rockhampton every three years, when the industry converges to educate, judge cattle and network. Rick and I are invited to attend the Beef Industry Awards evening. I am bubbling with excitement, delighted to be back in the game, renewing acquaintances in the industry mosh pit.

The awards get underway and the room is buzzing as the MC presents the first category. My attention is caught as I listen with amazement to the career highlights of the winner of the Young Beef Achiever Award – the similarities extend beyond coincidence. I turn to look at Rick, his eyes are glistening and his weathered rough hand reaches out to touch mine, he squeezes my hand and smiles, his eyes transfixed on the MC as the words stream past us like a familiar tale from a life lived a long time ago.

After completing an Agricultural Science Degree in 1995, this person worked for the past seven years in a beef extension role with Queensland Department of Primary Industries in the Burnett district. During that time, working with a small team of like-minded beef industry stakeholders and with limited budget resources, she initiated and drove the development of a series of industry forums and seminars in the region. These proved to be enormously popular with grassroots beef producers from a wide area of southern and central Queensland. Her enthusiasm, drive and dedication meant those producer information days became a benchmark for modern industry extension activity at a regional level.

Ladies and gentlemen, the 2003 Young Beef Achiever is Alice Greenup.

Rick leans forward and kisses me, his eyes moist with tears – it's something that happens a lot lately. With his signature stoicism gone he is in these moments unrecognisable as the laughing jackaroo who once tipped his hat to a backpacker. Instead, a more vulnerable and tender version has taken his place. This Rick is more reflective and remembers things he'd rather forget. As I pull back from the kiss I notice some grey specks in his dark hair and the deep creases stretching from his eyes to his temples and I wonder when they became so etched. I rise from my table and look at Peggy and Grahame, who, clued up by the organisers, are in attendance, clapping the loudest.

I look around the room filled with familiar smiling faces – government colleagues, industry giants, private consultants, mentors and role models – from all sectors of the industry supply chain. Some have known me since my earliest days as a backpacker apprentice, some have only known me in my professional career.

I take to the podium and thank my patient teachers who began this journey with me and forgave my ignorance and my unconventional ways; who answered my questions, guiding me and (most of the time) keeping me out of harm's way if a wayward cow charged.

The recovery is put on hold for a night and we head to the pub – I already have double vision, so how much damage can I do? Against doctor's orders – and good sense – we party on until the wee hours of the morning.

The expo lifts my spirits and reignites the fire in me. I want to get back into it. To do that, I need my independence. To have my independence, I need to drive again. To drive again, I need my eyesight back.

The ophthalmologists still have no ideas and no suggestions, so I make up my own eye exercises and do them at every opportunity. There is a small point of single vision very close to my nose. Basically I am already cross-eyed so I do the reverse of crossing my eyes: I hold my finger to my nose, where it is in single vision, and draw it away slowly, trying to hold the singular image. I do this every day, week after week. I gain a centimetre here and a centimetre there. It feels futile. I need metres, not centimetres! But I might as well practise, there is little else to do with my time.

One night I'm sitting in a bath of Epsom salts, relaxing my neck, playing eye exercises with the shower curtain rail, looking at something close up that is in single vision and then taking that line of sight outwards to the curtain rail ... and again ... and again ...

And then it happens: the rail comes into single view, just for a moment, then parts again. The rail has got to be at least two metres away!

I do it again. Another moment of perfect single vision.

I do it again. The single vision lingers tantalisingly for a couple of seconds. My head crumples forward into my hands in rapturous disbelief. I pull out the plug and get out of the bath. Rick is still out working even though it was dark hours ago. I float around the house with my secret, with indescribable immense elation and relief. I'm going to be all right!

I set a new goal, aiming for full recovery by branding, exactly twelve months after the accident.

I am keen to get back in the mix, doing what I love. Not confident to take on the onerous responsibility of paid employment I pursue voluntary work in the industry, accepting a position as a chair of a major beef industry event and another for a three-year term as a director of the Beef Australia Board. Rick supports and encourages me in both appointments.

Apart from my lack of contribution to our coffers, life begins to feel normal again. I start thinking about the next chapter. Even though pain, reduced mobility and fatigue are my regular companions, I figure they may never go away and we are as keen as ever to have children. I am realistic about the fact that the accident might have further compromised my ability to conceive. We make an appointment with Dr Twin Baby Maker.

Almost as soon as we are seated Dr Twin Baby Maker hands us a large document outlining the procedures for IVF, as he tells us that I have a very diminished capacity to conceive, given my history of irregular cycles, and that most likely I have severely polycystic ovaries. My inherent infertility has been exacerbated by the accident, which has caused damage to the pituitary gland, which regulates hormones, blah ... blah ... blah ... thus IVF would be our only option. Mind you, this diagnosis comes without performing any blood tests or scans and with minimal consultation.

I put the IVF manual in my bag. We thank him for his time, walk out of his office and never go back.

Until recently, my dilemma had been one of choice – motherhood versus work. Now, it seems, I'm both barren and unable to work – giving my newfound sense of self-worth a fair dusting up.

The naturopath that I am seeing for the accident recovery refers me to a second naturopath specialising in the field of fertility. She in turn refers me to an acupuncturist, who works miracles on my neck, getting my movement back and allaying the constant pain.

The fertility naturopath puts me on a course of herbal tonics and a restricted diet – mainly abstinence from champagne and carbohydrates (it wasn't too hard staying off the carbs) and implementing lifestyle changes to stimulate my pituitary, such as getting in tune with natural circadian cycles by going to bed when it gets dark and waking up with the sun – what a notion! I'm also taught to observe and chart my cycle – however aberrant it is. Each morning, I take my temperature.

It is a trying process of feigned patience. I wait for months just to have one cycle so we can have blood tests and see what is happening with my hormones. A normal cycle should last twenty-eight to thirty-one days and can be charted on a single A4 page. My charts go on for pages – each cycle taking months to complete. I stick A4 page next to A4 page, waiting for the rise in my temperature that indicates I have ovulated. There seems to be no improvement in my cycle, no pattern is emerging. Our goal of getting pregnant is replaced with our hope for some indication that I am ovulating and that my hormones are present and in some semblance of working order. My fertility naturopath told me at the beginning that she has never failed to get a pregnancy, but after six months of bland charts she admits that I might be her first client to not conceive. It's not a distinction I want.

It is well and good for people to say, 'Stop focusing on it and it will just happen.' 'It' must have come effortlessly for them, or they wouldn't say that. They haven't waited, wanted, wished. It's hard to not become obsessed when every morning the first thing you do is take your temperature and every trip to the toilet requires an observation to be noted on your charts.

Despondent as the months pass, I look at adoption options on the internet and throw myself into our business and voluntary work while continuing to take my herbs, do my charts and pretend it's no big deal. Life on the outside is busy; inside my emotions are stagnant and kept at bay by the full diary of things to do and places to be.

The early summer rains come, the calves are born and another season of branding will be upon us soon. My goal was to be recovered within a year of the accident, in time for branding in January 2004, but somewhere along the way I'd settled into my pain and sedentary lifestyle. With branding now just a month away, I'm not ready to spend two weeks in the saddle and cattle yards. I have been getting around like a closed pocketknife all year, avoiding exertion that will strain me or feel uncomfortable. It's time I got back on a horse.

Jem had been bushed to the back paddock after my accident. And until Rick's ready to look at him again and decide on his future, he will remain there. One thing Rick knows for certain: 'You will not ride that horse again, Alice.'

Rick gets in my old reliables, Skittles and Peppy's Fox, and shoes them. We all need to get into condition if we are going to handle a fortnight of mustering. I start riding in the arena and walk each day a little further. With eight border collies swirling around my feet, I look like a mad dog woman walking down Jumma Road. The forest is alive and the changing landscape is full of beauty in ways I've never noticed: the early morning fog settled in the gullies; dew droplets glistening on spider webs; marching caterpillars making their twice-daily migration; goannas scurrying up trees, tracks in the sand – the wriggles of a snake, the trace of a wallaby tail; and the cockatoos screeching from the uppermost branches of the tallest ironbark trees, twenty metres high in the sky. It feels wonderful to be back in the bush.

By the end of January I'm ready.

Out of a potential fifteen paddocks to muster, Rick inadvertently decides to begin with the same paddock and route of the previous year when I had my accident. My brain has wiped all memories of the accident, but my cellular and energetic fabric remember well. The demons are out there, lurking in the paddock somewhere among the blue gums, but they never reveal themselves beyond the shallower breathing that is nearly indiscernable. The cattle are mustered and we walk them back to the yards. Skittles pounds up the embankment of the last gully, triumphantly bringing up the tail. The old timber yards come into view. My head feels light – lighter than it has all year.

I nominate for a campdraft the following month.

It feels good to be back in a crowd of familiar faces. I am calm and unperturbed, warming up Skittles, waiting for my turn, no more anxious than usual. In the yard, I cut out my beast, call the gate and round the first and second peg at a reasonable pace; I come back around towards the gate, directing my beast into its final stage of the course. I don't quite get the gate, but wrap him up and will get a score.

I ride off the course at a canter. The emotion overwhelms me, blindsiding me. Tears find their way out of the seams of my eyes and escape down my face. At the edge of the arena I pull up my gentle old gelding and lie forward, hugging his big neck, drinking in his horsey smell. I am shaking. I'd been living with tightness in my chest and I didn't know it, until I felt it release. My heart breathes fully and deeply.

I have one final hurdle to clear before I can say I am recovered. I have to admit it. This should be the easy part, you might say, but sympathy is like a drug and after twelve months of constant outpouring of love, concern and consideration and emotional energy from others I have developed an addiction. I decide to go cold turkey to cure my addiction and tell the next person that asks about my condition that I'm recovered.

I hesitate when my moment comes. I want to speak of my ills and my pains. But more than that, I want to be healthy and I want to be defined by more than my accident.

'So, Alice, how are you going since your accident?'

'Thank you, I'm fine.'

'That's great,' they reply.

The identity that has stalked the halls of Cardowan for more than twelve months groans for attention, wanting to pull them back and say, 'But there are a few residual complaints – let's talk about me some more.' I crave to see the pity in their eyes and hear those treasured words, 'Is there anything we can do?'

But I resist, sealing my lips. I am ready to move on. Instead of me and my recovery, we talk about our favourite topic in the bush: 'How much rain have you had?'

Thirty-four

Pink lines. Two eight-millimetre pink lines. Who would have thought that teeny-weeny pink lines could bring such joy?

We have tried to be philosophical about not falling pregnant after two years of trying, but now we can bask in our bliss. Every bit of morning sickness is a welcome reminder. Nothing can diminish my pleasure. With my bump still negligible, fatigue grips me anew and aches and pains from the accident that had become memories come flooding back as healing takes a backseat to the greater biological mission, my body redirecting all its resources into cellular division. I want to sleep, but there is always so much to do. In the final stages of her restoration, in preparation for the new arrival, the Cardowan ironbark floors are polished to a gleaming reddish brown and the bedrooms are painted in fresh bright pastel colours, finally removing the last traces of the tan fifties lead paint that seemed to absorb all natural and artificial light in the rooms.

In April I put my most consuming project to rest. The Kingaroy Meat Profit Day is attended by 600 beef producers from around the state, forcing us to close registrations at capacity. The atmosphere is electric and inspiring and keeps me going despite the unaccustomed high heels. My growing belly strains against the waist of my skirt as the day wears on. I leave shortly after the closing address; the speakers and co-organisers can celebrate the success of the event without me. Rick takes me home. I curl up on the couch with a glass of red wine, barefoot, skirt unzipped, tummy lolling free. Satisfied, I hang up my navy suit for the rest of the year.

As a new life grows inside me, Rick's grandfather, the family's patriarch, George Alfred Greenup – Gaffer – passes away on 29 May 2004, aged eighty-six. Despite their properties still suffering the ravages of drought, beef producers come from all over Australia, travelling through the night to make the fifteen-hour-plus one-way drive from the far reaches of western Queensland to attend the funeral of this industry and community statesman, pay their respects, have a cup of tea and get back in their cars for the return trip.

Gaffer lives on in his children and grandchildren: his bold spirit and determination courses through their veins, leaving them his ultimate legacy, his spirit. He'd told me once that Rick was the most like him out of the grandchildren. I'd ruffled at the inference at the time, but I understand the truth of his words now.

Like Gaffer, Rick is impatient to grow our herd. In August we commence negotiations to implement a transition of tenure with the owners of Eidsvold Station, an iconic property and the oldest Santa Gertrudis stud in Australia. Eidsvold is a two-and-a-half hour drive north of Cardowan. Rick spends large blocks of time there, learning the run of the operation and assessing whether a long-term working relationship with the owners, Anthony and Sally, is doable, while I run the numbers to work out if it's viable.

It is a demanding time for us. Rick leaves the ute at Cardowan for me to use so I can check waters and run the cattle lick around. The VW Beetle is recalled from retirement to become our second work vehicle.

After a hectic weekend of trying to catch up on the work at Cardowan and Jumma, Sunday evenings Rick loads up the VW, squashing his Wranglers, boots, spurs and swag into the front boot. The saddle takes up the entire front passenger seat, stirrups tangling with the gear stick.

Five border collies line the back seat, packed in like furry sardines; the rest of the team stay behind with me, dejected. The chosen dogs' concern with this unconventional ute and fear of reprimand for getting into a car is overridden by their delight in being in such close proximity to their greatest love and master. They bound in past the inclined front seat and within seconds wet noses and panting tongues are streaking the windows with saliva. My precious Beetle is being sacrificed for the greater good. I squint and look past the slobber.

Rick tells me the sight of the powder-blue VW putting through the town of Eidsvold late at night draws unabashed stares from the confused locals. Rick and I laugh together, imagining their conversations: 'This can't be the bloke that Anthony is grooming for "The Station"?'

Week after week, Rick and the dogs maintain a gruelling schedule between Eidsvold and Cardowan. Rick works the dogs in teams, alternating their shifts to let their bodies recover. Our four-legged friends work to the point of exhaustion, doing long days in large paddocks, educating big mobs of cranky cows. Rick carts water on his back and saddle, stopping often to rehydrate the dogs, spitting the water into their mouths. The dogs get footsore, wearing the pads off their little feet. At night, Rick soaks their feet in Condy's crystals and cleans their eyes of grass seeds before feeding them and himself, rolling out his swag and collapsing asleep with his mates under the stars.

On the trip home from Eidsvold the dogs find any spot they can on the tiny back seat to slumber. They sleep sitting up, supporting each other's bodies, heads leaning over the seats - even the yellowed rubber hand strap that is suspended from the ceiling is comfortable resting place for a tired nose. No flea or stray breeze can arouse their attention on the return trip. The Beetle reverberates with doggy snores while Rick's mind races with thoughts about the limitations and potentials of the venture.

With my bump swelling, I wonder how we will do it all: baby, growing business and director of Beef Australia. I can't imagine what it will be like, so I just stop worrying. We will take it one day at a time and things will work themselves out. After dumping my obstetrician (Dr Twin Baby Maker), my first priority is to find somewhere to have this baby. I book into the Royal Brisbane Hospital Birth Centre; in the loving care of the same hospital that nurtured me after my accident.

Appointment for scans, blood tests and meetings with my midwife, Marion, fill my diary. Rick is unable to join me for most of the appointments and I try not to be disappointed. After nine years of marriage I have mastered the signature outback traits of self-reliance and stiff upper lip.

The crisp white marble floor of the hospital gleams with perfection and my footsteps echo anonymously into the glass ceilinged cavern as I stroll through the foyer towards the exit after my twenty-week scan. I can't believe it is already June and the baby is due early November. To my right, I glimpse a scale model of the hospital. It draws me in. Delighted by the intricate detail, I study the doll-house sized buildings.

And there it is. The helipad – a miniature helipad. My helipad. And miniature double doors. My double doors. Doors that swung over the threshold of my two lives; between this one and the previous life I took for granted when I thought I was immortal. My head begins to swim as I close my eyes, trying to regain my balance. Memories long forgotten come flooding back. Fears, long submerged in the cup-half-full of bravado, surface. I recall in a vivid flash the trauma staff racing towards me with a stretcher, blades whirring, the gentle drizzle of rain, overcast skies.

I open my eyes, a sob rising from deep within, like an unwelcome retch that will not be contained. I try to hold it together as I scuttle towards the large glass doors, pausing impatiently for them to lazily open.

I need to be alone. I round the corner of the building, race down a hedged path and find a deserted bench. The fear, angst and frustration that I had smothered since my accident bubble up. The lost time. The wasted time. The unacknowledged possibility that I could have died – I'd been so preoccupied in being thankful that I was not a paraplegic and assuring everyone that I was lucky, I'd ignored the fact that my soul had been shattered into fragments and terrified to its very core. I'd cheated death, and my inner spirit needed me to acknowledge the trauma it had borne.

Finally, my soul's ordeal honoured and empty of tears, I feel renewed and invincible about the impending birth. Even the knowledge that the baby is breech fails to disconcert me. I trust in my body and the process.

Rick is struggling with the birth as it draws closer. Actually, he is shit-scared. We are in the throes of calving season in the middle of another tough dry season, which is causing a large number of calving difficulties in the weakened heifers. We had pulled a number of calves already that year, mostly with poor outcomes and, although Rick is not inclined to liken me to a cow, the threats and complications of birth are all too fresh in his mind.

After twenty weeks of incubating our breech baby and trying every obstetric manoeuvre and old wives' tale in the book to turn it without success, I relocate to Sally's Brisbane unit a week before my due date. Rick spends the weekend with me and heads back to Cardowan on the Monday night. I am sad and anxious at his departure and would love Rick to stop working and stay with me. But we are still waiting on for the first rain of the season. Checking the waters is a priority, as is putting out supplement to sustain the cattle. Everything is on a knife edge: the cattle, the water, the risk of fire. He can't afford to be away for long. Life in the bush does not go on hold for anything.

Rick does an overnight round trip during the week to settle my nerves, returning to Cardowan at dawn. The following Saturday I am two days overdue.

I get a call around 9 p.m. from one of Ironpot's finest, Jetlag – the same Jetlag who scared the hell out of me when I was alone at Cardowan in the early days.

'G'day, Alice. Had that baby yet?'

'No, Jetlag. I'm still working on it. And to what do I owe the pleasure?'

'I'm ringing to let you know Rick's all right – he's with us. We're having a drought breaker tonight. If you go into labour call me and we'll bring him to the hospital.'

They put Rick on the phone.

'Hey there, how are you feeling?'

'Not as good as you, by the sound of it.'

'Jesus, they're funny bastards, Alice! Hook's set up deck chairs on the bank of Ironpot Creek with two fishing lines dropped over the bank into the sand. And he's got lobster pots sitting in the dry creek bed. There's a mountain of prawns here they're passing off as yabbies.'

'I get the picture. Have fun. I'll see you tomorrow.'

With no twinges or contractions, I know I'll be right for another twenty-four hours. Rick comes down the following day, Sunday, and decides to stay an extra day. At 2 a.m. on Monday 8 November 2004, five days past my due date, I awake to the first pangs of labour and call my midwife, Marion.

'You'd better come in, Alice, so we can monitor you since the baby's breech – just a precaution.'

I labour all day, walking the hallways and staircases of that hospital trying to strengthen the contractions. At 10 p.m., after a final five gruelling hours of intense labour, our beautiful baby girl – our special breech delivery – is born naturally. I have climbed my Mount Everest.

That night Ruby sleeps soundly, lying on Rick's bare chest, listening for the first time to her daddy's heartbeat. I sit in the chair next to the bed where my husband and daughter lie sleeping together. My heart swells with gratitude and a gradual acceptance that this miracle is not a dream.

The next day we are discharged and return to the unit. That afternoon I drive Rick to the airport, where he catches a plane to Rockhampton to complete two days with our business consultants while I stay in Brisbane.

Humans are habitual beings and slow to change, even when change is good. And it seems I am a slow learner, so still grappling with my addiction to adrenaline and the need to feel important, life continues at its former hectic pace. It's business as usual, baby in tow.

Thirty-five

It's hard. Harder than I imagined. Being a mum is constant, unrelenting. There is no break. I'm so tired. The dogs always bark just as I try to close my eyes. *Fucking dogs! I'll kill the next one that barks!*

Rick has been virtually missing in action since Ruby's birth, between working at Eidsvold and trying to keep our property running and cows alive. Each month, I attend directors' meetings in Rockhampton with Ruby, which is a three-day turnaround whether I fly or drive. We spread ourselves paper thin. In private the tears are frequent.

If those bloody dogs would just shut up I could get some sleep.

It's a late afternoon in February 2005. Rick is away again at Eidsvold. I'm sitting in bed feeding Ruby. Our bed faces a doorway opening onto the northern verandah, which is enclosed with metre-high vertical-join walls and eight-pane casement windows. Suddenly the blood runs from my hands, leaving them with tingling numbness as the fear–flight mechanism goes into overdrive in response to the two-metre brown snake sliding casually across the doorway, three metres from the end of my bed, quite at home. I interrupt Ruby's feast and silently slide first out of the bed and then out of the room with her pressed against my chest. Closing the door behind me I call a neighbour, Sam.

In ten minutes he is at Cardowan, shotgun in hand.

'Where's the snake now?'

'In my bedroom.'

'Are you sure you want me to shoot it? You'll have bullet holes in the floor.'

'I don't care what you do. Just get rid of it!'

Stealthily we open the door, trying to avoid making vibrations as we stalk the snake, first checking under the bed and in the immediate strike zone, and look up – too late, as his tail disappears out an open window. My floors and walls are intact, but my nerves are shattered. I tell myself it's just a freak one-off.

Until the next day. Ruby is lying on the kitchen floor for tummy time. I pick her up and put her down in the cot for a nap, returning to the kitchen to find a small brown snake skating across the polished floorboards where Ruby had been lying moments before.

Well-wishers and friends throughout the district hear of our close calls and speculation and advice is rife: 'Snakes can smell the milk', 'They love milk, especially sweet milk – like breastmilk', 'Oh, snakes will climb those stairs easily', 'Put tins of condensed milk outside and they'll go for that instead', 'What you need is some snake traps', 'The snakes will be coming inside looking for the baby'.

'Why?' I ask, when I'm told this last one.

'Because the baby smells like milk,' is the confident response.

I call a wildlife rescue service for advice on catching snakes.

'Did you see its underbelly?' is not the response I'm looking for.

'No I didn't see its underbelly, I was too busy removing my four-month-old baby from its reach! How am I supposed to see its belly?'

'Well, as it raises its body to strike, you need to be looking for the pattern of the scales on its underbelly–' Flabbergasted, I miss the rest of his explanation. '–Next time try and get a photo of the snake and email it to us for identification.'

I am alone with a baby and a brown snake in my house and he wants me to take its bloody picture?

'I don't want to know what it is, I just want to know how to catch it!'

'And then what? Kill it? You bush people try to kill everything,' he spews at me.

Unable to speak, I hang up and bawl with anger and frustration.

I catch possums in our ceiling and relocate them outside; scoop frogs out of toilets and rehome them in rivers and dams. We've preserved thousands of hectares of habitat; spent tens of thousands of dollars fencing off creeks and rivers to protect their ecosystems. But I draw the line at sharing our home with snakes. I order screens for the bedrooms and the living room. I'm told it will be a year before they can be installed.

I can't sleep. I'm haunted by the suggestion that snakes are attracted to the smell of milk, whether it's true or not. Every time Ruby has a nap I tuck a gauze net over her cot, ramming it firmly under the mattress, sealing all the gaps. I sleep with the windows and doors shut, even though it's the middle of summer and stifling hot. Neither of us sleep well in this self-imposed furnace. It is a long, exhausting, restless week waiting for Rick's return. Finally Rick comes home to a sleep-deprived, distraught wife.

I convince Rick that we need a break, so we pack the car and head to the beach for a week of rest. For seven whole days there will be no haunting images of snakes to unnerve me. As the rim of blue sea appears over the dash, I feel the weight beginning to lift off my chest, and breathe easier.

The mobile phone rings as we pull into the car park of our hotel. My body tenses. I watch Rick's face intently. He glances sideways at me, grimacing.

'It's where? Jesus! How far has it gone? Can we contain it? I can be there in three hours.' He hangs up and turns to me.

'There's a fire on Cardowan. They think it must have been a lightning strike.' My legs go weak.

Lightning from a barren storm igniting country as dry as tinder is beyond ironic – it's just plain cruel. The fire will ravage mercilessly throughout our entire property and those of our neighbours, wiping out the last remaining brittle stands of grass, unless it's fought with graders, dozers, backburning, water trucks and serious manpower.

'I'll head back and you can stay here. I'll be back in a couple of days.'

'Leave me here with no bloody car? I don't even know where I am!' I yell at him. I am furious, although arguing is futile. Always the property. Always.

My dreams of a good night's sleep and the occasional break from the constant demands of a newborn crumple in the car park.

Then the phone rings again. I lean to eavesdrop as Ricks listens and nods.

'Don't come back, Rick. It's under control. It's not as bad as they made out. The Ironpot and Kumbia Fire Brigades are here. We'll have it out by this afternoon. Stay where you are. If it gets worse, we'll call you.'

A week later we return to Cardowan and learn of the full extent of the fire and the effort our local community made to extinguish it. Dozens of Ironpot and Kumbia locals ceased their own work to attend it; stopping farming and cattle work; bringing their own staff, dozers, utes, water tanks and fire-fighting equipment. Someone made sandwiches and someone else brought thermoses of tea and coffee, and eskies of cold beer. Dozers put in firebreaks and the men backburnt into the fire. Some stayed most of the night monitoring the blaze and extinguishing small fires that escaped from stray sparks. Never a word of this was uttered to us while we were away.

We return refreshed. Rested. I feel able to cope with my world once again. So it's back to business and Rick resumes ferrying between Cardowan and Eidsvold.

The snakes must monitor when Rick's away. As soon as he leaves another slithering visitor joins me. I duck my head instinctively as I catch sight of a dark lump resting on a beam. This time it's a carpet python. Carpet pythons are non-venomous and prefer a diet of rats, possums, birds and lizards. But they still slither and have scales and are not my preferred housemates.

There had been a ferocious storm earlier – not enough rain to break the drought, but enough to settle the dust – no doubt he just wants a nice dry spot to rest, I tell myself. I assess the target and gather the necessary resources – mind you, I have little idea what the necessary resources are, but how hard can it be?

I use logic. I choose a pair of long barbecue tongs and a medium-sized saucepan as the appropriate receptacle to house my snake for the relocation. Holding the saucepan five centimetres under the snake with one hand and the tongs in the other, I try pulling it down into the saucepan. The snake rouses from its slumber and uncurls its body.

Bloody hell, I never thought of that.

The dark saucepan-sized lump turns into a metre-long yellow diamond python, sliding its way along the beam, offended by the awakening. Moronically, I persist with Plan A – trying to coax it into the saucepan. I flick it off the beam onto the floor and try to muster it into the pot as it slithers along. Although it always works on a cow, somehow flanking the snake's wings is proving less effective to direct it towards the stainless steel corral. I try to pick the snake up and place it in the saucepan one last time. In defiance, he rears up ten centimetres, warning me in no uncertain terms that, large as I am, he can take me on. I steel myself to remain calm and not think lethal thoughts. My brain eventually shifts gears and I come up with a Plan B. Loath to take my eyes off the slithery menace in case it disappears I race off to get a broom. With broom and tongs in unison I guide the visitor to the back door and watch it disappear into the paddock.

Once again my well-wishing friends are forthcoming with helpful advice: 'Snakes are *very* territorial. He's sure to be back.'

At least something has shifted in me – now I can listen to their crappy advice with some equanimity.

As a loving gesture, Rick surrounds the house and garden with netting as a physical barrier to my slithery housemates and gets me a shotgun – a .410, just like his mother's. As a sentimental gesture, it's right up there with the pocketknife and pliers and is the final rite of passage – I can now take my place alongside countrywomen everywhere.

Thirty-six

I had long ago accepted Rick's lack of romance, but now I discover that there is nothing as romantic as a husband that gets up at 3 a.m. to settle a baby, or a man who will change nappies without being asked. I no longer yearn for flowers and poetry – Rick's daily actions and encouragement of me to pursue my own interests are the epitome of love. He never questions the endless hours of unpaid work I do and the time it takes from our business, placing further pressure on an already heavily taxed system. So in the midst of our business and baby juggle, he encourages me to hold on to my dream for Beef Australia and follow it through. But between my responsibilities to our business and the monthly trips to Rockhampton on and off planes, in and out of hotels and meetings with a baby, I struggle with the commitment. He rallies me when I am on the verge of resigning – 'I think you should stick it out; you'll regret it if you walk away before the expo' – and even joins me on some trips to care for Ruby, bringing her into the boardroom for her feeds and getting me to the finish line.

Rick and I are keen for Ruby to have siblings. Given our history, I mentally prepare for a lengthy intermission between children and resume drinking foul-tasting herbal concoctions daily. However, by May 2006 I'm halfway through an uncomplicated breezy pregnancy as Rick, Ruby and I travel to Rockhampton to participate in the culmination of three years' work and sacrifice: Australia's largest beef expo, Beef06. The strain of the trip and constant activity causes some bleeding, which shakes me to my core. It is a reminder to slow down and have a little more respect for my body and the needs of our growing family, so, having completed my three terms and with a successful expo behind us, I resign as a director.

The smooth pregnancy continues. No surprises this time. The baby does plenty of backflips and somersaults throughout the gestation before settling into the preferred head down position and is due 17 September 2006, smack bang in the middle of the bull-selling season. Our bull sale is on Tuesday 26 September, which is to be our last joint sale with the family at Rosevale and coincides with the fiftieth anniversary sale. We'll hold our own on-property sale in 2007. With Rick attending multiple bull sales around the state for most of September, I relocate to stay with Sally in Brisbane again, a few weeks before my due date. I've had a lot of strong contractions and am positive the baby will arrive before its due date – a woman just know these things (hah!).

Sally is reassuring company for the first part of my confinement, but as the days roll into weeks and my due day comes and goes, she returns to Rosevale to help with preparations for the big day. In the event that I go into labour and need help with Ruby and getting to the hospital we prepare a list of back-up people – and back-up people to the back-up people. The days tick by. I just have to get through one more day and Rick and Sally will be back. I just have to get to Wednesday.

Wednesday morning, I'm spring-cleaning the unit to eliminate every trace that a 22-month-old toddler has taken over Sally's unit for a month. The physical activity stirs some good contractions, but considering the weeks of false labours, I ignore them.

I receive a call from the *Australian Women's Weekly*: I've been shortlisted as one of five Inspiring Rural Women and they'd like to interview me for a feature.

The journalist, Sue, gleans the story of how I came to work in the beef industry; my early days as Rick's apprentice; learning how to drive; being taught the differences between cows and bulls.

I struggle to remain focused as the blasted twinges gnaw in my back. The conversation drifts to family; Sue asks if we have any children.

'We have a little girl, twenty-two months, and we're expecting our second.'

'Oh that's lovely. When are you due?'

'Ten days ago. In fact I think I could be in labour now.'

'Do you think you should go?'

'If that's all right with you.'

I gather a few things. I call my first back-up person, Penny. She can't make it for a couple of hours. I call Rick and Sally. They'd left that morning and are en route.

'G'day, how's it going?'

'Please don't take your time getting here.'

'What do you mean?'

'I mean, don't be stopping off for milkshakes.'

'Why?'

A contraction tears through my body. Thirty seconds pass before I can speak again.

'Alice? Alice? Are you there? I think we've lost service, Sally. I can't hear her.'

I catch my breath, before another wave engulfs me.

'WHATDOYOUBLOODYMEANWHY?CANTYOUWORK OUTWHYYOURSELF? YOURBABYISTENDAYSOVERDUE ANDIT'SNOTSTAYINGINHEREFOREVER!'

'How far apart are the contractions?'

'IDON'TKNOWTHEY'REBLOODYCLOSEJUSTGET HERE!'

'Okay, we're an hour and a half away. Who's coming to help with Ruby?'

A momentary lull from the spasms flooding through my core allows a civil sentence to escape. 'I can't get hold of anyone and I think I need them right now,' I pant into the phone, tears brimming in my eyes.

'Just get to the hospital. We'll find someone to meet you there.'

In between contractions I pad around the unit packing my bag and Ruby's. Rick calls back. 'Margo will be there in an hour.' Margo was the back-up person to the back-up person.

'I haven't got an hour, Rick.'

I hang up and call my midwife, Marion, to let her know I'm coming. I'm realising too late that our contingency plans aren't brilliantly thought through and our laissez-faire birth plan has some weaknesses when put to the test.

A taxi arrives. I painstakingly load Ruby, my bag, her snack bag, her toys, the nappy bag, a bag of rubbish and myself into the elevator. I had planned to whip around the back of the building and throw the rubbish into the skip, but by the time I unload Ruby, my bag, the snack bag, her toys, the nappy bag, the rubbish and myself out of the elevator in the lobby, I might as well have planned to fly to the moon.

After two stops for contractions I make it down the twenty-metre path. The taxi driver takes the bags and I ease into the front seat, Ruby on my lap, the bag of rubbish at my feet. All rationality has abandoned me.

The trip to the RBH is one I have done many times and I know the fastest way without a doubt. We can be there in seven minutes. But oh no – the driver decides to take the scenic route and gets us stuck in a traffic jam on the city fringe.

I remain composed as the contractions roar through my body.

I'm using all my strength to remain quiet, otherwise I could redirect him or challenge the route, but I'm a mute witness to his folly as I try to ignore this baby's rapid descent through my body. I'm devastated that my longed-for water birth is about to be forgone in favour of a public birth at the St Paul's Terrace intersection with a nonchalant middle-aged taxi driver in attendance, a toddler on my lap and a bag of rubbish at my feet.

After a gruesome twenty minutes we arrive at the hospital. I open the taxi door and lift Ruby out onto the kerb; she trips on her blanket and starts crying, so putting my pelvic floor muscles into reverse I lift her up. We walk through the huge glass door into the foyer of my big white-walled sanctuary. Just a few more minutes, a small shuffle and a quick trip in the elevator and I will be in the care of my angel, Marion. I can hang on. The driver dumps my bags at the information desk.

'This woman is having a baby. Can someone take her upstairs?' A young girl takes one look at me, gasps and bustles us towards the elevator.

I step through the door into my birthing suite, my dim cocoon, and fall into Marion's arms. Soon I'm undressing and climbing into the warm bath they've prepared. Relief. Minutes later Rick bursts through the door. Ruby runs to him. 'Daddy!'

'Rick, this baby is ready to be born. I think you better get into the bath and catch your baby,' Marion instructs. Rick glances sheepishly around the room.

'I don't have any shorts.'

Marion laughs. 'That's all right, Rick, we've seen plenty of men's underpants around here.' His eyes widen in concern.

'Marion, I don't wear jocks. All I have on are my jeans.'

There is a moment of stunned silence as Marion composes herself, rifling through her mind for options. 'Can you borrow a pair of Alice's undies then?'

'I s'pose,' he mutters reluctantly.

Rick rummages through my bag and emerges moments later from the bathroom in women's red jockey briefs. He climbs into the pool and minutes later our baby is born into Rick's hands. Rick's eyes fill with tears watching our little man come into himself as we coax him from his foetal slumber – the pinkness spreading across his back and up to his head.

And so it comes about that on 27 September 2006 my cowboy is in a birthing pool wearing my red undies, with Ruby standing on the edge of the bath nibbling Tiny Teddies as her brother James is brought into the world.

'Geez, we're proper hippies now,' Rick announces.

A few hours later, Rick takes Ruby back to the unit, gives her dinner and settles her to sleep in the care of his sister before returning to James and me. Just like Ruby, our little man spends his first night sleeping on Daddy's bare chest, listening to a new heartbeat as his lungs learn to breathe and his body acclimatises to this foreign outside world. I sit and watch them in silent, grateful wonder.

With a new child and a new phase in our business underway, we farewell the last of our connections to Rosevale and prepare for our first bull sale at Cardowan in 2007. Even the unrelenting drought cannot diminish the hope we see for our future. And with a new full-time stockman appointed to share the load at Cardowan and Jumma, it seems that our dreams for our family and business are finally coming together.

On 12 December 2006 we get a call that shatters those dreams.

Thirty-seven

'Rick, I think you better get down here, some of the bulls are dead and there's a heap circling.' It's Cam, the new stockman, on the phone.

Dreading what he'll find, Rick tears out to the paddock. The bulls are blind and out of control. One hundred and fifty-six bulls are in the mob: our entire 2007 team of sale bulls is affected.

I put my detective hat on, drawing on every shred of physiological, toxicological and nutritional knowledge I ever possessed, and rely on my professional network to get to the bottom of this inexplicable tragedy. The findings are a bombshell. Because of the drought we are buying in feed for the bulls. The ration turns out to be high in sulphur and toxic levels have been consumed. The bulls have developed hydrogen sulphide toxicity, affecting their pulmonary system, and sulphur-induced polioencephalomalacia (PEM). In other words, they have brain damage. We postpone our inaugural sale until 2008.

Putting down the worst of the affected animals, carting away their dead bodies and watching our dreams decompose, rocks our world to its foundation. The beasts that survive are downgraded to butcher meat. We cope by keeping our blessings front of mind: our two precious children, our health and our love; but his spirit is sapped and it takes Rick more than a year to recover from the tragedy.

As James starts walking and Ruby heads to kindy, I notice there is someone missing from our family. I begin to take my herbs again and two months later, there they are – those amazing pink double lines.

The year 2008 shapes up to test our stamina and endurance. We commit to running an on-property field day in April as a marketing tool, which is attended by more than 200 beef producers. I'm planning speakers, catering and publicity, as well as getting Cardowan to her shiny best, all while six months pregnant. As well as the baby due in July we are also preparing for our two inaugural bull sales: one on-property at Cardowan and the other at the Eidsvold Saleyards in September.

We build a sale complex at Cardowan which includes catering facilities, grandstand, bull ring, auctioneer's box and toilets. I develop, design and prepare the sale catalogues and in the middle of it all we hold a jazz day for the local kindy and Cam, our stockman, resigns for health reasons. We are understaffed again, spreading Rick thinly across the properties. Distractions from routine like dinner parties and campdrafting are distant memories. But with my favourite drug, adrenaline, coursing through my veins I blaze on, setting myself up for another fall.

For the record, this is stupid behaviour. It's just that sometimes we get in deeper than we intend and don't know how to get out. And I can't see just how stupid I'm being, until a dream forces me to …

Tracy had told me in confidence that she'd hired an imposter to act in her role as mother and wife, while she went out and worked and lived with free abandon. While on a business trip Tracy died in a car crash. The imposter continued playing the role, so that all those who loved Tracy were oblivious to her death and their loss. They didn't know to grieve. Only the imposter and I knew the truth; that the real Tracy had died.

'We've got to tell them,' I insisted.

But the imposter's response was blunt and accurate: 'If you tell them then they'll be angry with Tracy, because she lied about her double identity and let me take her place. They will feel cheated. It's best if they go on thinking she is alive and I continue living as the real Tracy.'

I was devastated, grieving Tracy's death in secret. The real Tracy had died and this fake Tracy was here in her place, but no-one would ever know except for me and the imposter.

Tracy is one of my closest friends, and someone whose life often runs in parallel with my own. I call her first thing in the morning and tell her about the dream.

'I don't know if it is about you or whether you are a metaphor. What you think?' I say to her.

But I already know the truth. My world is a function of choices I'm making for myself, but in the depth of self-pity and the blinkered grip of motherhood, I can see no way off the hamster wheel: round and round it goes – business activity statements, breastfeeding, drought feeding, swimming lessons, budgets, herd recording, NLIS transfers, toilet training, tantrums, wages, sick animals, paying bills, superannuation, work cover, absentee husband, cleaning, washing, cooking, weight recording, profit benchmarking, advertising, organising speakers, presentations, industry meetings, cleaning up vomit, reading books, playing dress-ups, wiping bottoms, sandpits and swings ... all conducted in the hazy fog of sleep deprivation and the occasional bout of mastitis.

I was eighteen when Rick and I met, and Rick's passion for his world was electrifying. I'd been directionless when I'd left Melbourne to find myself. I found direction – and a whole new life. A great life. But somewhere along the way, that life started to live me.

I know things have to change. So I begin looking for a solution in the obvious place and do what all self-respecting wives do – I blame the husband. I launch a full-throttle attack, accusing Rick of not 'making me a high enough priority ... I do so much for everyone, I have dreams too, you know, blah, blah, blah.'

In his characteristic non-combative style, Rick takes the kids out for a drive to check waters. I get out some paint and a canvas that I had purchased about eighteen months earlier in a flash of inspiration as I'd sought the Alice of yesteryear. The canvas has sat there week after week, taunting me as the dust accumulated on it. The longer the canvas accused me with its stark whiteness, the more I'd simmered at my inability to find time for myself.

But now I put paint to canvas. I paint, and paint – and paint. Onto that canvas I unleash the frustrations of putting so many things on hold: trips to Europe, campdrafting, friends, lazy days just spent reading, career choices, maternity leave ...

As the white disappears under a heavy layer of pigment, something is emancipated. I don't know what inspires it, but in the ensuing weeks I begin collecting pictures of things that excite me: mosaics, children swimming, fresh vegies, the Greek islands, a woman meditating and another painting her toenails. With these images I create murals.

As the days go by, the murals remain to remind me of my dreams and goals. I begin to understand what they mean by putting your own oxygen mask on first on aeroplanes, and I start saying no. By saying no, I may deprive the Australian Tax Office of receiving their paperwork on time, but I give to my husband and children the gift of my sanity and my laughter. By saying no, I may not get the Martha Stewart award for neatest house and the floors may feel neglected, but I'd rather the floor feel it than my kids and my soul. I do bake cakes for smoko when it suits me and I also have a pantry of ready-mades for when it doesn't.

The weeks roll by and life continues as the day-to-day pressing demands consume our time, and at last, *at last*, it rains, an amnesty from the financial haemorrhage and the strain on physical resources. The biggest burden, of keeping cattle alive with water and supplements, is behind us for now. Rick reminds me that it is a start and no more: 'The rain gauge will have to fill a heck of a lot more times before we can say the drought's over.' I know what he means now – the land is so depleted of moisture that any rain is sucked up into her dry earth and leaves nothing for the rivers or the trees. It is rain, but it is the bare sustenance. Nevertheless, we are grateful as we watch the dams top up, the grass grow, and the cows' protruding hips disappear for the time being under a thin layer of fat.

The rain creates a space in our time and our minds. I think about where and how we are going to have this third baby. With no employee appointed yet at Cardowan, Rick can't leave the property for any length of time. I don't want to go through another period of confinement away from Rick, especially with two toddlers.

I am thirty weeks pregnant, two months away from D Day, and I start to panic – I don't have a birth venue or plan. I go through my options in my head, again. Nothing feels right. Until I consider homebirth – it's not perfect, but it means no travel and I can have another water birth.

We find a midwife, Sonya, who specialises in homebirths and who agrees to deliver our baby at our home despite the 150-kilometre distance between us. Sonya must have a sixth sense about Rick, handing him a book on our first visit entitled *Homebirth – Not Just for Hippies*. 'In fact, Rick, the truth is I've never even delivered a baby for a hippie,' Sonya assures him.

At thirty-six weeks she provides us with an inflatable birthing pool and a list of preparations to make. Our close friend Natasha, who is also an experienced midwife, agrees to be our doula.

As the due date (July 7) approaches I race against time to complete our first bull sale catalogue. I fantasise about stopping work; about taking maternity leave doing yoga and having a rest just like all the books say.

On our baby's due date Rick leaves at 3 a.m. for Eidsvold and is out of contact all day, returning at 10 p.m. It's a long and anxious day.

Three days later he returns to Eidsvold – another day of crossed legs waiting for his return. Natasha leaves a care pack in case the baby is born before either midwife arrives. We have on hand: vitamin K for the baby in the event of a traumatic delivery, umbilical pegs, Syntometrine and Syntocinon in the event of haemorrhaging, a baby ventilator and an assortment of medical paraphernalia. Natasha takes Rick through the essentials: how to resuscitate, how to administer drugs, how to peg the cord and so on. Both of us hope that all this preparation is unnecessary.

The blue inflated birthing pool takes over our bedroom. I look at the pool. It stares back at me.

What in God's name are we doing? The repressed memories of the biting, searing pain of labour course through me. My heart thumps rapidly.

'Rick, I want to be in Brisbane! I want to be at the birth centre with Marion!'

'No you don't, Alice,' he assures me.

'Yes I do!'

'No you don't. You're just scared.'

'Are we mad?'

'It'll be fine.'

'I don't know if I can do this.'

'Alice, you can do it. You know you don't want to pack up the kids and go to Brisbane.'

'Yes I do!'

'You couldn't even get into the birth centre now and Marion wouldn't be able to deliver you.'

My mind races with how I can pull a swiftie: get to Brisbane ... turn up at the RBH at the last minute – giving them no choice but to admit me – then call Marion.

Apart from being a woman with a large belly that squirms of its own accord and a blow-up pool in her bedroom, I feel totally unprepared for the birth. For the next few days, I walk past the pool with one eye closed, giving it sideways glances, trying to become accustomed to its presence without getting palpitations. Gradually I accept its presence in our bedroom. By Sunday I'm at peace with the inevitable and want to meet our baby.

Rick is planning another day working out in the paddock on Monday morning. Our new manager, Philip, who started five days before, is just beginning to get the run of the place.

I pull Rick up as he heads for the door 'Can you hang around? I think we might have a baby today.'

'Okay, we'll just go for a drive around and I'll show Philip some things. I'll be back in a few hours.'

'*Please* don't. You need to stay here!'

He gets it. He goes outside, has a talk with Philip and is back in fifteen minutes. Then he takes one look at my expression and calls Sonya and Natasha. I set up for the birth, pausing regularly as the waves of contractions move through my body. Peggy collects Ruby and James for a playdate.

Natasha arrives. She assesses the baby's heart rate and helps Rick fill the pool with the twenty metres of new hose he'd bought to run the length of the house from laundry to bedroom. The tepid liquid supports my body and the gentle pressure takes the edge off the contractions. Sonya arrives two hours later, sets up her equipment and begins monitoring the baby's heart rate. Just thirty minutes later and seven days overdue our baby is born in water, into Rick's arms. Our third miracle, Rory. Two hours later and we are eating homemade mince and pasta around the kitchen table.

Two days later we go for our first drive as a family to check the stock waters around the property. We buckle in our three special people. I look into the back seat and my heart fills with joy. Everyone is here.

Thirty-eight

Hugging the side of the hill, the newly built terraced amphitheatre overlooks our horse-training arena, yet it looks as if it's always been there – the thick matt of couch grass is mown and trimmed in anticipation of our inaugural spring bull sale. Wide beams of ironbark from the floor of the old Jumma hut form the facade of the auctioneer's box, their roughly hewn slabs polished to a smooth grey under decades of dust and boots.

With fifty bulls and two horses up for auction, it's the culmination of Rick's dream and a testimony to his dogged perseverance. The horse-training arena has been divided into small yards with portable panels for pre-sale viewing of the bulls. An encouraging crowd swells and the yards are filled with people inspecting the bulls, but it won't be until the end that we'll know if they're serious or window shopping.

The auctioneers declare the opening: 'Sale-O, sale-O,' they call, as the crowd is seated.

The bulls come into the ring in pairs. The crowd tries to control the bidding, and the auctioneers work to build the energy, sweat dripping from their foreheads as they squeeze each bid from the crowd.

'Eight thousand. Sold.'

'Six thousand. Sold.'

'Four thousand. Sold.'

'Nine thousand. Sold.'

One by one the hammer falls as the bulls are knocked down. The sale gets tougher as we go down the line. In the end, six are unsold and the rest average $4100. The week before at Eidsvold we sold 53 bulls to average $3500. Both are solid results: not ground-breaking and not as good as we'd hoped, but a start.

There's only the horses to go now. As I watch Rick ride the gentle bay mare into the sale ring, I'm filled with nervous joy for him. He trots his mare in front of the 300-strong crowd. He stops and turns her; she rolls smoothly back through herself. He canters off slowly in the other direction. The auctioneer picks up the rhythm and the bidding starts. There are a number of active bidders and the auctioneer has the crowd eating out of his hand. 'Do I hear two thousand? ... Yes. We have two thousand ... Do I have three thousand? ... Yes! Four ... Five ... C'mon, she's worth her sugar, ladies and gentlemen. I have six, six thousand ...'

The momentum builds. Rick clicks her up into a fast canter, displaying the mare's balance and athleticism in front of the crowd. He's put himself and his vision out there to be judged and bid upon and my heart swells with love and admiration. The hammer falls.

'*Sold* – for eight and a half thousand dollars.'

Those first sales seem like an eternity ago. It's already December again and the 2009 calves are sprinkled across the paddock. Like signposts reminding us that another summer is here, the angophoras are losing their bark, peeling back to reveal their new bright orange-pink underbelly, as if showing off in front of their more austere ironbark cousins. The grass at their feet is dry and crisp, fragile as tissue paper. It should be long and green by now; the dogs should be getting lost in the mat of grass, rearing on their hind legs to look over it, to get their bearings on the herd and master. But the season has turned against us again and it is dry. Dry again.

At night I look to the heavens, and the greying brittle stalks of grass underneath my feet can be forgotten in the moment. The stars are so beautiful – the sky is clear and uninterrupted. But I crave the inky, impenetrable darkness that bodes a storm front and would settle for even a smudge of cloud shrouding the stars; something, anything, to show that there is some moisture and variation in the system.

Our skills in managing the land and coping with dry seasons have improved. Our development of infrastructure ensures we still have water for the cattle, and the fences and our pasture spelling is protecting the grasses, so there is some dry feed, which we can use with supplements to keep the cattle going. Our greatest challenge is no longer physical but psychological; to divorce our emotions from the erratic occurrence of rain. We draw on our reserves, mental skills honed over the years to manage the extended dry seasons. We preserve our sanity with our ability to focus our attention on our health and good fortune; a roof, comfortable beds, safety from persecution, wholesome food, children, love.

Yet the vitality missing from the land drains the soul, eroding even the strongest mind. I try to bolster Rick in preparation for the visual onslaught he is going to encounter when he rides through the paddock. I feel like I'm patching up a soldier each night and sending him back out to war.

'It's going to be tough, Rick. It's dry. Accept it now before you ride out into that paddock. We can't change it. Just do what needs to be done. Make the decisions and manoeuvre through and around the obstacles and daily challenges. We will emerge on the other side.'

'Yeah, I know.'

While I am bathing the kids one night, Rick walks through the door. I see the thin smile he has put in place to disguise the emotions below the surface. The kids bumble on oblivious to his reduced span of patience for their stalling antics of wriggling while getting dressed, fighting over which book he will read them – standard bedtime stuff. Once they are settled I ask him, 'Do you want to tell me what you're feeling?'

'I'm fine.'

'Are you sad about going to Eidsvold this week?'

'No.'

'Then what is it?'

'It's all good.'

'Then why do you close your eyes or look away when you answer me?'

'Do I?'

'Yes.'

'*If it would just bloody well rain!* For Christ's sake, Alice, we've just started to recover from the last ten years of drought and it's taken us two seasons to catch up, and now—' he breaks off, his lip quivering '—to watch the cows slipping and falling behind again and all our progress lost—' he breaks off again, shaking his head before it comes to rest in his hands.

I'd seen this coming. It was inevitable. Even the most stoic has to succumb at some point.

In my mind I ask, *Why? Why are we so beholden?* The cattle and the land and the horses and lifestyle are wonderful, but it comes with so much pain – it's like having a lover whose affection is hot and cold, unpredictable: nurturing today, beating you tomorrow.

There are no guarantees in agriculture, but the probability of rain is high now, as Christmas approaches. And that will keep us going. Tomorrow he will get back in the saddle. Tomorrow he will get back on the merry-go-round and go to Eidsvold to begin branding.

I've glimpsed what a paradise this country can be. For two consecutive seasons I saw how abundant this land is when it rains and dared to imagine what it was like – I've heard them speak of it, like folklore – back when it rained every year without fail, like clockwork. The dams were full and the cows and calves fat, even in the forest country. Back when the creeks never ran dry, the men spent most of the summer putting up creek crossings – sometimes eight times in one season. Our kids don't know what a creek crossing is. But in spite of the drought we have built a business and are raising a family. And as long as there's enough water for washing grubby faces and filling the wading pool, then life goes on with relative jubilance.

The genie in me is quiet. I'm careful to check that her lid is secure when I feel down, so she can't make things worse. I've learnt to recognise her deceptive murmur and am quick to remind her that if she hasn't got anything nice to say, then she should just keep quiet.

So I am grateful, as I sit in the cool late-afternoon shade of our garden with my 'babyputer' – as the kids have come to call it – on my lap, watching them jump on the trampoline under a sprawling tipuana tree. The garden is shaded by two poinciana trees with their wide sweeping branches and exquisite flame-red flowers in summer and, courtesy of the jacarandas, the lawn is a blanket of purple. Planted as seedlings when we first arrived, now they stand as semi-mature trees, providing a good canopy and shelter for more tender species. I'm amazed at how well the garden has grown despite the lack of rain, replacing the hot barren plot that once surrounded the homestead.

I drag my attention back to the words I've just written:

Nature changes. Effortlessly. Yielding. Succumbing. Cyclic.

Forgetting we are part of nature, change makes humans uncomfortable. We resist against the physical changes occurring in our body, with resentment or denial. We adhere to the familiar, often beyond its use by date.

If we must endure change, we prefer premeditated change arising with reflection and preparation – still discomforting or disorientating, but acceptable. Imposed change is like dozers coming through the landscape and we rail against it.

Some changes are glacial, barely visible, yet monumental and discernible only when seen with the distance of time: the shifting of tectonic plates, the accumulation of rings on a tree and grey hairs on a head.

And some things never change: who we are; that essence inside, that vitality that never ages, that dreams and glows with blinding brightness when we are inspired. And by turning our attention to that unwavering part of ourselves the external changes no longer seem so frightening—

I close my laptop, smiling as the rumble of Rick's ute pulling into the driveway causes a mad scramble off the trampoline and six pint-sized pink legs hurtling towards the gate. *That chapter will have to wait.*

Life is like that now. A series of interruptions. Colourful strands interrupting each other, taking precedence in their turn, all as vital as each other, to weave the rich fabric of life. The more strands, the stronger and more beautiful the final garment.

Scooping up a wobbly, lagging Rory into my arms, I run to catch up with Ruby and James.

Rick has been away for the week, working at Eidsvold. The older kids get to him first, smothering him with cuddles. He kisses them and lifts them up onto his hips, one on each side; his eyes and smile are mine. He kisses me with a soft kiss that becomes hard as he tells me with his lips how much he loves me and missed me and the kids. His face is unshaven and covered in dirt and Ruby laughs and crinkles her nose at Daddy's prickly face. He smells musky, like a man who has been working, the odour of sweet sweat mingles with traces of branding – scents of smoke and burnt hide. My head spins. I am conscious of our audience, so return his affection modestly. Rick climbs onto the trampoline with the kids and together we all sing 'Ring o' Roses'. I act like nothing's changed, because I don't want the kids to think that life is better when Dad is home and less complete when he's away, always waiting for him to make everything perfect, but we're all delighted and overjoyed to see our man come back.

We start branding the Cardowan and Jumma cattle the following day. Drafting the calves is one of the best jobs of the year – a satisfying fruition of years of genetic selection. The new sires have done a good job and by the looks of these large, muscular calves, the future looks bright.

I'm amazed how easily I slip back into the routine. It feels good to be back in uniform: Wranglers, old work shirt, leather boots, belt and knife. My brown hair is in desperate need of a trim, but no-one can tell; it's pulled back into the usual ponytail, smelly and sweaty under my filthy work hat that's speckled with blood from dehorning and hued with a decade of dust.

Philip and I load the cattle into the race and drop the first one down in the cradle. Rick works the head: tattooing ears and dehorning, and Philip vaccinates before bringing up another pen of calves while I pull the brand out of the glowing coals and leave my mark. After ten years I still feel proud watching our brand, wings over nought, leave its golden singed mark on the hide of our calves.

The kids are still too little to be working alongside the men in the yards, but they sit in the adjoining feed trough, watching intently, drafting stick at the ready for when Daddy says it's safe to have a go. In the midst of the bellowing calves and heat and dust

I see Rick pause from branding and look over at them, shooting them his characteristic grin. The kids beam and their faces light up. I know how they feel; they are the centre of his world, and they know it. He stops and explains to the kids what we are doing.

'... and then we put a letter and a number on.'

'Why?' they reply in unison, echoing the voice of a girl I knew twenty years ago ...

Epilogue

Another three years have passed since 2009 – that mother of all dry years, which took us to the brink. Even with the chance of rain increasing with each passing week of December that year, we still sold 300 cows and calves on the eve of Christmas to protect our pasture and spread out the remaining stock to give the land the reprieve it needed. Three years on and we are still rebuilding our herd from the setback of that season.

In January 2010 it rained again and good solid rain continued through autumn. It was too late for the mating season and to help the cows and calves, and a long way off what would be considered drought-breaking rain, but it set us up for the best winter we'd had in years. As summer 2010 arrived the El Niño weather pattern finally slid aside for its counterpart, La Niña. Floods covered Queensland and much of the state was declared a natural disaster area. Our dams filled and we did creek crossings every other day for three months. Dams and roads and fences were destroyed in the wake of the floods and it would take another six months to rebuild our infrastructure, but for us the benefits outweighed the losses immeasurably.

With her memory jogged, Mother Nature continued her downpours for the remainder of 2010, through 2011 and into 2012. After two decades, the drought had finally broken.

The bull sales have gone from strength to strength and, as part of our philosophy of simplifying life, we combined them, holding our inaugural combined sale at Eidsvold in 2011, selling 95 bulls to average $5750 each, and another 250 bulls 'out of the paddock'.

Ruby and James attend the fabulous local school at Kumbia, which has ninety students in total, and Rory does 'cowboy kindy' whenever Dad can take him. The washing line is filled with pint-sized Wranglers and checked shirts, and lines of midget brown boots crowd the back steps.

I finally got to Europe with Rick and the kids to celebrate my fortieth, doing my best to resurrect the EU economy with my consumption of French bubbles.

In 2012 Rick bought three little camp stretchers and a little truck that could fit three ponies, alongside five horses, and we got back into campdrafting. The kids are sad for me that I don't 'bring home ribbons like Daddy', but I'm just happy to be riding ol' Fox, and my new mare, Venus. Skittles is retired from competition (for now).

Jem was sold to a friend who knew his background, has gone on to compete successfully at campdrafts and is now ridden by a nine year old and is the 'quietest, gentlest horse' they've ever owned.

There was a time in my twenties when I was living the dream and bulletproof. Now I'm forty, I'm still living the dream, albeit a slightly modified dream. No longer do I believe I am bulletproof, nor the people around me. Since finishing this memoir, our darling John O'Shanesy has passed away and around the same time so did wonderful Lachlan Hornery, who was helping us that fateful day of my accident, and who could make Rick laugh and relax when he thought the world was too serious a place. And, as much as it saddens me to write it, our gorgeous Sally, our sister and our best friend, passed away suddenly on 2 April 2010, having contracted bacterial meningitis. So it is in deference to their spirits and the way these incredible people lived their lives: with joy, a sense of adventure, and pursuit of knowledge – their parting gifts to us all – that I remember to have fun, notice and be thankful for the little things, and enjoy the journey of discovery.

Acknowledgements

The journey of writing bears some resemblance to that of parenthood, and not just in the patience and love required, but in that it also takes a village to raise a book from birth to maturity. There are many people to whom I am very grateful for the part they've played to nurture *Educating Alice*.

My HarperCollins publisher Fiona Henderson and Agent Selwa Anthony steered the book from conception to publication and I am thankful for their patient and firm guidance. Selwa's passion for Australian stories ensures distinctly home grown tales are captured for present and future generations. Fiona's constant assurance of 'every book in its day' gave *Educating Alice* the time to evolve into a narrative that I hope speaks more broadly about life and growing up. Allowing me several years to write, edit, cull and rewrite while raising a family and running a business has resulted in a better rounded manuscript. I was blessed from the start having Fiona and Selwa in my corner.

'To write is human, to edit is divine' said Stephen King, and I have had some divine editors to guide me. Thank-you Kim Swivel and Jody Lee for structural and narrative guidance, Katie Stackhouse for sublime line editing and for 'just getting me' and Rochelle Fernandez as project editor. Thank-you Kelly Fagan, my publicist and all the team at Harper Collins - working with you is like hanging out with mates, you have made me feel very comfortable and welcome and I am honoured to be part of your legacy.

Thank you Drew Keys for being the first bloke (other than Rick) to read EA and give it the big thumbs up – that was a breakthrough moment. Thanks also to Terry Underwood for your considerate forward and for being a constant source of inspiration to me.

The determination and commitment to edit and develop a manuscript can be traced back to my grade eight teacher Mrs Magasanik, who encouraged her students to resubmit essays, refining the craft. I acknowledge her and all the teachers I have been blessed with for shaping my life in many wonderful and inspired ways. To teach and to inspire are two of the greatest callings in life and I honour teachers everywhere who do both.

Writing with a young family and business has been a challenge and I have had some help along the way. Thank-you June Lee, Prue O'Shanesy, Hannah Routledge, Taylah Teschner, Jamie Davies, Eri Carey and the irreplaceable Les Koy, for keeping our home and lives intact.

Greenup Eidsvold Station has grown more than ten-fold since its inception and Rick and I are very grateful to the people that have made it possible and so much fun: Glenda Rogan, John Meeks, Lachlan Hornery, Mark Buttsworth, Shane Cullen, Sandy Douglas, Daniel Cheers, Cam Webster, Victor Bligh, Ronnie Bligh, Warren Sturt, Philip Mathews, Peter Scholl, Matt King, Grant Nagal, Trish Richardson, Ken May, Anita Martin, and Anthony and Sally Coates

Rick and I have had the incredible privilege of working with some of the industry's wisest teachers in life and business. They have been a constant source of challenge and extension for us, and have become family along the way. Terry and Pam McCosker and the RCS team, Jill Rigney and Dave Hanlon, The Right Mind International and Patrick MacManaway, Dragonlines, thanks for keeping the path lit.

We are blessed to have a bunch of old and new friends that share a generosity of spirit when it comes to putting up with our long absences from social life when we get beavering into work. I love that when we resurface you are waiting with a big hug, a long yarn, a bellyful of laughs and a glass of bubbles.

Rick's parents Peg and Grahame have always given unwavering support for all of Rick's and my ventures, and are a constant reassuring presence in the good times and bad.

My mother Jill has been a lifelong source of inspiration and encouraged for me to tackle anything and take on whatever the world offered, which is no doubt how this whole journey started. Thanks Mum.

Special mention must go to our easygoing kids who have grown up with a fourth sibling, my 'babyputer'. After four years of them asking 'is it done yet?' I can happily say, 'It's done'. Ruby, James and Rory, thank-you for being so patient with mummy.

Rick, my good-natured man, who believes in my dreams as much as his own — I would choose you over and over and over again.

Namaste.

Alice